ESSAYS ON
BIOETHICS

D0140928

ESSAYS ON
BIOETHICS

R. M. Hare

CLARENDON PRESS · OXFORD
1993

Oxford University Press, Walton Street, Oxford OX2 6DP
Oxford New York
Athens Auckland Bangkok Bogota Bombay
Buenos Aires Calcutta Cape Town Dar es Salaam
Delhi Florence Hong Kong Istanbul Karachi
Kuala Lumpur Madras Madrid Melbourne
Mexico City Nairobi Paris Singapore
Taipei Tokyo Toronto
and associated companies in
Berlin Ibadan

Oxford is a trade mark of Oxford University Press

Published in the United States by
Oxford University Press Inc., New York

First published 1993
First issued in paperback 1996

British Library Cataloguing in Publication Data
Data available

Library of Congress Cataloging in Publication Data
Hare, R. M. (Richard Mervyn)
Essays on bioethics / R. M. Hare.
Includes bibliographical references and index.
1. Medical ethics. I. Title.
R724.H236 1993   174'.2—dc20   93–16302
ISBN 0-19-823983-1
ISBN 0-19-823678-6 (Pbk)

Printed in Great Britain on acid-free paper by
Biddles Ltd., Guildford and King's Lynn

PREFACE

In this volume I am offering to interested readers a number of essays of mine in the general field of bioethics, understood as covering not only medical ethics, but other related topics. In all of them I attempt to apply a coherent ethical theory, worked out in my other writings, to these practical issues. Those more familiar with the philosophical writings of my colleagues than with my own may be surprised to find that the theory that I use incorporates substantial elements drawn from Kant as well as from the utilitarians. The two kinds of moral philosophy are generally thought to be irreconcilable. One of my main aims has been to illustrate the affinity between them by applying them to practical problems and getting the same conclusions whichever kind, Kantian or utilitarian, is used. My own theory, which is a combination of these two elements, will not itself be defended here, though it is briefly summarized near the beginning of the first essay and, where necessary, elsewhere; for a full exposition and defence I must refer the reader to my books *Moral Thinking* and *Essays in Ethical Theory*, and to a forthcoming paper on Kant (H 1993a).

The other main theme that recurs throughout the book may also surprise some people. It is that we can harm people's interests, and thus perhaps fail in our duty to them, by stopping them coming into existence. This view is generally thought preposterous, but it is nevertheless easier to defend than the opposite view, that we do no harm to anybody by denying him (or her) existence. If true, it puts the current disputes about abortion, embryo experimentation, the treatment of defective neonates, population policy, and the like in an entirely new light, which might greatly increase our understanding of these issues, and put an end to some very bad arguments that encumber most popular writing on these subjects. However, this thesis does not entail a conservative view about abortion, because, as well as making us respect the interests of the person that the present foetus would turn into, it makes us also consider the interests of other future people who might be born if this person is not. This theme is most prominent in essays 5 to 12.

The first two essays are introductions to the application of ethical theory to the practice of doctors and especially psychiatrists. The third is a conceptual enquiry into the notion of health, fundamental to the discussion of the duties of doctors. The fourth is about behaviour control by medical and other means, and the ninth about the ethics of experimentation on human children. The last three essays deal with the free will problem, with the just distribution of scarce resources in health care, and with some of our duties to non-human animals.

When one is making similar moves in the hope of illuminating a lot of different problems, one cannot avoid some repetition, because the moves have to be explained every time if the papers are to be readable independently, as is my intention. I have cut out some overlaps, but in general have been content to put in ample cross-references to help the reader find his (or her) way about the volume. I have done this in a way that avoids all footnotes; this is explained at the beginning of the bibliography.

The changes I have made to previously published essays are nearly all stylistic, for the sake of uniformity. I have not, in general, tried to bring them up to date, though I have done so in some places, and have added some new references. I still adhere to the philosophical views appealed to in these essays, though for the readership for which this volume is intended I did not think it right to put in all the detailed qualifications that are needed.

Many of the papers were written before 'non-sexist' language (so called) became 'politically correct'. I have not altered them in this respect, although more recently I have found a way of conforming which is stylistically just tolerable. The contortions which would have been necessary to make the older papers conform illustrate very well what the feminists are doing to our style. I do not think in fact that the current fashion does much for the welfare of women in general, pleasing as it may be to a few intellectuals; and it certainly makes good clear writing more difficult. The Germans and others, the structure of whose languages makes it well nigh impossible to follow this fashion, are perhaps fortunate. And sometimes I feel like abandoning any attempt to do so, as a protest against the tyranny of 'political correctness'.

I am grateful to the original publishers for giving permission to reprint where necessary. The place of first publication is given at the foot of the first page of each paper. My thanks are due to the many people who have by their writings helped me understand these questions better; to the medical professionals who in numerous working parties and seminars have made me familiar with the kinds of case in which these moral problems arise; to Rory Weiner, for many discussions on Kant and on health care policy; to Marin Smillov, who put all these papers through the optical reader to convert them to the computer program I now use; and above all to my wife, without whose devoted efforts and constant encouragement I could never have got these papers together in a form that could be given to the printer.

R.M.H.

Gainesville, Florida

CONTENTS

1. Medical Ethics: Can the Moral Philosopher Help?   1

2. The Philosophical Basis of Psychiatric Ethics   15

3. Health   31

4. Moral Problems about the Control of Behaviour   50

5. Possible People   67

6. When does Potentiality Count?   84

7. *In Vitro* Fertilization and the Warnock Report   98

8. Embryo Experimentation: Public Policy in a Pluralist Society   118

9. Little Human Guinea-Pigs?   131

10. Abortion and the Golden Rule   147

11. A Kantian Approach to Abortion   168

12. The Abnormal Child: Moral Dilemmas of Doctors and Parents   185

13. Prediction and Moral Appraisal   192

14. Health Care Policy: Some Options   209

15. Why I am only a Demi-Vegetarian   219

References and Bibliography   237

Index   243

I

Medical Ethics
Can the Moral Philosopher Help?

1.1 If the moral philosopher cannot help with the problems of medical ethics, he ought to shut up shop. The problems of medical ethics are so typical of the moral problems that moral philosophy is supposed to be able to help with, that a failure here really would be a sign either of the uselessness of the discipline or of the incompetence of the particular practitioner. I do not want to overstate this point, however. It could be the case that, so far as practical help goes, philosophy is at the stage now at which, not so long ago, medicine was. It has been said that until fairly recently one was more likely to survive one's illnesses if one kept out of the hands of the doctor than if one allowed oneself to be treated—and this was at any rate true of the wounded on battlefields, because the surgeons' instruments were not sterilized. Yet all the same medicine *has* now progressed to a stage at which it saves lives. The change came when certain *methods* got accepted: I mean, not merely such things as aseptic surgery, but also the application to medicine of the scientific method in general, which meant that firm and reliable procedures were adopted for determining whether a certain treatment worked or not; and also the relation of medicine to fundamental knowledge about physiology and biochemistry, which made possible the invention of new treatments to be tested in this way.

The same could be true of philosophy. There have been great philosophers in the past, just as there were great doctors before the advent of modern medicine; but it is only very recently in the history of philosophy that general standards of rigour in argument have improved to such an extent that there is some hope of our establishing our discipline on a firm basis.

From *Philosophical Medical Ethics: Its Nature and Significance*, ed. S. Spicker and H. T. Engelhardt, Jr. (Reidel/Kluwer, 1977), 49–61. © R. M. Hare 1977.

By 'standards of rigour', I mean such things as the insistence on knowing, and being able to explain, exactly what one means when one says something, which involves being able to say what follows logically from it and what does not, what it is logically consistent with, and so on. If this is not insisted on, arguments will get lost in the sands. Even now it is insisted on only in certain parts of the philosophical world; one is very likely to meet philosophers who do not accept this requirement of rigour, and my advice is that one should regard them in the same light as one would regard a medical man, whether or not he had the right letters after his name, who claimed to have a wonder drug which would cure the common cold, but was not ready to submit it to controlled tests. It is undoubtedly true that many patients will feel much better when they have taken his drug; but since we simply do not know whether it is the drug that has made them feel better, or his personal charisma, or natural causes, he has not contributed to the advance of medicine.

I do not want to give the impression that nobody insisted on rigour in argument until recently; indeed, it was the insistence on knowing what one meant that really got philosophy started. Socrates, Plato, and Aristotle, as well, probably, as some other great men of their time whose works have not come down to us, knew how philosophy ought to be done and made great progress in it; and there have been other periods in which philosophy in this rigorous sense has flourished; but they have always been succeeded by periods of decline in which a kind of superficial excitement was prized above rigour in argument, and so philosophy got lost. It is very important not to let this happen again. For the true philosopher the most exciting thing in the world—perhaps the only exciting thing—is to become really clear about some important question.

I said at the beginning that if philosophers could not help with the problems of medical ethics they might as well shut up shop. But *how* can they help? Not in some of the ways that many people seem to think. The failure to help in *these* ways is indeed the reason why it is thought that philosophy can never help at all. But we must not look for elixirs.

It is very important, for example, to understand that the relation between a philosopher and somebody who is troubled

about a question in medical ethics can never be like that
between an old-fashioned general practitioner and his patient.
Philosophy is much more like the teaching of remedial exer-
cises. Philosophers cannot give their patients pills which the
patients can just swallow. Philosophy itself is the medicine, and
it has to be understood, to some degree at any rate, by the
patient himself, in a way that medical science does not.

Nor does philosophy try to prove to people that they must
think this or that, by deducing conclusions from premises
which cannot be denied. Some philosophers have thought that
they could do this; some still do. What I am now saying is
controversial; but I can only say what I think in the present
state of the controversy. Claims to prove moral conclusions,
starting from premises which we cannot deny, always turn out
to fail in one of the following ways: either the premises can,
after all, be denied; or the argumentation is simply invalid; or
it is expressed in an ambiguous way, so that if one takes the
words one way, the premises can be denied, but if one takes
them in a way in which the premises cannot be denied, the
conclusion does not follow from them.

I.2 I will give an example connected with the problem
about abortion (10.1 ff., 11.1 ff.). People sometimes think that
they can prove that abortion must be wrong by using the following sort of argument. We know that murder is always
wrong; we know that killing (sc. intentionally) another innocent
human being is murder; we know that the foetus is a human
being, and innocent; so we know that killing it is murder, and
therefore wrong. There are at least two points at which this
argument can be assailed. The first concerns the word 'murder'; the second, the word 'human'. Another word that could
give us trouble is 'innocent', and so could 'intentional'; but I
shall not have room to discuss those. It is perfectly true that on
one definition of 'murder' it means something like 'wrongful
killing'; and in that sense murder must be wrong. But that is
not how the word is being taken in the second premise of the
argument, that killing another innocent human being is murder. For this premise is being claimed to be undeniable, and to
make it so we should have to *define* 'murder' in such a way that
it must be true. Some people have indeed defined 'murder' as
'the intentional killing of another innocent human being',

though there are difficulties about this definition. But if we used this definition of 'murder', we should make the argument invalid; for it does not follow logically from the fact that someone has intentionally killed another innocent human being that he has done wrong. So even if we were to accept without question that to kill a foetus is to kill an innocent human being, we cannot prove that it is wrong; it is, certainly, murder in the sense defined, but not in the sense in which murder logically has to be wrong.

More interesting is the expression 'human being'. There is no doubt a sense in which the foetus is already a human being; and there is another sense in which it does not become a human being until it is born (8.7, 10.3, 11.1). How are we to decide in which of these senses the words 'human being' are being used when murder is defined as 'the intentional killing of another innocent human being'? Is this meant to cover foetuses or not? If it is, then it is not so self-evident that the killing of *any* innocent human beings, including foetuses (which is what 'murder' will now mean), is wrong. That, indeed, is what we were trying to decide, and we cannot beg the question by *assuming* that it is wrong. On the other hand, if 'human being' does not cover foetuses, then killing foetuses will not be killing human beings, and so will not be murder, and so will not be wrong just because murder is wrong.

At this point it may be objected that deciding to call the foetus a human being is not just an arbitrary decision. Foetuses, it may be said, are *like* human beings in certain important respects. But the question remains, are these respects sufficient to make us include foetuses under the prohibition of murder? On this question, no light has been shed by these verbal manœuvres. Philosophers spend a lot of time talking about words; but at any rate the good philosophers do this precisely in order to *avoid* being deceived by words into evading the substantial questions. The thing is to get the words straight—to decide what you are going to mean by them—and then get on to the real business.

This brings me to what I think is the main—perhaps the only—contribution of the philosopher to the solution of these problems. He comes in because moral problems, of which problems in medical ethics are an example, cannot be discussed without using many words whose meaning and logical properties are not at all clear. These include, in particular, the moral words such as 'wrong'. Moral philosophy is a training in the study of such tricky words and their logical properties, in order to establish canons of valid argument or reasoning, and so enable people who have mastered them to avoid errors in reasoning (confusions or fallacies), and so answer their moral questions with their eyes open. It is my belief that, once the issues are thoroughly clarified in this way, the problems will not seem so perplexing as they did at first. The philosophical difficulties having been removed, we can then get on with discussing the practical difficulties, which are likely to remain serious.

1.3 So much for the place of philosophy in this business, as I see it. I shall now expound two rival philosophical approaches to problems of medical ethics (both of them consistent with the view about the role of philosophy that I have just been advocating). I am going to call these two approaches the 'absolutist' approach (2.1, 7.6) and the 'utilitarian' approach. These names are not particularly helpful ones, and can be misleading; but they are current in philosophical discussions and so I do not want to introduce new names. 'Absolutist' is not here being used in the sense in which it is the opposite of 'relativist' (that is a quite different controversy which need not concern us); and there are a great many different versions of utilitarianism, some of which are very easily demolished, but others of which are at least extremely plausible. After I have set out these two rival approaches, I shall suggest a way of looking at the matter which combines the virtues and avoids the faults of both of them.

Either of these approaches could be represented as in line with common sense and our ordinary opinions, although they look inconsistent with each other. This is a sign that common sense and our ordinary opinions may not be entirely self-consistent. I shall be trying to show that, when the issue is fully clarified, we can still go on holding the important parts of our common-sense views, and that this will not land us in inconsistency. But before we can understand this, we shall have to do some fairly difficult philosophy.

Absolutists will often say something like this: there are certain kinds of actions (for example, killing innocent people) which are wrong, and nothing can make them right. The kinds of action in question are specified in fairly simple, general terms, and this, as we shall see, is the most characteristic feature of this approach. Utilitarians, on the other hand, are likely to say that one has to do the best one can in a given situation—to act for the best. It is easy to see how the two approaches can conflict in unusual or difficult cases. For example, absolutists will say that because killing innocent people is always wrong, if you are in a situation in which if you do not kill one innocent person twenty other innocent people will die (though not by your hand), then you ought to be prepared to let the twenty die rather than become guilty of the death of the one. But utilitarians will say that you have to act for the best in the circumstances, and save the twenty at the expense of the one. To use an example that is commonly used in philosophical discussions of this subject: twenty-one potholers are coming out of the cave that they are exploring when the front one, who is fatter than the rest, gets stuck in a narrow place; there has been sudden heavy rain and the water is rising in the cave behind them, so that they can only survive if they use such force (e.g. explosives) to remove him as will in fact kill him. I have used this example because it is a particularly clear one; the literature about abortion and other questions in medical ethics is of course full of similar examples.

1.4 Let us first look at some of the arguments that are used on both sides of this kind of controversy. Some of these arguments are theoretical and some practical. On the whole it is the theoretical arguments of the utilitarians which are convincing, and the practical arguments of the absolutists. This, as we shall see, points the way to a resolution of the conflict, because a more sophisticated utilitarian theory can absorb enough of the absolutist approach to retain its practical merits.

As an example of a practical argument which is used by absolutists, consider the following. It is variously called the 'slippery slope' or 'thin end of the wedge' argument (7.3, 10.6, 11.7). If one once allows abortion in some admittedly very difficult cases, then one has breached irrevocably the principle that it is wrong to kill innocent human beings. One will then find oneself unable to condemn abortion in any cases, or infanticide, or even the plain murder of adults when it seems to be 'for the best'. Or, to take another example: if one is prepared to allow the bystanders to kill the driver trapped under the blazing petrol tanker to save him from roasting to death, how can one say it is wrong to kill *anybody* who seems to have a greater likelihood of unhappiness in life than of happiness (which perhaps includes a great many of us). And if we can kill somebody when it is for *his* greater good, ought we not in fairness to kill him when it is for the greater good of all, considering their interests impartially? I have heard of a doctor who said, 'We shall start by administering euthanasia to put patients out of intolerable suffering; we shall end up doing it because we want to get away for the weekend' (1.5, H 1975).

What the absolutist is here appealing to is the sanctity of a very simple and general (and, most people will think, a very important) moral principle. We feel that if we once loosen our hold on this principle, anything goes. The utilitarian may reply by saying that life is not so simple as that. In the general run of cases this simple principle that it is wrong to kill innocent people is the one to follow; its general abandonment would have disastrous consequences for people's well-being; we should go perpetually in fear of our lives. So we should very seldom indeed be acting for the best if we did anything to weaken the hold of this principle upon our society or upon ourselves. It is extremely easy to persuade oneself that in one's own particular case it would be for the best to breach the principle; but, just because it is easy to persuade oneself of this, we ought to be on our guard against doing so when, perhaps, an impartial spectator, who knew the facts and the future better than we do, would warn us that we were deceiving ourselves. And that is why most of us think, when we are considering the moral education of our children or the formation of our own characters and of the generally accepted mores of society, that it is very important to establish a secure place for these good general principles (2.3, 4.3, 6.4, 10.6)—principles like the one about killing, or the principle that it is wrong to tell lies or break promises. And we think, most of us, that if it would take a very great deal to make a person break one of these principles, he is a better person than somebody who will break them without a qualm if he can convince himself that it is the best thing to do in the circumstances.

1.5   If all this is so, then there are sound *utilitarian* reasons for doing all we can to preserve the good principles by which the absolutist sets store. I want to illustrate this by considering a move which is extremely common in arguments about euthanasia. Medical people often say, 'Our whole training and our attitudes are directed towards the saving of life; how can you ask us to kill people?' Here it is a question of the attitudes that we think doctors ought to have in general; it is certainly true that unless, in general, a doctor is devoted to the saving of life, he is likely to be a bad doctor. So if a doctor is asked to end a patient's life, or even (though this is not euthanasia strictly speaking) to refrain from saving the life of a patient whom it is far better to let die, he will, if he is a good doctor, feel the greatest reluctance; to do either of these things goes against the grain—the 'grain' being his training as a doctor in the saving of life. If the advocates of euthanasia or of letting people die in certain cases are right, the doctor ought to overcome this reluctance, provided that he is certain that this is a case in which the patient will be better off dead (*MT* 177). But there is a practical danger that, if it is overcome in these particular cases, this will lead to a general change of attitude on the part of doctors and perhaps also of patients; doctors will stop being thought of, and will stop thinking of themselves, as devoted to the saving of life, and will come instead to be thought of as devoted to doing what *they* think is best for the patient or even for people in general, even if it involves killing him; and this development might not be, taken all in all, for the best.

So here again we might have a *utilitarian* argument for preserving the absolutist principle. I say that we *might* have such an argument. It might, on the other side, be said that the new state of affairs that I envisaged would be better than the old. That would be a matter for investigation. But I have done enough, perhaps, to illustrate the general point that, if we allow the absolutists the practical importance of their good general principles, we can do something to reconcile their position with that of the utilitarians; for we can say that it might be better, even from a utilitarian point of view, in our medical training and in our legislation to seek to preserve the general respect of doctors for the lives of their patients, than to endanger this respect in order to do the best thing (apart from considerations about endangering respect for life) in some relatively rare particular cases.

It will be disputed whether this is true: it will be argued on one side that the cases calling for euthanasia or letting die are very numerous and that therefore it would be better to *change* our attitudes; and on the other side that these cases are relatively few, and that they can be looked after in other ways, and that therefore the present attitude is the best one. Or there may be a half-way position (one which is now extremely popular, but which I do not myself find altogether logical) which says that the best attitude to adopt is that killing is absolutely ruled out but it may be all right to let patients die in certain cases. The difficulty here is with the extremely tenuous distinction between killing and letting die—a philosophical problem with which I shall not have room to deal (see Glover 1977). But at any rate we seem to have reached a point in the argument at which we can investigate, with some hope of discovering the answer, what is the best attitude for doctors to adopt to this kind of question. For we can ask what it would be like, in hospitals and in the homes of dying patients, if one attitude or the other were adopted, and which would be the better state of affairs. So the philosophical exercise would have resulted, as all good philosophy should, in returning the problem to the non-philosopher for further investigation, but in a form in which it is better understood, clearer, and therefore easier of solution.

1.6 However, I did not really go deep enough into the philosophical aspects of the question. For I left unexamined the problem of how we would decide which state of affairs was 'for the best'. In order to be clear about this question, I shall have to assume for the sake of argument the truth of a theory about moral reasoning which I hold and have argued for in *MT* and elsewhere, and apply it to the present problem; I shall not have room here to defend it. But my position is not quite so weak as might appear from what I have just said. For in fact it can be shown that for the purposes of this practical argument my theoretical position has the same effect as a great many of the most well-supported views on how we should argue about moral questions.

Before I put the matter in my own way, I will just give a list of these views which I say lead to the same results as my own. There is first of all the Christian (and indeed pre-Christian) view that we should do to others as we wish should be done to us (2.4, 7.6, 10.4, 11.5 ff.). This means, done to us if we were in precisely the position of the person we are dealing with, including having his desires and interests. Then, secondly, there is the Kantian view that we should act only on that maxim through which we can at the same time will that it should become a universal law (Kant 1785: BA52 = 421). This entails that it is a law to be applied also if we ourselves were in the position of our patient or victim. Thirdly, there is the so-called 'ideal observer' theory, according to which we should do what would be recommended by an impartial spectator who knew all the facts and had the interests of all the parties equally at heart (for a good recent exposition see Haslett 1974). And fourthly there is the so-called 'rational contractor' view (see Rawls 1971, Richards 1971). This holds that we should do what is required by the principles which a set of rational and self-interested people would accept for the future conduct of the society in which they were going to live, if they did not know what particular role in that society each individual one of them was going to fill. Though Rawls does not think that this view yields the same practical results as the others, I have tried to show elsewhere that it does (H 1972c, 1973).

What is common to all these positions (the logical bones of all of them, we might say) is that they require us to adopt certain *universal* principles or prescriptions, to be applied impartially to whoever is affected by them—ourselves or other people. This logical kernel of all these positions is what is stated in its simplest and most economical form by my own theory, which says that in making a moral judgement what we are doing is prescribing universally for all cases of a given precisely specified kind. If we realize that this is what we are doing, and that therefore our prescriptions would have to be followed also in cases in which we were at the receiving end of the actions which we are considering, we shall be led to give equal weight to the equal interests of all the parties in the situation (because in other precisely similar cases we would occupy the roles now occupied by the other parties). And this, in turn, will lead us to a form of utilitarianism (though Rawls does not think so); for the essence of utilitarianism is that we should do the best we can to serve the interests of all the parties affected by our actions, treating the equal interests of each of them as of equal weight. That is what 'acting for the best', as I have been using that expression, really means.

Now there are a great many different varieties of utilitarianism, as I said; and this is no place to try to say what they all are. The variety which I think is generated by a careful application of the theories I have just been listing is one which, fortunately, enables us, in the way I have indicated, to incorporate the important practical insights of the absolutist. Let me try to say as clearly as I can how this comes about.

Suppose that we are wondering what universal principles to adopt for the conduct of ourselves and others, and that we are therefore, as I have said, led to seek to do the best we can for the interests of all the parties considered impartially. This at first sight looks as if it will lead to arguments which many doctors will find repugnant. Imagine a doctor who is told that if he gives a patient of his a bottle to kill his wife with, the patient will give him a very large sum of money; the wife is going to have a pretty miserable time if she lives anyway; the husband will benefit enormously if he is rid of her; the doctor himself will spend the money on buying a yacht and thus get a lot of healthy enjoyment; and if he puts in the death certificate that she died of heart failure, nobody will know there was any foul play. So, it might be argued, the doctor has very good utilitarian reasons for supplying the poison. This sort of example can be used to create the impression that utilitarianism is a thoroughly disreputable creed.

But the utilitarian can justly reply that the argument has been altogether too superficial. We have to ask, not only what is for the best on this particular occasion for the parties affected, but what is for the best for society as a whole. All the members of society are likely to be gravely harmed if doctors are brought up with such attitudes that they can even contemplate such an act. The interests of all are therefore best served if doctors simply put such thoughts out of their minds. This sounds like an absolutist sort of thing to say; but there are good utilitarian reasons for saying it. The doctor who would even think of such a thing is a bad doctor and a bad person, and he or anybody who had a hand in his upbringing was doing something enormously harmful when he allowed such ideas to be entertained. The good doctor by contrast will put such thoughts out of his mind altogether; and it is in the interests of all of us that our doctors should in this respect be good ones.

The point I am trying to make is that, even on the utilitarian view, there are certain principles which we ought all to try to preserve, and that anything which damages the general acceptance of them is always harmful; and that even though in some rare particular cases it might be more in the interests of the parties, taken as a whole, to break these principles, the good doctor and the good person simply will not consider doing it. If he were going to consider it, he would have to be a worse doctor and a worse person, and to have such doctors is worse for society in general than to have the sort that, on the whole, we do have.

1.7 However, all this does not answer for us the question, *What are* the good general principles whose general acceptance by doctors would be for the best? How are we to tell what these principles ought to say about killing? Ought they to ban all killing of patients, for example, or ought they to permit euthanasia? And if so, precisely under what conditions ought they to permit it? To deal with these questions clearly, we have to distinguish between two kinds of moral thinking—two levels or two occasions of moral thought; and correspondingly between two sorts or two uses of moral principles (2.5, 4.3, 6.4, 10.6).

There is first of all the kind of thinking that we ought to do when we are considering a particular case before us with all its difficulties and temptations and uncertainties—a patient, say, has just collapsed and we are wondering whether we ought to try to revive him. And secondly there is the kind of thinking that we ought to do when we are not faced immediately with a particular problem, but are trying to decide what principles or attitudes doctors ought to have, what guidelines the disciplinary bodies of the medical profession should follow, or what laws the legislature should enact. In this second sort of thinking, too, we are allowed to think about particular cases, but in a rather different way. We are not confined to actual cases before us, but can consider hypothetical, even fantastic, cases, like the one about the potholers that I mentioned earlier. And, since we do not have actually to act in the cases which we consider, we can take them at our leisure, find out all about them including what happened *after* the crucial decision was made; or, if we cannot find out, *invent* particular details to illustrate particular points. And about each of these cases, when we have been into it in detail, we can decide what ought to be done, or to have been done, in these precise circumstances. So we shall end up with a lot of very *specific* principles (though still universal ones) which say that in all circumstances just like this one ought to do just that.

But this ought not to be the end of this kind of thinking; for, as I said, the purpose of it is to give some sort of general guidance about the attitudes of doctors and others, who are not going to be able to give the cases in which they find themselves involved nearly so much thought, because they will not have the time or the information. The principles the doctors will need are not highly specific ones, but, rather, general ones which give the best guidance in the ordinary run of cases, and which, therefore, are the best principles for doctors to adopt almost as second nature—though of course in very peculiar cases they may find themselves constrained to depart from them. So now we come to the question which I said I had not dealt with—the question of how to select those good general principles which absolutists rightly say we should follow (though they say next to nothing about how the principles are to be *selected* or the selection *justified*). What I have to say about this will make it doubly clear that there is a place for such principles in a utilitarian system and that the reasoning which leads to their selection is in fact utilitarian.

First of all, when we are doing the selection, we ought not to pay too much attention to particular cases, actual or hypothetical, which are not at all usual or which are unlikely to recur. For we are selecting our principles as practical guides in the world as it actually is, and not as it would be if it were composed of incidents out of short stories, or out of philosophers' examples. So it makes a difference if, for example, the

number of people who die in agony of terminal cancer either
is very small, or would be very small if proper care were taken
of them. This is the point of the maxim that hard cases make
bad law. If we give weight to the cases in proportion to the
probability of occurrence of cases of precisely that type, we
shall be more likely to adopt principles whose general adoption
and preservation will lead to the best results, on the whole, for
those who are affected by them.

And we should not be put off if somebody comes along and
tells us about some highly peculiar case and says, 'In this case,
in which it would obviously be for the best to depart from
these principles, either you must agree that we ought to depart
from them or you are not really a utilitarian' (of course it does
not matter very much what we *call* ourselves). What we should
say to him is, 'All right, then, if the case really is so very peculiar and really occurs, we ought to depart from the principle.
But since it is so easy to deceive oneself, and since in actual
cases we never know enough and never have enough time to
think about it, it is very hard to be sure that this *is* a case in
which we ought to depart from the principle. Maybe it is; but
maybe, on the other hand, the case actually before us, which
we have to deal with here and now, is not really so peculiar
after all; we are only trying to persuade ourselves that it is
peculiar because we want to get away for the weekend. But
even if it is peculiar—even if in this case we ought to break
the good general principle—we shall do so with the greatest
misgiving, because it goes against our whole upbringing as
doctors; and the occurrence of this case does not in the least
mean that the good general principles are no good. They still
ought to be our main standby as doctors, and we ought not to
do anything to weaken them.' This, I think, would be a sound
attitude, and fundamentally a utilitarian attitude, for doctors to
preserve, because it is for the best that they should preserve it.

2

The Philosophical Basis of Psychiatric Ethics

2.1 I have already in the preceding paper outlined the way in which, as I think, the moral philosopher can help with the problems of medical ethics, and I shall not repeat all that I said there. There are some problems, however, which afflict the psychiatrist in particular, and not only illustrate the method well, but deserve a more extended treatment.

I distinguished two ways of thinking which I called 'absolutist' and 'utilitarian' (1.3). It is evident that psychiatrists, like most of us, think from time to time in both these ways. But it is also evident that cases can and frequently do arise in which the two methods seem to yield different results. For example, in a case involving treatment against the wishes of the patient, a psychiatrist might well think that the treatment was clearly in the patient's best interest and in that of everybody else concerned and yet think that he had no right to impose it if the patient did not want it. To this question we shall return.

Because of these apparent conflicts between the approaches, philosophers and others have suggested various more or less clumsy ways of combining them so as to avoid the conflicts. One way would be to say that the duty to do the best for the patient and others (the so-called duty of beneficence) is one duty among many, and that, as in all cases of conflicts between duties, we have to 'weigh' the relative urgency or importance of the duties in the particular case; in some cases we may decide that the duty of beneficence is the more weighty, in others the duty to respect some right. This way out is utterly unhelpful, relying as it does on a weighing process of which no explanation whatever is given (see *MT* 34).

Another equally unhelpful suggestion is that the duties in

From *Psychiatric Ethics*, ed. S. Bloch and P. Chodoff (Oxford UP, 1983).

question, including that of beneficence, might be placed once for all in an order of priority, sometimes called 'lexical ordering' (from the practice of lexicographers of putting first all the words beginning with 'a', whatever other letters they contain, and then those beginning with 'b', and so on). So we should, for example, fulfil duty *a* in all cases in which it existed, whatever other duties might also be present, and only then go on to consider duty *b*. This suggestion is unhelpful for at least two reasons. The first is that, as before, no account is given of why the duties should have this order of priority rather than some other. The second is more subtle: will it not be the case that on some occasions duty *a* ought to have priority, on others duty *b*? In terms of the same example as before, ought we not sometimes to treat the patient against his will if the harm to which he will otherwise come is very great, but in others respect his right to refuse treatment? No lexical ordering of the duties could allow us to say this, and yet we might often want to say it (see *MT* 32–4). Nevertheless, the idea of lexical ordering has been quite popular.

These suggestions are handicapped by their failure to distinguish between the different levels of moral thinking (2.3). It is indeed hard to see how any one-level account could solve the problem of moral conflicts; for if conflicts arise at one level, they cannot be resolved without ascending to a higher level. That we have a duty to serve the interests of the patient, and that we have a duty to respect his rights, can both perhaps be ascertained by consulting our intuitions at the bottom level. But if we ask which duty or which intuition ought to carry the day, we need some means other than intuition, some higher kind of thinking (critical moral thinking) to settle the question between them. And this kind of thinking has also to be brought to bear when we are asking what intuitions we ought to cultivate, or what our duties at the bottom level are (our prima facie duties, as philosophers call them).

2.2 It may help to give an illustration of the difference between the levels, and of its relation to that between the utilitarian and absolutist approaches. A simple case is that of our duty to speak the truth. A common example in the philosophical literature, which goes back to Benjamin Constant's well-known objection to Kant (see Kant 1797), is this: a madman is seeking out a supposed enemy to murder him, and I know where the proposed victim is; do I, if I cannot get away with evasions, tell the truth to the madman? Most of us, as well as the duty to speak the truth, acknowledge a duty to preserve innocent people from murderers, and here the duties are in conflict. An absolutist will have to resolve the conflict by calling one of the duties absolute and assigning some weaker status to the other. Let us suppose that, as some absolutists have, he calls the duty to speak the truth absolute and therefore requires us to sacrifice the life of the victim to it. A utilitarian, by contrast, is likely to say that neither duty is absolute; what we have to do is to decide what would be for the best in the particular case. In this case it will presumably do most good to all concerned, considering their interests impartially, if I tell a lie. But then it is objected that the utilitarian is making a solemn duty, that of truthfulness, of no account; he simply maximizes utility, and might as well not acknowledge any other duties.

The dispute is easily resolved once we distinguish between the levels of moral thinking. At the intuitive level we have these intuitions about duties, and it is a good thing that we do. A wise utilitarian, bringing up his children, would see to it that they developed a conscience which gave them a bad time if they told lies. He would do this because people with such a disposition are much more likely to do, on the whole, what is best than somebody who does cost-benefit analyses on particular occasions; he will not have enough time or information to do them properly, and will probably cook the results to suit his own convenience. Firm moral dispositions have a great utility. So the utilitarian can let the absolutist operate at the intuitive level in much the way that he proposes. But when conflicts arise, or when the question is asked, *what* intuitions we ought to have, or *what* duties we ought to acknowledge, or *what* would be the content of a sound moral education, then intuitive thinking is powerless; for if intuitions conflict or are called into question, it is no use appealing to intuitions to resolve the difficulty, since they will be equally questionable.

A utilitarian can therefore let the absolutists have their say about the intuitive level of thinking, and ask them in return to keep their fingers out of the critical level at which intuitions themselves are being appraised. That the method to be used at the critical level has to dispense with the appeal to intuitions seems on the face of it clear; that there is no other method than the utilitarian which can achieve this is more controversial, though I myself know of no other. But it is at any rate clear that *if* the utilitarian is given the monopoly of the critical level, he can readily explain what happens at the intuitive level; we form, in ourselves and others, for good utilitarian reasons, sound intuitions prescribing duties, and the disposition to feel bad if we go against them; the content of these intuitions is to be selected according to the good or bad consequences of our acquiring them; when they conflict in a particular case, we have to apply utilitarian reasoning and do the best we can in the circumstances; but when the case is clear and there is no conflict, we are likely to do the best by sticking to the intuitions.

2.3 This is not the place to give a full account of these two levels of moral thinking, the intuitive and the critical (1.7, 4.3, 6.4, 10.6, *MT* chs. 2 f.). For our present purposes it will be enough to characterize them briefly. The intuitive level, with its prima facie duties and principles, is the main locus of everyday moral decisions for the psychiatrist as for everybody else. Most of us, when we face a moral question, decide it on the basis of dispositions, habits of thought, moral intuitions (it makes little difference what we call them) which we have absorbed during our earlier upbringing and follow without reflection.

It is sometimes suggested that this is a bad thing, and that we ought to be more reflective in our moral thought even about these everyday decisions. But it is easy to see that this is not so. One of the qualities we look for in a good man is a readiness to do the right thing without hesitation. A man would not, for example, have the virtue of dependability if, when the time came to fulfil some undertaking he had made, he first had to spend some time thinking about whether he ought, after all, to fulfil it. Not only do we seldom have time for such thought (especially if we are doctors); but, if we do engage in it, it is frighteningly easy to deceive ourselves into thinking that the case is a peculiar one in which our ordinary moral principles give the wrong answer, when in fact we would do better to stick to them. Our ingrained moral principles are therefore not merely time-saving rules of thumb, but necessary safeguards against special pleading. On the whole we are more likely to err by abandoning one of these principles than by observing it; for the information necessary in order to be sure that this is a case where the principle gives the wrong answer is seldom available.

Most of us get these sound general principles in the course of our normal upbringing and acquire what is called a conscience, which makes us very uncomfortable if we break them; and this too is a good thing. However, those philosophers are mistaken who think that these moral feelings which we have are by themselves certificates of correctness in the moral judgements which they prompt. For the upbringing which led to our having them might have been misguided; if, in the old South, a typical white felt bad about being friendly with blacks, because he had been brought up to believe in keeping one's distance from them, we should not regard that as a proof that he had a duty to keep his distance, but rather condemn his upbringing. In the medical and other professions the prima facie principles which apply especially to their members have been to some extent made articulate, if not in codes of conduct, at least in the consistent practice of disciplinary bodies like the General Medical Council in Britain and the medical licensing authorities of each State in the USA. But even more obviously in this case it is possible to ask whether the particular practices which at any one time have this official blessing are the right ones.

That is one reason why the intuitive level of moral thinking is not self-sufficient. Another is that the prima facie principles, to be of much use, have to be fairly simple and general, or they could not become second nature, as they have to. This has the consequence that cases can easily arise in which the principles conflict and thus yield no determinate answer. It is good for doctors to strive always to save life, and to strive always to relieve pain; but what if the only way to relieve pain is to kill? Or what if we can save one life only by destroying another? Such cases are the main fuel of controversy in medical ethics.

2.4 For these reasons a full account of moral thinking will include an account of the critical as well as of the intuitive level. The critical level is that at which we select the principles to be used at the intuitive level, and adjudicate between them in cases where they conflict. But how is this to be managed, and how do we know when to engage in critical moral thinking? For, as we implied above, it is sometimes even dangerous to do so.

To answer the first question I should have to survey almost the whole of moral philosophy. Good brief general introductions to ethical method are to be found in the opening chapters of Singer 1979 and Glover 1977. *MT* provides a full-scale account. All I can do here is to state my own view briefly, recognizing that other moral philosophers might not share it. My view is based on an analysis of the moral concepts or words, such as 'ought' and 'wrong', in order to determine clearly, first their meanings; and then, as part of these, their logical properties; and thus, as a consequence of their logical properties, the rules for arguing about questions formulated in terms of these concepts. This is really the only sound basis for an account of moral reasoning. I am perhaps unusual among moral philosophers in insisting that at the critical level no appeal should be allowed to moral intuitions. Such appeals are bound to be viciously circular; for if intuitions are in dispute, no appeal to intuitions could settle the dispute. To this one exception can be made; some of our intuitions are not moral but linguistic or logical, and can be shared by people with the most diverse moral views. Logical intuitions are acquired when we learn our language, not as part of our moral upbringing; they are expressed, not in moral judgements (e.g. that it would be morally wrong to force the patient to submit to treatment), but in statements of logic (e.g. that to say such and such would be to contradict oneself). The failure to distinguish between these two kinds of intuition is one of the main sources of confusion in moral philosophy (*MT* 10 ff.).

It seems to me that it can be established on the basis of logical intuitions alone that whenever we make a moral judgement of the typical or central sort we are prescribing that something be done in all cases of a certain (perhaps minutely specified) kind, i.e. prescribing universally for a given *type* of case. We cannot consistently claim that some particular individual has some duty, but that some other individual, however like the first in his character, circumstances, etc., might not have it (1.6, 7.6, 10.4, 11.5 f.). The thesis that moral judgements represent universal prescriptions can be made the basis of an account of moral reasoning which supports most of our common moral convictions (though it would be quite wrong to quote this fact in support of the account itself—for how are we to know that the moral convictions, implanted in us by our upbringing, are the ones we ought to have?). An example (which is all there is space for) will perhaps help to make clear how this can be done. We most of us accept the principle that it is wrong in general to confine people against their will. If 'wrong' expresses a negative universal prescription, or universal prohibition, this is easy to explain. For then in saying that it is wrong to do this, we are prescribing that it never be done. And the reason why we are ready to prescribe this is that we imagine ourselves in various circumstances in which other people might wish to confine us against our will, and unhesitatingly prescribe that they should not. There are some complications in the logic here which would need to be gone into in a full treatment; but it is not difficult to see intuitively that one who is prepared to prohibit involuntary confinement in all hypothetical cases in which he would be the victim will be prepared to assent to a general prohibition.

2.5 The same kind of reasoning can be used to establish exceptions to the general principle. In some cases the patient, if not confined, is likely to kill some other person. If we put ourselves in the place of this other person, we find ourselves ready to prescribe that the patient *should* be confined. It is a question of balancing the interests of the two parties: presuming that the interest of one in not being killed is greater than that of the other in being at liberty, we shall, if we put ourselves in the places of both in turn and respect their interests impartially, allow the confinement of the patient, because this would promote the greater interest of the other person. So by this means we can build up a set of universal principles, each with the necessary exceptions written into it, to cover all contingencies.

At least, we could do this if we had complete information, superhuman powers of thought, and infinite time at our disposal. Since we are not so endowed, we have to do the best we can to arrive at the conclusions to which such a gifted being would come. That, indeed, is why it is necessary to separate moral thinking into two levels. By doing the best critical thinking of which we are capable, when we have the leisure for it, we may be able to get for ourselves a set of fairly simple, general, prima facie principles for use at the intuitive level, whose prescriptions for particular cases will approximate to those which would be given by a being who had those superhuman powers. This is really the best that in our human circumstances we can do.

In practical terms, what this means is that psychiatrists should, when they have the time, think about the ethics of their profession and try to decide what principles and practices would, on the whole, be for the best for those affected by their actions. In this thinking, they should consider a wide variety of particular cases and think what ought to be done in them, for the greatest good of those affected. And then they should select those principles and practices whose general acceptance would yield the closest approximation to the actions which would be done if all cases were subjected to the same leisured scrutiny. It is important to notice that cases have to be weighted for the likelihood of their occurring. In deciding whether people ought to wear seat belts when driving, we should be more moved by the huge majority of cases in which this increases the chances of survival than by the small minority where this is not the case (see *MT* 47).

2.6 I wish now to take some more particular problems that often face psychiatrists (drawn mainly from the editors' introduction to Bloch and Chodoff 1983, in which this paper first appeared) and ask how this method might be applied to them. We shall, I hope, see that the distinction between the intuitive level of thinking, at which an absolutist stance is appropriate, and the critical level, at which we should rather think in a utilitarian way, enables us to find a path through the philosophical difficulties, and at least pinpoint the empirical, factual questions which we should have to answer in order to solve the practical ones.

I will start with a problem which illustrates especially well the value of the separation of levels: the problem of the medical man's peculiar duty to his *own* patient (4.3). As we saw, it is natural for a psychiatrist to regard himself as owing a special duty to his own patient, to safeguard his welfare—a duty which ought to override any duties he may have to the public at large. If, for example, he has as a patient somebody who he knows will be a great deal of trouble to anybody who is so unwise as to employ him, has he any duty to reveal the fact when asked for a medical certificate? Here, as before, it is obviously no use treating the duty of confidentiality to the patient and the duty of candour to the employer as duties on the same level but ranked in order of priority; for it may depend on the case which duty should have precedence. If the patient is an airline pilot and his condition will cause him to lose control of the plane, we may think the public interest paramount; if he is a bank clerk and is merely going to turn up late to work from time to time, we may think that his condition should be concealed. Other good examples of such conflicts between duties to patients and duties to the public are given by Rappeport in Bloch and Chodoff 1983.

It looks at first as if a utilitarian, who is required to treat everybody's equal interests as of equal weight, can find no room in his system for special duties or loyalties to people standing in special relationships to oneself (e.g. that of patient). And indeed this has often been made the basis of objections to utilitarianism. But the two-level account makes it easy to overcome them. At the critical level of moral thinking we are bound to be impartial between the interests of all those affected by our actions. So at this level, we shall have to give no special edge to our own patients, but simply ask, in each case we consider, what action would produce the best results for all those affected, treated impartially. A superhuman intelligence, given complete information, might be able to provide specifications, in this way, for all cases that could possibly occur. But if this gifted person were asked to draw up some simple ethical principles for the conduct of psychiatrists, which they ought to cultivate as second nature, it is obvious that he would not give them the single principle 'In every case, do what would be in the best interests of all considered impartially'; for mortal psychiatrists are seldom going to know what this is. It is much more likely that the principle to do the best one can for one's own patients will figure among the principles he recommends. Why? Because if psychiatrists absorb this principle as second nature it is much more likely that the interests of all, even considered impartially, will be served than if psychiatrists think they have to do an impartial utilitarian calculation in every case. This is because the relationship between a psychiatrist and his patient, based on mutual trust and confidentiality, has itself immense utility, and the destruction of this relationship is likely, except in extreme and rare instances, to do much more harm than good. So we have the paradoxical result that a utilitarian critical thinker would recommend, on utilitarian grounds, the cultivation of practices which are not themselves overtly utilitarian, but appeal to such notions as the patient's right to confidentiality.

However, this right to confidentiality is not the only right which will be entrenched in the principles of a good psychiatrist. There will be other rights there too, including the right of the public to be protected. All these rights are important; yet they will sometimes conflict. A one-level account of moral thinking based on rights is powerless to deal with such conflicts. The two rights, of the patient to confidentiality and of the public to protection, ought to be respected; but if that is all we say, we can say nothing about cases where one of these rights has to be overridden. In such cases, the psychiatrist will have to do some critical thinking; and it may have different outcomes according to the severity of the impact on the various parties' interests.

2.7 Next, let us take the right to liberty (3.7, 4.4, 9.6, 13.6, 14.2). As we saw, some sort of prohibition, in general, of forcible deprivation of liberty is likely to be part of the moral armoury of nearly everybody, because liberty is something we all value highly. For this reason, the good psychiatrist will be extremely averse to confining anybody against his will unless there is a very strong reason. But sometimes there will be. The right of the public to protection comes in here too. So here too we have the same picture. A superhumanly well-informed critical thinker who had considered all possible cases on utilitarian lines might be able to arrive at the right answer in all of them without saying anything about rights; but if he were asked to draw up a set of principles to be imbibed by mortal psychiatrists, which would lead them in the course of their practices to the nearest approximation to his ideal solutions, he would certainly place high on the list of such principles that which protects people's right to liberty. For to confine people against their will does them, normally, such enormous harm that any psychiatrist who makes light of this principle will be a public menace.

Two particular cases of this kind of problem require special consideration. The first is that of when a psychiatrist may justifiably confine somebody *for his own good* (e.g. to prevent suicide). It is the case that *in general* people who kill themselves are not acting in their own best interests (as is shown by the later thoughts of most of those who have been prevented). However, it may be that some suicides are doing the best for themselves and others (for example, some who face miserable senility and have no close friends or kin). So here too the right to liberty has to be balanced against a duty to preserve the patient from great harm to himself. Both are very important and will be recognized as such by good psychiatrists; and this recognition can be justified on utilitarian grounds at the critical level. But at the intuitive level a psychiatrist will do well to respect *both* these principles without thinking in a utilitarian way at all—until they conflict; and then he will have, perhaps at the cost of a great deal of mental anguish, to think critically and ask what, in these particular circumstances, is for the best.

The other problem is that which arises when the patient is incapable of judging for himself what is in his own interest. This may be because he is a young child, or because he suffers from some mental disability. Our ideal critical thinker would no doubt, in some of the cases he reviewed, come to the conclusion that the best interests of such people would be served if they were treated without their consent. These would be cases in which the patient is unable to grasp the facts of his own case, and in particular facts about the prognoses with and without the treatment. The psychiatrist may be better able to make such prognoses. But it is terribly easy to stray across the boundary between prognosis, on which perhaps he can claim authority, and judgements of value about possible future states of the patient, on which he cannot. Suppose that the patient, if subjected to brain surgery, will become placid and contented, but lose all his artistic flair; but that if he is not, he will remain an artist of genius, which is what he wants to be, but suffer miserably from recurrent depression and perhaps in the end kill himself after enriching the world with some outstanding masterpieces. An exceptionally gifted psychiatrist might be better able than the patient to predict that these would be the respective outcomes of treatment and of no treatment; but that would not give him the authority to override the patient's preference for the second outcome over the first.

Looked at in terms of our two levels, the picture becomes clearer. At the intuitive level, the patient's right to decide for himself what sort of person he wants to be will seem very important; and we can justify at the critical level the entrenchment of this right by pointing out that in the vast majority of cases patients are the best judges of what will in the end suit them, and also that psychiatrists are very subject to the temptation to impose their authority beyond its proper limits, i.e. to stray over the boundary above mentioned. On the other hand we can also justify at the critical level the entrenchment of the duty to preserve patients from the consequences of their inability to grasp what their own future states are likely to be. In most cases there will be no conflict between these principles; but where there is, it can be resolved only by an ascent to the critical level in the particular case. However, there is danger in a too ready ascent; for it is easy to persuade oneself that there is a serious conflict between the principles, when what is really happening is a conflict between the patient's right to liberty and our own propensity to meddle (4.4).

2.8 We may next consider a group of problems about consent, which are closely related to the problem we have just been considering. One of the rights on which great emphasis is properly laid is the right not to be treated without one's own informed consent. The justification, at the critical level, for the emphasis on this right is the same as before, that patients are on the whole the best judges of their own interests, and their interests are normally much more severely affected than anybody else's; so the ideal outcome from the utilitarian point of view is much more likely to be realized if this right is normally allowed to 'trump' any considerations of utility which might seem strong in particular cases (the 'trump' metaphor comes from Dworkin 1977: xv). But if we wish to entrench the right in this way, we have the difficulty on our hands of saying what counts as informed consent. Can people who have neither practised psychiatry, nor actually been in the state which they will get into if not treated, ever be *fully* informed about what they are letting themselves in for? If they are really pretty mad, could they not make crazy choices even if they did grasp the alternative prognoses? And would not this make their refusal of consent not fully informed? These are familiar problems. What our critical thinker will try to do is to find some principles for deciding what criteria of informed consent, if absorbed into the practice of psychiatrists, are likely to lead them in the majority of cases to do what is for the best.

An especially difficult subclass of these problems afflicts psychiatrists who have to deal with patients who are already confined in a mental institution or in prison. In either case the psychiatrist may be in a position to force treatment on patients (for example, aversion therapy or psychotropic drugs); and it has sometimes been thought that this presents an ideal opportunity to do good to the patient (and also serve the public interest) against the patient's will. 'Force' need not mean 'physical force'. If the psychiatrist says to the patient that he is likely to get out much earlier if he submits to the treatment, this is not force in Aristotle's strict sense (1110^a1) of 'that of which the origin is outside [a man], being such that in it the person who acts, or [to be more exact] is acted upon, contributes nothing'; but it is certainly duress, which Aristotle treats of in the next few sentences; the patient is faced with alternatives such that he is highly likely to do what the psychiatrist wants. It has therefore been denied that people in confinement can give meaningful consent, and it has been held, accordingly, that it is always illegitimate to use such treatments on them (3.7, 4.1 ff.). But this doctrine too could lead to less than optimum results if it caused offenders to languish in prison who might, if given suitable drugs, be safely allowed out.

This could be a consequence of the failure to distinguish between our two levels, and a resulting rigidity in the application of the principle guaranteeing the right to freedom of choice to be treated or not treated. The principle is immensely important as a safeguard against abuses; if psychiatrists can break it without a qualm, they are not to be trusted with prisoners or even with patients confined in institutions. But in order to determine the limits of the principle, what is needed is not a lot of casuistry about the precise meaning of 'consent', but a set of practical rules whose general adoption will lead to the best decisions being made on the whole.

One such rule would be to insist on the separation of decisions about confinement or release from decisions about treatment (4.6). In the case of prisoners, decisions to confine would be left to judges, and decisions to release to the civil authorities; decisions about treatment would be the province of the psychiatrist, who, therefore, could only say to the prisoner that he might be able to improve his condition enough to enable the authorities to release him, and not that he (the psychiatrist) would release him if he successfully underwent treatment. Certainly any mixing up of the roles of judge and doctor is likely to have bad consequences; for a decision on medical treatment requires careful observation over a period of an individual patient, which courts cannot undertake; whereas the sentence of a court aims at consistency and fairness between different offenders, and, subject to this, at the protection of the public, and the psychiatrist has neither the experience nor the expertise nor even the habits of mind required for this judicial role. Sound critical thinking would be likely to insist on such a separation of roles, and thus prevent many abuses. But whether this is so or not, the general point stands: *what* rights ought to be enshrined in *what* rules should be decided in the light of the consequences of making those the rules rather than some others.

2.9 Lastly, we may consider a related problem: How are we to decide which conditions are mental diseases and which are merely deviations from the currently accepted social or political norms (3.6 f., 4.5)? This is the problem raised by the political abuse of psychiatry in the Soviet Union. For example, is homosexuality a disease; and if it is, is 'revisionism'? Where do we draw the line? The term 'disease' is above all a ticket giving entry to what has been called 'the sick role'. It is an evaluative term, implying that the person with the disease ought, other things being equal, to be treated in order to remove it. If we classify homosexuality, or 'revisionism', as a disease, what we are doing is subscribing to such an evaluation. So it is no use hoping by mere conceptual analysis to settle the question of whether homosexuality is a disease. We shall call it one if we approve of the treatment of homosexuals to remove their homosexuality (if this is possible); and the same with 'revisionism'. The crucial decision, then, is whether to approve of this. And it should depend on whether the approval, and therefore practice, of treatment to remove homosexuality will on the whole be for the best for the homosexuals and others. Confining ourselves for the moment to voluntary treatment, it would seem that sound critical thinking might arrive at the following principle: if the patient wants not to be a homosexual and asks for treatment because he wants to have sexual relations with the opposite sex, he should be given what he wants; on the other hand, if he wants not to be a homosexual only because of the social stigmas and legal penalties attached to homosexuality, it might be better, if we could, to remove the stigmas and penalties. The reason why critical thinking would arrive at this conclusion is that in the first case the interests of the patient and others are advanced by 'cure', whereas in the second they would be better advanced by the removal of the need for it. If the situation is thus clarified, it becomes less important whether we call the condition a disease or something else.

But if *compulsory* treatment for homosexuality or 'revisionism' comes into question, the right to liberty again becomes of the first importance. Since having things done to one against one's will is something that nobody wants (this is a tautology), it is in itself an evil; it can only be justified by large countervailing gains (e.g. as above, the protection of the public from dangerous mental patients). It is hard to see what these gains could be in the two cases we are now considering. In both of them the general good would be much better advanced by removing the political institutions which make 'revisionism' something that the authorities feel impelled to suppress, or by removing the habits of thought which make people want to persecute homosexuals. It will be better all round for everybody if this comes about.

I have perhaps done enough to indicate in general how problems of these kinds are to be handled. In all cases what we have to do is to find a set of sound principles whose general acceptance and firm implantation in the habits of thought of psychiatrists will lead them to do what is best for their patients and others. In the general run of their professional lives, they need not think like utilitarians; they can cleave to principles expressed in terms of rights and duties and may, if they do this, achieve better the aims that an omniscient utilitarian would prescribe than if they themselves did any utilitarian calculations. But if that is all they do, their thought is still defective; for, first of all, it is a matter for thought what these principles should be; and second, we have to know what to do when they conflict in a particular case. And thought about both these questions will be best directed if it has as a target the good of those affected by the application of the principles.

3

Health

3.1 The concept of health is one the understanding of which would help with both theoretical problems in philosophy and practical problems in medicine. The theoretical problems arise because philosophers, at least since Plato and Aristotle, have used what may be called the medical analogy when discussing morality; they have claimed that expressions such as 'good man' behave in some ways like the expression 'healthy man', and that if we have no difficulty in applying the latter, we should have no more difficulty in applying the former. Thus advocates of descriptivist ethical theories often claim that since 'healthy' is a descriptive concept, so may 'good' be. The obvious reply, for those who reject descriptivism, is to ask whether 'healthy' is purely descriptive either; and that is what I shall be doing in this paper.

That this discussion is of practical importance should be clear to anybody who reflects on the bitter disputes that have been going on recently about what is called 'mental illness'. We have, for example, psychiatrists in the Soviet Union arraigned by their colleagues from other countries for classing as mental illness, and treating by allegedly inhumane methods, what is really only political deviancy (Bloch 1981); and we have 'anti-psychiatrists' like Thomas Szasz (1961) accusing their colleagues even in the West of treating what they call 'mental illness' as if it were the analogue of physical illness, whereas, he says, it is nothing of the kind. We shall never be clear about these disputes until we are clear about the meaning of the term 'illness', whether applied to mental or physical conditions, and about its opposite 'health' and its near synonyms 'disease' and 'disorder'.

But even if we confine ourselves to physical health, there are severe practical problems which would be easier to handle if

From *Journal of Medical Ethics* 12 (1986).

we were clearer about the concept. Take, for example, the treatment of children born with spina bifida, which has been much discussed recently. Spina bifida is in the ordinary sense a disease and I suppose an illness; but what counts as 'treatment', let alone as 'cure' of it? If medicine is the art of healing, how near to normality has the patient to be brought before it can be said that the exercise of the art was justified? And how could we answer that question, without deciding what we mean by 'heal' and therefore by 'health'?

3.2 I will start, as Aristotle used to (he was the son of a doctor), by looking at some of the conceptual difficulties (the symptoms of our ignorance of what we are saying when we call a person healthy). Is health perhaps the absence of disease or illness? But is illness the same thing as disease, and health just the absence of these, or is it something more positive? A patient can have a disease (say diabetes), and yet not be ill if the disease is well controlled. He will *become* ill, if he does not observe the prescribed diet and take the prescribed remedies; but he is not ill now. Also, we say that there are two different diseases, if there are two different causes (for example, when it was discovered that some dysenteries were caused by amoebae and some by bacilli, it was said that there were two different diseases, amoebic and bacillary dysentery); but are there two different illnesses? The whole notion of counting or classifying illnesses, as opposed to diseases, in this way is a bit strange. As we shall see, some philosophers have made more even than this of the difference between the concepts of disease and illness. Professor Boorse (of whom more below) considers the interesting suggestion that illnesses are particulars, diseases universals (1977: 552).

Doctors tend, in fact, to use neither of these words, but the more non-committal word 'condition'. They do this because it is useful to be able to describe the patient's condition without committing oneself about its aetiology, and by saying that he has a certain disease one may so commit oneself. Secondly, not all conditions are pathological, but all diseases are, by definition. If a doctor says that his patient has a certain condition, he does not presuppose that it is a bad condition to be in (the condition might, for example, be pregnancy, both normal and desired). As we shall see, this is very important for our understanding of the concepts.

Not all the conditions treated by doctors are diseases, there-fore. There are even bad conditions which are not diseases, such as injuries and wounds. If I am bitten by a dog and go to the doctor for repair, I am not suffering from a disease (assum-ing that the dog did not carry rabies). The same is true if I am knocked down by a lorry (assuming that I have got over the shock and just require a few stitches). But if it is a virus that has attacked me, I do have a disease.

Why do the attacks of viruses count as diseases, but not the attacks of larger animals or of motor vehicles? Is it just a ques-tion of size? Or of invisibility? I believe that doctors call the attacks of intestinal and other worms diseases, though there are also more precise words like 'infestation'. If I have a tape or a guinea worm (which are quite large), do I have a disease? Does it make a difference if the worm can be seen but its eggs cannot? Or does it make a difference that the worm, although it can eventually be seen, is in some sense, while active, *inside* the patient, whereas dogs and lorries, and also lice and fleas, whose attacks are likewise not called diseases, are always out-side the body? Does a disease have to be something *in* me? And in what sense of 'in'? Some skin diseases such as scabies are so called, although the organisms which cause them are on the surface of the skin, and do not penetrate the body. Is the difference between these organisms and fleas merely one of size? Or of visibility?

Or is it simply that our conceptual classification of these terms grew up before we knew as much about the causes of diseases as we do now? Now, we can actually see viruses and bacilli through microscopes; but the diseases they cause came to be called diseases before we could do this. On the other hand we could always see dogs. So perhaps we use the word 'disease' for conditions whose cause was not visible before the invention of microscopes. We must note, though, that in order to identify a condition as a disease we do not have to *know* what its cause is (think of cancer, for example). But we do have to commit ourselves to there being a cause, ascertainable in principle, of the same general sort as the causes of diseases whose aetiology we understand. Thus the names of diseases are what logicians call 'natural kind' terms (H 1984 = 1989a: 76 ff.).

3.3   Fortunately the puzzle about why dog bites are not diseases does not affect our main problem very much, because, whether they are diseases or not, they can certainly claim the attention and care of doctors. The patient, if he is in the Army, will be 'on the sick list'. However, the puzzle that I am now coming to *is* crucial to our understanding of the role of doctors. Before we classify something as a disease, does it have to be something *bad*? Could there be a wholly beneficial disease, or one which was neither beneficial nor harmful? It seems not. But we have to be careful. If a soldier is prevented by a mild attack of malaria from being sent back to the battle in which he is very likely to be killed, it was in his interest to have the disease. The device which philosophers use for dealing with this complication is called the '*ceteris paribus* clause'. Malaria can be classified as a disease because *other things being equal* or *in general* it is a bad condition to be in; that does not prevent its being a good condition to be in, in this soldier's particular circumstances.

But there are worse complications. Who or what does the disease have to be bad for? Consider the diseases of plants, and in particular of weeds. Let us assume for the sake of argument that the word 'disease' has the same meaning when applied to plants as it has when applied to dumb animals and to man. If I have in my garden a bad infestation of ground elder, and the ground elder plants get a disease and die out, I shall be pleased; so the disease is not a bad thing *for me*. (The same applies if in a battle the *enemy* has an outbreak of disease like the army of Sennacherib, or like the Greeks in front of Troy.) In what sense is the disease a bad thing for the ground elder? Do plants have interests, so that things can be good or bad for them (see H 1987*b* = 1989*b*: 244)? The same problems that afflict the concepts of health and disease afflict also the more general concepts of good and bad; philosophers who discuss these issues are deeply divided, as we shall see.

Conversely, there is a mildew of vines (and mildews are classified in most gardening books as diseases and not as pests) called *pourriture noble*, which actually improves the taste of the wine. Do we rightly call it a disease, because it is bad from the vine's point of view? But does the vine *have* a 'point of view' if it cannot think about the question?

There is said to be a tribe in South America in which the disease of dyschromic spirochetosis, marked by coloured spots on the skin, is so prevalent that it is accepted as normal, and those without the spots are regarded as pathological and excluded from marriage (Sedgwick 1973: 32, citing Mechanic 1968: 26). In that tribe, is dyschromic spirochetosis a disease? Recently I had a painful boil removed from the middle of my back, and the report from the laboratory said that it was caused by an organism which exists normally in the bowel, but if it gets into the bloodstream causes this sort of trouble. So whether this organism is pathogenic seems to depend on where it is. Are we to say that whether the spirochete I have just mentioned is pathogenic depends on whether it is on the skin of a South American Indian of that tribe or on that of a European?

If, frightened by such puzzles, we try to define the notion of disease without bringing in the notions of good and bad, we get into other difficulties. We might try, without mentioning the goodness or badness of the conditions, saying that they were diseases if they had, or were likely to have, certain specified alternative effects. For example, we might say to begin with that a condition is a disease if and only if it has a tendency to cause either pain or death or both. This obviously will not do, because a condition would be called a disease if it had a tendency to cause not pain or death but, say, blindness. It may be said that if a disease causes blindness, it can tend to cause pain or death indirectly, because the blind are more likely to hurt themselves; but this indirect causation is irrelevant to our problem. We do not want to have to say that courage is a disease because it leads to the greater likelihood of being killed in battles.

Perhaps, in view of the blindness example, we should be moved to extend the definition a bit and say that a condition is a disease if it has a tendency to cause *suffering* (which will include pain and other kinds of suffering) or *incapacity* (which will include, as the extreme case, death; for only the dead are totally incapacitated). But then we are on a 'slide'. For what is to count as suffering or incapacity? Can we define *those* notions without bringing in the requirement that to count as an incapacity or as suffering, a condition has to be the cause of some effect which is thought of as *bad*?

Health

I have raised enough problems, in this more or less unsystematic way, to make us think twice before swallowing too easily the arguments of writers like Szasz (1961; see 4.4 below). He says that what has been called 'mental illness' is a 'myth'; physical illness, he says, is an established and acceptable concept, but the concept of mental illness has been invented by a false analogy with it. Szasz's ideas have led some psychiatrists to make drastic alterations in the way they treat patients; but we cannot know whether they are well founded unless we know whether we can share his assurance that the concept of *physical* health is a clear and uncontestable one. I have been trying to cast some doubt on this assurance, not because I think that the concept of physical health is not perfectly viable, but rather because it may well be that, in the process of showing how it is viable, and what its definition should be, we shall discover that the notion of health so characterized is, after all, extensible to include mental health, for all that Szasz says. And that might make a very big difference to the practice of psychiatrists.

3.4 It is time now to be more systematic. I shall achieve this by considering first the approach to this problem of one of the parties to the philosophical dispute, and then, after pointing out some difficulties in this approach, giving my own view of the question, which is favourable to the other party, though with qualifications.

The approach I shall consider rests heavily on the notion of *natural function*. This is supposed to be a purely descriptive notion—i.e. we can, it is claimed, say which functions are natural without committing ourselves as to whether they are good or bad for the organism or for anything or anybody else. Professor Boorse has suggested a definition of 'health' which well expresses this approach (1976: 62 ff.). I cite Boorse's definitions in these earlier papers because they well illustrate our problem. I shall not have room here to discuss his arguments in full detail, nor his later writings, in which he has developed his views in the direction of treating *both* illness *and* disease as purely descriptive concepts, and has defended them further (1981, 1986). But it will be instructive to consider his earlier definitions. They are as follows:

An organism is *healthy* at any moment in proportion as it is not diseased; and a *disease* is a type of internal state of the organism which:

(i) interferes with the performance of some natural function—i.e., some species-typical contribution to survival and reproduction—characteristic of the organism's age; and (ii) is not simply in the nature of the species, i.e. is either atypical of the species or, if typical, mainly due to environmental causes. (Boorse 1976: 62)

He later gives a partial defining characteristic of 'illness' which distinguishes the meaning of this term from that of 'disease':

A disease is an *illness* only if it is serious enough to be incapacitating, and therefore is (i) undesirable for its bearer; (ii) a title to special treatment; and (iii) a valid excuse for normally criticizable behaviour. (ibid. and 1975: 61)

Boorse thus distinguishes 'illness' from 'disease' by including evaluative terms like 'undesirable', 'valid', and 'title' in the definition of the latter. I have already indicated that the two terms are to be distinguished; but I do not agree with Boorse that this can be done by treating 'illness' as evaluative while keeping 'disease' descriptive; for, as I shall argue, 'disease' is evaluative too. But quite apart from this, Boorse's definition of 'health' presents difficulties, of some of which he is aware.

What does 'internal' mean? As we have seen, a skin disease may be in no literal sense *in* (i.e. inside) the organism. It is, indeed, a condition *of* the organism; but this wider description will not bear the weight put upon it by Boorse's definition. Being hung in a noose is also a condition *of* the organism; it, likewise, interferes with species-typical contributions to survival and reproduction. The same is true of the condition of being tarred and feathered, and of being bitten by dogs or run over by lorries. None of these is a disease.

The difficulty is not overcome by clause (ii). If to qualify as a disease malaria has to be 'not simply in the nature of the species', then being tarred and feathered satisfies this condition. And if malaria, though typical, counts as a disease because it is due to environmental causes, then so would being hung. There might be a sense of 'typical' in which malaria was typical but being hung was not; but this would not help Boorse, because then being hung would be 'atypical of the species', and so would not be excluded by clause (ii), and so, if it satisfied clause (i), as it does, would be a disease. We shall return in a moment to these problems about what is species-typical, and shall see that the expression 'environmental causes', like 'internal', is too imprecise to bear any weight. A person is tarred and feathered by other people; he is caused to have skin diseases or malaria by fungi or other organisms; but where precisely is the difference? Boorse has not explained either what he means by 'internal' or what he means by 'environmental causes'.

However, as we saw, such difficulties with the definition of 'disease' are not going to affect the question of whether doctors should be professionally concerned with a condition. Whatever the cause of the condition, and whether it is inside or outside the skin, if it is a condition of the organism, and interferes with some species-typical contribution to survival and reproduction, doctors will be professionally concerned with it.

The expression '*state* of the organism' also presents a difficulty, albeit, perhaps, a somewhat pedantic one: are not some diseases processes rather than states? In so-called functional disorders, for example, there may be no state of the organism which causes the malfunction; there may be just the malfunction. But this difficulty I shall not press; it looks fairly easy to surmount.

Looking again at the numbered criteria (i) and (ii) in the definition of 'disease': they both contain the expressions 'species' and 'typical'. These terms have already given us trouble. What is the species, and what is typical of it? Species are subject to mutations; evolutionary changes occur. Some of the mutations give rise to what are called hereditary diseases; others alter the species, or produce a new strain of it, so as to cause that species or strain to multiply at the expense of others. Bacteria develop resistance to penicillin, and rats to the poison warfarin.

How are we to say which of the changes due to mutations are diseases and which are not? Suppose that the change which makes rats resistant to warfarin is *in itself* (apart from producing this resistance) a minor impediment to reproduction and survival: in an environment free of warfarin, that is, the rats that had not been affected by this change would be more likely to survive than those that had; whereas, of course, if there is warfarin around, the ones that have mutated survive and those that have not are killed by the poison. A somewhat similar situation obtains in the case of sickle-cell anaemia and malaria: if there is malaria around, one is more likely to survive if one has sickle-cell anaemia, but if there is no malaria, those who have sickle-cell anaemia are a bit less likely to survive and reproduce.

Does it depend on the presence or absence of warfarin in the environment whether we say that the rats who have suffered the mutation (if the latter is in itself a minor impediment to reproduction or survival) are the victims of a hereditary disease? In both cases the mutation will be, by definition of 'mutation', atypical of the species. So it will satisfy condition (ii). So if, given the warfarin, the mutation is conducive to survival, but without the warfarin it is inimical, we might think that it does so depend. However, Boorse can escape this difficulty in the same way as we escaped the difficulty about the soldier with malaria. He can say that the mutation is a disease because *other things being equal* it is inimical to survival and reproduction; but the presence of warfarin makes other things not equal.

Another difficulty with the expression 'species-typical' is this: there are certain diseases which *are* typical of certain species. Only elm trees get Dutch elm disease. So, if Boorse had not put in the phrase 'or, if typical, mainly due to environmental causes', he would have been open to the objection that, on his definition, Dutch elm disease would not be a disease, because it *is* typical of that species, or in the nature of that species.

Actually, however, the phrase does not help him out of the difficulty. For it is hard to say what is or is not due to environmental causes. Ultimately, I suppose, everything is. An individual is literally produced by its environment, including, first of all, its parents, i.e. their reproductive mechanisms; secondly the other causes, such as nutrition, water, air, warmth, and so on, which are necessary for its growth and survival. So everything that happens to it is due to environmental causes. What Boorse seems to mean is that, given an already existing individual at a certain stage of its development, changes which are to be called diseases have to be produced by *new* environmental factors at that stage. But even this will not do to make the distinction. Nearly everything that happens to the organism at a given stage in its development is due to an interaction

between the organism and its environment. So Boorse's definition might count as diseases some conditions which are not
diseases. It might also exclude some which are. A hereditary
disease which became apparent, without any further damage
arising from the environment, at a certain age, would not
count as a disease.

A further difficulty is raised by the expression 'characteristic
of the organism's age'. Boorse's purpose in putting this in must
be to avoid the objection that some natural changes, for example the menopause, are inimical to reproduction but are not
diseases. He can get over this difficulty by saying that it is not
characteristic of ages over 50 to bear children, and therefore
the menopause which prevents this is not a disease unless it
occurs at an unusually early age—when no doubt it *would be*
called some kind of pathological sterility, and any condition
which resulted in this would be likely to be called a disease.

The same applies to survival: species have a natural life-
span, and to die what is called a 'natural death' after that span
is over is not disease. But this might be contested. It might be
said that nobody dies literally of old age; we all die of one disease (or injury) or another. So there is no age of which, for
example, breathing, which is a natural function, is not characteristic. Yet it might also be said that it is uncharacteristic for
someone to be breathing at the age of 120, so that a man who
survived to the age of 119 and on his next birthday contracted
pneumonia would not, on Boorse's definition, be entitled to
call it a disease, since it did not interfere with any natural
function characteristic of that organism's age.

Let us, however, waive these subsidiary difficulties in
Boorse's definition, some of which, as we have seen, he might
overcome, and some of which would affect other definitions
besides his—even those which introduced evaluative concepts
like 'bad', as I shall later be doing. We must now come to the
most difficult phrase, 'natural function'. How are we to tell
whether functions are natural or not? Boorse glosses 'some natural function' by the phrase 'some species-typical contribution
to survival and reproduction'. But this will hardly do. There
are some functions which, though natural enough, do not contribute to survival or reproduction. The growing of hair on the
legs seems to be a natural function, and it seems that a condi-

tion which prevented it might, if caused by some organism, be called a disease (though in a moment we shall find reason to qualify this suggestion). But how does hair on the legs contribute to survival or reproduction? I do not believe that the ladies who shave it off find it harder to find boy-friends.

It may be that such a condition would be called a disease by analogy with one causing baldness, which would naturally be so called. But baldness too is not inimical to survival or reproduction. The reason why we call conditions causing it diseases is simply that people do not *like* being bald. It is evident from this example that at least part of the differentia between pathological and non-pathological conditions is that the former do, and the latter do not, result in something *bad* for the sufferer.

Suppose that the genetic engineers developed an organism, guaranteed not to spread from one part of the body to another or to other people, which had this effect of preventing hair growth; and suppose that it came to be sold commercially as a depilatory for use on women's legs. Would we then, or would we not, call the condition which it induced a disease? I suspect that, if we did, we should put quotation marks round the word, and would hesitate to say that the skins of the ladies who used it were not healthy. Doctors would probably not concern themselves with this condition if it were thought *harmless*.

3·5 If it is true that we would call the condition producing baldness a disease, but would hesitate to use this word of the depilatory-induced condition, this may be an indication that the differentia between pathological and non-pathological conditions is the *badness* of the effects of a condition, and not its interference with survival or reproduction, nor with natural function. For in neither example is there interference with survival or reproduction; and in both there is interference with natural function in the ordinary sense of that expression. It is the fact that the ladies want to get rid of their hair, but balding men want to keep theirs, that makes the difference.

There seems, then, to be missing from Boorse's definition of 'disease' as cited, and thus of 'healthy', an element which he did include in his original definition of 'illness': the evaluative element. He is compelled to rely so heavily on the rather wobbly notion of natural function because he wishes to avoid saying that what makes us classify conditions as diseases is that *in general*, though not always in particular cases, they are *bad* things for the patient to have. This in itself is not enough; for otherwise, as we have seen, we should have to call dog bites diseases. But given that the other criteria are satisfied (and I have not been able to give more than hints as to what they are) we seem to classify conditions as diseases if and only if they are bad things for the patient, in general.

At this point it may strike us that one is perhaps being over-ambitious if one thinks that one will be able to capture our understanding of words like 'health' and 'disease' in cut-and-dried definitions. Wittgenstein has made us familiar with the idea that a word may have a spread of meanings; there are a whole lot of conditions for its use, and perhaps none of them is necessary or sufficient. On a particular occasion the word will be understood although one of these conditions is absent. So although, for example, a word like 'disease' is used of humans and of other animals and of plants in the same sense, in a way, yet in another way it is being used in subtly different senses. Understanding its use consists, not in being able to pro-pound a hard-and-fast definition which will work for all cases, but in having learnt to recognize all these conditions, and when they are present or absent in a particular case. Doctors should not need reminding of this, because they will often agree that a patient has, say, dengue, even though one of the common symptoms of that disease is absent, provided that he has the rest.

So I shall not insist that in every case where we call a condition a disease it has to be in general bad for organisms to have it. I shall merely claim that this is one of the standard con-stituents of the notion: a person who did not know that it was would not understand the notion. And this gives the clue to the importance of the concepts of disease and health, which is more than theoretical or academic.

'Bad' is what moral philosophers call a normative or evalua-tive word (I myself often use the term 'prescriptive'). To call a thing bad is to imply that it has qualities which, other things being equal, *ought* to be avoided or remedied in things of the kind in question. If I have bad eyesight, for example, I ought to go to the oculist and he ought to prescribe spectacles if they will make my eyesight better. So if 'illness', 'disease', and 'health' involve standardly the notions of 'good' and 'bad', the classification of conditions as diseases is going to have great practical importance. It will determine what actions we think we ought to take with regard to people who have them. If a person has a disease, and we know, and can remove, its cause, or in other ways cure the disease, then, other things being equal, we ought to do so.

This explains the attraction of the expression 'mental illness'. It came into fashion at a time when people began to be more optimistic about *curing* such conditions, because they thought they were on the way to discovering their *causes*. The present reaction against the notion is due to a disillusion, in certain quarters, about both these dreams. The actions which seemed to be called for, once we had classified certain mental conditions as diseases, turned out to be either unsuccessful in curing them or objectionable for various reasons, or both.

3.6 We can perhaps begin to understand the point at issue between the two sides in this dispute by considering the following form of argument:

(0)   *A* (a person) exhibits observable features $F_1 \ldots F_n$
       So *A* has condition *C*
       But *C* is a disease
       So *A* is not healthy
       But *T* is the treatment most likely to remove *C*
       So *A* ought to be given *T*.

This, it might be thought, gives the form of the inference which all doctors make when they decide what to do to their patients. $F_1 \ldots F_n$ might be, for example, high temperature at two-day intervals, and the presence of a certain organism in the blood; *C* might be malaria; and *T* might be the giving of quinine or one of its more up-to-date successors. The inference then becomes:

(1)   *A* has a high temperature at two-day intervals, etc.
       So *A* has malaria
       But malaria is a disease
       So *A* is not healthy

But giving quinine etc. is the treatment most likely to
   remove the condition
So *A* ought to be given quinine.

But now suppose that we use the same form of argument in
some cases which are not physical but mental 'diseases'. We
then have, for example:

(2)   *A* is at recurrent periods intensely dejected, apathetic,
       wakes early, etc.
      So *A* has depression
      But depression is a (mental) disease
      So *A* is not (mentally) healthy
      But giving tryptazol is the treatment most likely to
         remove the condition
      So *A* ought to be given tryptazol.

This looks all right; and one wonders at first sight what Szasz
and his supporters find to object to in it. We may perhaps be
able to find a clue if we consider, not this example, but some
others which look more dubious:

(3)   *A* is unable to conform to certain expected patterns of
       behaviour
      So *A* has schizophrenia
      But schizophrenia is a (mental) disease
      So *A* is not (mentally) healthy
      But giving ECT is the treatment most likely to remove
         the condition
      So *A* ought to be given ECT.

(4)   *A* is sexually excited only by members of *A*'s own sex
      So *A* is a homosexual
      But homosexuality is a (mental) disease
      So *A* is not (mentally) healthy
      But aversion therapy is the treatment most likely to
         remove the condition
      So *A* ought to be given aversion therapy.

And lastly, for good measure:

(5)   *A* goes round criticizing the regime
      So *A* is a political deviant
      But political deviancy is a (mental) disease
      So *A* is not (mentally) healthy

But confinement in a mental hospital with frequent
doses of apomorphine is the treatment most likely to
remove the condition

So *A* ought to be confined in a mental hospital and
given frequent doses of apomorphine.

Most of us, I suppose, have qualms about (5), and for some
of us these qualms extend successively to (4), (3), and even (2).
We have here another 'slide'. The trouble is that we cannot
find any firm line on which to dig in our heels and stop. Szasz
wants to stop the slide right at the beginning, at the transition
between physical and mental illnesses. If we find this unacceptable, we shall have to look for some other stopping place, and
what is much more difficult, give reasons for stopping there.

3·7 The earlier part of this paper ought to have suggested
to us a factor which, if we pay attention to it, enables us to
stop the slide fairly easily and on good grounds. This is the
evaluative character of the term 'disease' on which I have been
insisting. The third line of each of the above inferences says
that a certain condition is a disease. Supposing that the condition has been descriptively defined by an enumeration of the
observable symptoms which are necessary and/or sufficient
conditions for diagnosing it, this third line will be the first
value-judgement in the inference. It does not follow in strict
logic from the previous lines (which is why I have begun the
third line with 'But' and not with 'So'). We are introducing a
new, independent, and in this case evaluative, premiss.

The important thing to notice is that, when we introduce an
evaluation into an argument, it makes a difference *whose* evaluation it is. In inferences (1), (2), and possibly (3) it is fairly clear
that it is going to be an evaluation made by the patient. It is
the patient who deems it bad that he should be in the condition in question. So those inferences rely on a third step to
which the patient may be presumed to agree, and therefore
their conclusions, given the truth of the factual premisses in
the first and fifth lines (on which the doctor is the authority),
are likely to secure his agreement too.

I say 'are likely to' because the operation of the *ceteris paribus*
clauses mentioned earlier has to be allowed for. If the patient
is a soldier who, if cured, will be sent back to the battlefront

and killed, he may agree that the skin infection he has *is* a disease, because it is *ceteris paribus* and in general bad for people to have; but he may not think the doctors ought to give him whatever would cure it, because this will result in harm to him. In this case, where all are subject to military discipline, it might be held that all have a *military duty* to co-operate in the cure of the disease; but this has nothing to do with the duty of the doctor *qua* doctor, as can be seen by considering a civilian patient with the same disease who for some reason does not want it cured. In that case the doctor would be doing wrong to cure it against the patient's wishes, unless there is a serious danger of harm to others through his infecting them.

There is also the possibility, ignored in the above schematic inferences, that the treatment might have side-effects which the patient did not wish to undergo. Mention of these (perhaps by including them in the fifth premiss) would make this premiss evaluative, if they were specified in evaluative terms. If, on the other hand, they were specified in descriptive terms, we should have to add an additional premiss saying that these side-effects were preferable to the continuance of the condition. In either case, we should have an additional evaluative premiss to which, also, the patient would have to agree if the conclusion were going to follow for him. This complication could be dealt with, but in the interests of simplicity I shall ignore it. It is likely to affect the later inferences more than the earlier, and provides an additional reason for a reluctance to follow them. But the main ground for distinguishing them, and thus stopping the slide, is the evaluative character of the third premiss.

Attention to this evaluation will enable us to differentiate clearly between inferences (5) and (1). The 'patient' in (5) will not agree that political deviancy is a disease, because he will not agree with the evaluation of members of the regime who so label it. So the psychiatrists will be doing wrong to try to 'cure' it against the patient's wishes; it will be a breach of *another* principle, that of political freedom, to which we all attach importance. Inference (1) does not breach this principle, simply because the patient agrees with the evaluation in the third line.

This sheds light on inference (4). If the patient agrees that homosexuality is a bad condition to be in, he may agree that it be labelled a disease; and then, if he takes the doctor's word for the fifth line of the inference, he will agree with its conclusion, and willingly undergo aversion therapy (2.9). But if he does not mind, or even likes, being in that condition, he will not agree, and it will then be an infringement of liberty to make him submit to aversion therapy (see 2.7 and refs.).

A difficulty is presented by the fact that there are two distinct reasons why he may think it a bad condition to be in. One is that he would like to fall in love with members of the opposite sex and detests his abnormality as such. The other is that he suffers social or even legal disabilities because of the condition, and, though he does not in the least mind being a homosexual as such, wants to avoid these disabilities. In the second case his predicament could be made tolerable, without altering the condition, by altering the law or social attitudes. It is a political and moral question, not a medical one, whether this ought not rather to be done. Doctors should be grateful to a philosopher who makes this point clear; for he thus relieves them, *qua* doctors, of the responsibility for answering this moral and political question, while, of course, leaving with them the responsibility which they share with all other citizens for answering it.

Now consider (2). Having clarified the evaluative character of the third line, we see that patients are just as likely to agree to it as they are to the corresponding line in (1), and therefore to welcome the treatment. So we can perhaps, in standard cases where such agreement will be forthcoming, classify (2) with (1).

In inference (3), there is often a difficulty in ascertaining the wishes of the schizophrenic patient; and this makes the case more problematic than (2). In the film *Family Life* (Loach 1972; see Taylor 1972) it was suggested that it was not the patient that made the necessary evaluation, but the patient's parents, backed up by society and its agents the doctors. If that were so, then the liberty of the patient would be being wrongly infringed. But the makers of the film and the anti-psychiatrists who inspired them were hinting that this is *always* the case where ECT and other strenuous treatments are given. I believe this to be a gross exaggeration. Indeed, it has been widely held (see e.g. Wallace 1985) that the latest Mental

Health Act, which was partly motivated by the sort of thoughts which the film aims at engendering, may have gone too far in the direction of protecting individual liberty. It has been suggested that in some cases schizophrenic patients cannot get the help they need because psychiatrists are too reluctant to do anything which would incur a charge of undue interference.

But the main trouble still is that we do not know enough either about schizophrenia (which may not be a single disease at all but a family of diseases), or about the effects of ECT. If we knew more about both these things, we might be able to be more certain about the first and fifth lines in the inference, and thus form a sound judgement about whether the treatment ought to be used in a particular case; these difficulties are the concern of the medical researcher rather than of the philosopher.

3.8 However, one difficulty, already mentioned, would remain. Many mental patients are in no state to give an opinion as to whether their condition is a bad one to be in. In many cases the psychiatrist, if he is to care for the patient at all, cannot avoid judging *on behalf of the patient* whether it is bad. The case resembles that of children. If a child has an incipient but so far not painful disease, his parents and the doctor may rightly begin treatment in the assurance that if the patient knew the facts about what would happen if the treatment were not given, he would agree in accepting the third line and therefore the conclusion of the inference.

It is an attraction of the move I have made that it deals with inference (2), but cannot be extended to inferences (4) and (5), because in those cases, we may presume, the 'patient' already knows all the relevant facts. Case (3) is harder. If we were better informed about the causes and cure (or cures) of schizophrenia, we should at least be able, with more confidence than at present, to set out in factual terms the prospects for the patient, if one or another treatment were used. This would, however, leave us in ignorance as to what the patient would wish done, were he in possession of this information.

I should guess that a great many schizophrenic and other mental patients could, if the information I have postulated were available, give the doctor an idea of what they wanted;

and this should be respected. Cases where this is not so have to be assimilated to those of children. If the patient is unable to form a correct factual picture of his own situation and prospects, there is nothing that the doctor can do, if he is going to care for the patient, but judge, in the light of the patient's situation, what the patient *would* wish if he were able to form such a picture. I stress that by 'factual' I mean 'factual'. It is not within the doctor's province to import his own evaluations into the patient's supposed judgement of his situation.

There is obviously a lot more to be said about this. I have tried only to show, from the point of view of a philosopher, how we might *begin* to handle questions like these. I hope I have said enough to indicate why I think that the wholesale rejection of the concept of mental illness, and of psychiatry with it, was too hasty. Mental health and disease have enough in common with physical health and disease to make them proper fields for the exercise of medical skills. But in order to show this I have had to examine the concepts of health and disease in greater depth than might have been thought necessary—though in fact I have only scratched the surface.

4

Moral Problems about the Control of Behaviour

4.1 Behaviour control, whether voluntary or compulsory, is an area of medical and also of penal practice which rightly arouses much moral discussion, not only in the professions but in the newspapers. It has also been the subject of films such as *A Clockwork Orange*. But it is best to take real cases. Most of mine will come (some of them verbatim) from an excellent paper by Professor David Wexler (1975), delivered at the same conference for which I wrote an earlier version of the present paper.

Here, to set the scene, are some examples. In 1973 a prisoner-patient called *Mackey*, at the California penal institution at Vacaville, was given the drug anectine in connection with a programme of 'aversive treatment' (at least it was so alleged), when he engaged in inappropriate behaviour. 'Anectine is a relaxant drug which induces paralysis and respiratory arrest. It is ordinarily used, together with anaesthesia, as an adjunct to electroconvulsive therapy, in order to minimize the possibility of bone fracture.' If given without anaesthesia (as it allegedly was to Mackey), it produces a sensation of suffocating, or drowning, or of dying. The appeal court ruled that proof of Mackey's allegations could raise 'serious Constitutional questions respecting cruel and unusual punishment' under the Eighth Amendment or of 'impermissible tinkering with the mental processes', presumably in violation of the First Amendment.

In the same year staff at the Iowa Security Medical Facility

Not published before. Revised version of paper given to conference at Reed College, Portland, Oregon, 1975, in reply to paper by David Wexler (*Criminal Law Bulletin* 11, 1975). I am grateful to Professor Wexler and to Research Institute of America, Inc., Warren Gorham Lamont Professional Publishing Division, 210 South St., Boston, Mass. 0211, which holds the copyright in that paper, for giving permission to cite excerpts from it. They reserve all rights in Wexler's paper.

(an institution for the 'criminally insane') administered the drug apomorphine (which induces vomiting) to a prisoner-patient called *Knecht*. According to Wexler, 'armed with blanket orders from physicians, nurses . . . apparently administered the drug whenever they determined—either first hand or through hearsay remarks of other inmates—that institutional codes had been transgressed. Under the Iowa scheme, an incident of swearing could trigger an injection of apomorphine. On those facts, the Eighth Circuit ruled squarely that the administration of apomorphine without the informed consent of a patient contravenes the constitutional proscription against cruel and unusual punishments.' But it held 'that the drug could be constitutionally administered to *consenting* patients, so long as each injection was authorized by a physician, and . . . so long as the rule violation was witnessed personally by a staff member'.

Also in the same year there was a decision in Michigan which disallowed the performance of experimental psychosurgery on involuntarily confined patients. The plaintiff was called *Kaimowitz*. The ground of the decision was that consent was lacking, because the patient was neither competent to give it, being 'too affected by the "institutionalization syndrome" to be able to competently make the serious and complex decision to undergo psychosurgery', nor informed, because the outcome of the proposed operation was profoundly uncertain, nor was the operation voluntary, because 'the lure of possible release from the institution [was] so powerful that it would coerce patients into consenting'. Wexler, in my view rightly, holds that the decision of the court was correct, but that the grounds given for it were much too wide, and that the notion of consent needs much more careful definition in such contexts.

Among other forms of behaviour control in American institutions which have attracted attention are the so-called ' "token economies"—where patients earn tokens for appropriate behaviour, and are then permitted to cash the tokens in to purchase desired items or events; and "tier systems"—where privileges increase hierarchically and where patients are promoted or elevated to higher tiers upon engaging in appropriate behavior'. These 'often involve severe states of *deprivation*, which in effect force patients to earn their way to improved living conditions'.

Shortly after the cases I have mentioned, there was a juicy scandal concerning a State retardation training centre in Florida. 'The abuses, reported by the press (and confirmed by a blue-ribbon Resident Abuse Investigating Committee) included, among many other things, forced public masturbation and forced public homosexual acts as punishment for engaging in proscribed sexual behaviour, beatings with a wooden panel for running away, and washing the mouth with soap for lying, for abusive or vulgar language, or sometimes for speaking at all. Further, food, sleep and visitation privileges were withheld as punishment; incontinence was punished by requiring residents to lie in soiled sheets and to hold soiled underwear to their noses; a resident accused of theft was addressed by staff and residents as "The Thief" and was required to wear a sign so designating him; and one boy was required to walk around publicly clothed only in female underpants. . . . The incidents were carried out by staff members, who recorded them in great detail in well-kept records, with the encouragement, or at least the acquiescence, of the Chief Psychologist (who held a Ph.D. degree, though not in psychology). Moreover, the Committee believed the participants to be generally well-meaning and hard-working, and attributed the problem generally to an unscrutinized and unsupervised system run by poorly trained personnel.'

4.2 I have perhaps said enough to illustrate the nature of the questions we need to ask. The scandal in Florida led to the setting up of a Task Force, on which Wexler served, to draw up a set of psychological and legal principles for the appropriate use of behavioural procedures in State facilities for the retarded. The Task Force consisted of psychologists and lawyers. They had, obviously, two different methods at their disposal for preventing such abuses. The first Wexler calls the 'administrative model'. It consists in adopting certain administrative procedures *within* institutions, laying down what those in charge of patients may or may not do. The second he calls the 'judicial model'. It consists in enacting state laws binding upon all those in such positions, so that aggrieved patients can sue them if they think their rights have been infringed, or even cause criminal charges to be brought against them. The Task Force had to decide what mixture of these two methods to recommend. It actually inclined more towards the administrative model, recommending the setting up of two committees: a Peer Review Committee composed of highly regarded professionals in applied behaviour analysis, and a Committee on Legal and Ethical Protection, consisting of one professional, one lawyer, and informed laymen. All proposed procedures would have to be sanctioned by both these committees in general terms, and the more intrusive procedures in individual cases. I shall be commenting later on the merits of these two models.

In all the cases I have mentioned, the discussion has been couched to a great extent in terms of the *rights* of the people subjected to these procedures. I see no harm in this, provided that we have some idea of how to decide *what* rights ought to be preserved to them (see H 1989*b*: 79-147, *MT* ch. 9, and Sumner 1987). I deprecate, however, a decision-procedure which relies on ever vaguer analogies between proposed rights and already acknowledged rights. This kind of creeping extension of a right which in its narrow interpretation can well be defended is particularly evident with the so-called 'right to privacy'; it seems sometimes as if this right could, if we so wished, be extended to prohibit doing anything to anybody that we wished to prohibit. We need to know whether the alleged analogies between one case and another of this supposed right really will bear the weight that is being placed on them; and no secure way is given of deciding this.

4.3 I am going, therefore, to start afresh and discuss how the method of argument that I have advocated (*MT*, H 1976, and 1.6 ff. above) might help to decide such questions. It allows us to have general principles, enshrined in the law and enforceable in the courts, some of them safeguarding the rights of patients. It also allows us to have general administrative procedures laying down what doctors and others may or may not do. And it allows us to establish *moral* guidelines for them, so that it is not merely a matter of following the right procedures, but of developing the kinds of attitudes to their patients and their work that they ought to have. But the criterion for the choices of all these things—laws, administrative procedures, and moral attitudes—is: Which would most further the interests, all in all, of all those affected, treated impartially?

Any decision, in a case such as those Wexler considers, is going to affect the interests of a number of people. We have, say, a prisoner-patient who, it is thought, might be improved in his behaviour by the use of some kind of behaviour therapy, perhaps to such an extent that he could safely be released earlier than would otherwise be the case. Here we have to consider the interests, first, of the prisoner himself; secondly, of the staff in the prison in which he is confined, and of the other prisoners; thirdly, those of the people outside the prison whom he may harm (or help) when he gets out; fourthly, those of members of the public who may be harmed, not by him, but by others like him if the law is not enforced strictly enough to deter law-breakers; and fifthly, those of taxpayers who meet the costs of penal institutions. And no doubt there are other interests too; but those are the most important. We have to do the best we can for them all, giving equal interests equal weight, as impartiality requires.

This obviously complex problem can be simplified a little if we make use of an idea mentioned already (1.7), that it would be unwise to try to work out every individual case in complete detail. Although, so far as the medical aspects go, doctors do approach this ideal, even they have guidelines, and when it comes to the moral aspects such guidelines are also required. It is in connection with these guidelines that words like 'just', 'fair', and our old friend 'rights' are often used (because principles of justice and principles determining rights are among the general principles which any viable society will have to incorporate in the structure of its moral thinking). In moral matters the guidelines have to be firm, or there will be all sorts of special pleading; it is not a question of mere 'rules of thumb' (an expression which ought never to have been introduced into this discussion) but of deeply ingrained convictions, to err against which excites the strongest compunction (see *MT* 38, H 1988: 223).

Such intuitive principles, however admirable in general, will conflict with one another in particular cases. For this reason among others, a structure of such principles cannot be self-supporting but needs a more fundamental kind of moral thinking to sort out these conflicts. Another principle, especially relevant here, is that requiring a scrupulous devotion by doctors to their own patients (2.6). It is for the best that such a principle should be given a high priority by doctors, including prison psychiatrists, for otherwise patients will be less well looked after. The case of the patient in prison is no different in this respect from that of the patient outside. The interests of the patient are likely to be more affected than those of any other single individual, and that is why they are so important. Doctors in general tend to give extra weight to the interests of their own patients, just as parents tend to give extra weight to those of their own children; and this is a good thing, for the same reason in both cases, namely that the acceptance of this principle by doctors and parents leads, all in all, to patients and children being looked after better. If they all felt equal obligations to everybody else's patients and children, it is likely that the obligations would prove so daunting that none of them would be attended to and the patients and children would suffer more from neglect than they do now.

There is therefore only an apparent conflict between this principle and that mentioned earlier of giving equal interests equal weight. Paradoxically, a careful moral thinker who was selecting the best general principles for the conduct of doctors and parents, and was himself giving equal interests equal weight, would select a principle that the doctors and parents should *not* give equal interests equal weight. Himself impartial, he would recommend partiality, because only thus can the interests of those whom he has impartially at heart be best served. The solution of this paradox, as of many others, depends on the distinction between these two levels of moral thinking (1.7, 6.4, 10.6, *MT* 135–40).

Among the other general principles that he would select would be principles of justice. Because these may conflict with that of partiality to one's own patient, which we have just been considering, society, understanding the importance of both, has wisely assigned to different classes of people the safeguarding of the different principles (2.8). Doctors are charged with looking after the interests of their patients; judges and their instruments the prison administrators are charged with the preservation of justice, and also of order. Our present problem arises partly because of a blurring of these distinctions of role. But even if they are not blurred, the difficulty will remain of so demarcating the roles of the two classes of people, in a viable system, that the best overall situation will be achieved (that is, the situation nearest to what would be achieved if some omniscient being were to direct our actions so as to secure the greatest possible realization of the interests of all, treating equal interests as of equal weight).

4.4 It is because of the importance of seeking to serve the interests of the patient in all the doctor does that *consent* is thought to be required for medical treatment (2.7, 9.6, 13.6). The ordinary patient is thought to be able, after his condition has been explained to him, to decide for himself whether a proposed treatment and its predicted results are in his interests. This is, no doubt, an oversimplification, because, unless the patient is himself a doctor, he is unlikely to be able to understand all the details of the prognosis. So what he is consenting to is not a treatment whose precise consequences he can accurately and reliably foresee (even the doctor cannot often do that); rather, the patient, in giving consent, is backing his own judgement as to the professional skill of the doctor, a judgement based on past experience and on what the patient *can* understand about his present case.

It may be objected that the doctor might know better than the patient himself what was in the patient's true interest. I suppose that in theory he might (I return shortly to the question of what 'interest' means); but I also believe that in practice giving additional powers to doctors (especially of the more self-confident kind) to override the consent requirement in the case of competent patients would not conduce to the interests of patients in general (2.8). This opinion is based, not on an intuition about the rights of patients, but on (I hope) a shrewd observation of what goes on in the medical world.

In this relatively simple, ordinary case, both the patient and the doctor are presumed to be seeking the interest of the patient (which normally lies in recovering from his illness or at least preserving his life or his freedom from pain; the controversy about euthanasia, however, reminds us that even this is a nest of problems (1.5, H 1975)). I shall not have room to go fully into the problem of how it is to be determined what *is* in a person's interest. This is a complex function of his preferences, actual and hypothetical. A rough approximation would be to say that what is in his interest is what he would prefer if he were fully informed about his preferences in actual and possible situations, and about the probability of these situations occurring, and gave no priority to present over future desires. This might be summed up by saying that it is what he would desire if he were perfectly prudent (*MT* 105, H 1988: 217).

The best way of tackling our present problem will be to ask how the cases we are considering differ from the ordinary case, and in how many different dimensions, and what moral difference this makes. First of all, the ordinary patient is competent to give consent, but some of the patients we are considering may not be. Secondly, the ordinary patient I have been speaking of is a free man, whereas some of the cases we are considering are cases of patients confined in, or threatened with confinement in, institutions of various sorts. Thirdly, the ordinary patient has, say, appendicitis, whereas the patient we are concerned with may have any of a wide range of what (*pace* Szasz, 1961) are called mental illnesses, or manifest other deviancies, some of which are called criminal and some merely objectionable in other ways to either the patient or other people (3.6 f.). And fourthly, the patient, or subject, or whatever we are to call him, may or may not have been found guilty by a court and sentenced to some legal penalty involving confinement in a prison. If we multiply all these dimensions together, we shall obviously get a very large number of possible cases, probably approaching a hundred, depending on precisely how one does the classification. And the matter is made worse by the fact that what I have represented as simple dichotomies are in fact not that at all: in each dimension there are many gradations which shade into one another—take for example the question, raised by Szasz, of whether so-called voluntary mental patients really are voluntary.

4·5 Perhaps the simplest way of dealing with these complexities will be to take the distinctions one by one, and see whether each, taken by itself, makes a moral difference. It does not follow that if we were thereafter to put them together the result would be a simple function of the conclusions we reach about them separately; but even our simplified procedure will be quite complex enough. Take first the distinction between competent and non-competent patients. Since the reason for requiring consent is to protect the patient, we must, in cases where the patient is not competent to give or withhold consent, do our poor best (and it is a second best) to achieve the same end by some other means. I agree with what Wexler says is the prevailing view that 'the patient may be subjected to certain procedures if it is determined . . . that less onerous alternative therapies are or have been unsuitable and that, in an anticipated cost-benefit sense, the proposed procedure is in the best interest of the patient'. So the absence of competence to give consent does not exactly make a moral difference to the decision that ought to be taken; it makes a difference to the method of taking it, since one method (simply asking the patient whether he consents) is not available.

What difference does it make if the patient is not a free man? There is a prior question of when it is right to take away people's freedom, if ever. Let us assume for the sake of argument that it is all right to confine in prison people who have offended against laws which impose the penalty of imprisonment for their breach (on the justification of punishment in general, see H 1986). And let us also assume that non-criminals who, because of their mental condition, are likely to harm others by outbreaks of violent and irrational aggression, may also rightly be confined. Even Szasz might agree to this. The difficult cases are ones where people are confined in their own interest, for example to stop them committing suicide. It sometimes is in people's interest to be prevented from killing themselves; sometimes they are very thankful that they were prevented.

Suppose, then, that the patient is rightly confined. What difference does that make to the moral question? It certainly puts more power into the hands of the psychiatrist, which *could* be power for good (the patient's good). To what extent is it right to use this extra power? I have already to some extent answered this question by implication in what I have said about consent. If the patient is competent to give consent, his consent must be sought, even if he is confined, because that is the best way of protecting his interest. If he is not competent, then we have to do the best we can to safeguard his interest. That he is confined makes no difference to this; it simply makes the question more important, because what we can do to him is more far-reaching. I agree with Wexler that confinement in itself does not remove competence.

Next, does the difference between physical ailments and so-called mental illnesses make any difference? It seems to me highly probable that all mental illnesses, and indeed all mental states whatever, have a physical correlate, and that with the advance of physiology we shall ultimately be able to find out what this is. This makes no difference at all to the necessity for deciding moral questions (it is a simple mistake to suppose that predictability of mental processes by physiological means is incompatible with the 'freedom of the will' that is necessary before we can judge acts morally—see 13.2 ff.). But it does, if true, to some extent cut the ground from under Szasz's feet (for how is he going to maintain his position that so-called mental illnesses are not real illnesses because they have no physical correlate?). There is this much of truth, though, in what Szasz says: some deviant patterns of behaviour like homosexuality have been classified as illnesses simply because the behaviour was contrary to the current mores, and 'therapy' has been practised on the deviants in order to get them to conform (3.6 ff.). It certainly needs to be asked when, if ever, this is legitimate. This can be admitted even by somebody who thinks that there really are some mental illnesses, as I do.

If the patient can give consent, and is a free man, the question is not so difficult. His interest, which is paramount, demands that treatment not be given without his consent. But what if he *wants* the treatment? Suppose, for example, that he has a potentially happy heterosexual marriage, and his homosexual tendencies are in danger of ruining it. Why should he not seek the assistance of the behaviour therapist? On the other hand, if the patient is quite content to be a homosexual, his interest is not going to be advanced by compelling him to undergo treatment which will change him into a heterosexual (assuming such treatment to be possible). The position is analogous to that of the person who has misshapen and therefore ugly, but otherwise healthy teeth: if he *wants* to have them extracted and a set of false teeth substituted, then the dentist should do it; but if he prefers his own teeth, no dentist would want to force him to have them out.

To justify forcible treatment in the homosexual case, it

would have to be shown that, if it were not given, *other people's* interests would suffer, and to an extent which more than balanced any harm to the patient's interests. But suppose that the homosexual is especially attracted to young children, and cannot keep away from them, and suppose that this does the children great harm. Or, since this is disputed, let us change the example and suppose that what his deviancy makes him do is not rape children but murder them. Then even Szasz might agree that this would be a justification for doing *something* to him by force, even if it is only confining him (2.8).

4.6   At this point we have to face the fourth of the distinctions I mentioned: that between people who have been found guilty and sentenced to imprisonment by a court, and those who have not. The law very strictly regulates compulsory confinement of non-criminals. The justification for this is that it would be very much against the interests of people at large if they could be locked up, other than in emergencies, without legal recourse. If the law did not protect us in this way, we should all go in fear of being locked up at the whim of policemen or psychiatrists.

But after someone is put into confinement, what can legitimately be done to him? Here it does make a great difference whether he has been imprisoned as a penalty for a crime, or certified and confined as mad. If he is a criminal, the question arises, and has to have been settled by the legislature, of how rigorous the imprisonment is to be. This is largely independent of psychiatric questions. It depends on one's theory of punishment. I am myself a utilitarian on this question as on others (H 1986); I think that penalties ought to be no more severe than is necessary to attain the ends of punishment. These ends are complex (they go beyond mere deterrence), and can be summed up by saying that the purpose of punishment is to maintain the rule of law, in the public interest.

In the United States, unlike Britain, the scale of punishments is limited by the Constitution: punishments are not allowed to be 'cruel or unusual'. But this does not make much difference in practice; for, first of all, the British Parliament is unlikely to impose penalties which the general public thinks barbarous, and, secondly, the phrase 'cruel or unusual' has been interpreted so flexibly that it has come to mean little

more than 'what offends current enlightened public opinion'.
Thus capital punishment, which has been usual from time
immemorial, may *become* 'cruel or unusual' if enough people
start to be squeamish about it. I too am against it, but I like to
have reasons for my attitudes.

Given, however, a certain degree of rigour in prison conditions as laid down by the legislature, what can a prison psychiatrist legitimately do? Can he legitimately do any more to a
convicted offender than he could to a certified madman? I
think the answer is, when the question is rightly understood,
'No'. Both are the patients of the psychiatrist. He should be
concerned with *their* interests, for the reasons I have given.
Punishment is not his job; punishment and treatment should
be kept separate, and psychiatrists are not judges, nor legislators, nor prison officers. They have their own job to do, which
is to serve the interests of their patients (2.6). And judges, legislators, and prison officers are not psychiatrists. It is not their
business, nor do they have the expertise, to prescribe a method
of treatment (2.8).

I will try to amplify these remarks, and show how this division of labour is justified by my general theory, which is based
on doing the best to serve people's interests, that is, to satisfy
their preferences or (as Kant might put it) further their ends. I
have said already that we shall all go in fear, and our interests
will therefore be severely damaged, if confinement can be
imposed otherwise than as strictly regulated by law. The same
applies to the punishments that may be imposed on us once
we are behind bars. It is a very important feature of good laws
that their operation is predictable, so that we know where we
stand. What was most objectionable about old-fashioned
despotisms of the Arabian-Nights sort, in which one could be
hauled up in front of the Grand Vizier and sentenced to
absolutely anything, was that it greatly increased anxiety,
which is one of the most tormenting of mental states. That is
why I say that the legislature and the courts, following a consistent practice, and not psychiatrists following their own opinions about particular cases, should determine penalties.

On the other hand, judges and legislators do not examine
criminals medically (on a couch or off it). Nor can they follow
their progress and modify the treatment accordingly. They are,

moreover, properly concerned for the public good and therefore for justice (which is necessary for the public good), more
than for the good of the person in the dock. The psychiatrist,
on the other hand, is properly concerned for the good of his
patient. What, then, are psychiatrists doing in prisons? They
are there to do what they are there to do everywhere else: to
look after their patients medically, in the patients' interests. But
the fact that their patients are convicted prisoners makes a
difference to those interests. To begin with, the prisoner will
normally have a strong interest in getting out of prison as soon
as possible, and in becoming the sort of person who will not
be put back in again. So it is in his interest if the psychiatrist
can alter his behaviour in a way which will make possible his
earlier release and make recidivism less likely.

4.7 A perhaps extreme example will illustrate this. Dr
Stürup, the Danish psychiatrist (1968), has carried out castra-
tions of sexually violent offenders with this sort of motive.
Although Danish law at the time allowed compulsory castration of some sexual offenders, it was not under this law that he
proceeded. Nor did he even say to patients at his hospital at
Herstedvester 'Allow me to castrate you, or you won't get out
for years'. Castration, he says, was never made a condition of
release. Instead, he tried to explain to patients the probable
prognoses, given the alternative courses of castration and non-
castration; and, just as with any other therapeutic choice, the
patient and the doctor decided between them what was best
for the patient.

I am not going to pronounce on the medical aspects of this,
which will certainly have been altered by the discovery of new
chemical treatments. I am not qualified to say whether castration is in fact likely to help people avoid repetition of sexual
crimes, as Dr Stürup thinks is true in selected cases. I wish
merely to draw a parallel between that therapy and the case of
non-surgical behaviour therapy. I would think it wrong to
make it one of the legal penalties, to be inflicted by courts for
violent crime, to be subjected to behaviour therapy. Judges, as
we saw, are not doctors, and do not have the medical knowledge to decide when this should be done and when not, nor
are expert witnesses likely, in many cases, to have the time to
examine the prisoner and inform the judge on such matters.

And certainly the legislature is not a doctor, and cannot lay down in the laws what conditions are to incur this penalty and what are not. It seems to me that legislators and judges act rightly in confining certain offenders so that they cannot go on harming others. Given that the confinement is legitimate, the question then arises of what can be done for the good of the patient. It then becomes a medical question. If a certain course of treatment is likely to make it safe to release the patient sooner than he would otherwise be released, then it seems sensible to say to the patient that this is so, and seek his consent to the treatment, and, if it is successful, to release him. If he is in an ordinary prison, release will have to be at the discretion of the usual authorities, though the law might usefully be altered to give them greater flexibility. If the patient is confined 'at Her Majesty's pleasure' in a psychiatric prison such as Broadmoor, the release is administratively easier.

But I would follow Dr Stürup's practice in *not* saying to the patient 'Have the therapy or else you'll be in here a long time'. Do doctors say to patients 'Have this leg amputated or you'll be in for some excruciating pain and you'll lose it in the end anyway'? Doctors do not, and should not talk like that. They should be concerned for the good of their patients, seeking to know their mind as much as possible, and giving them as much information as they can understand. There may not seem to be much difference between saying the things I mentioned just now, and saying 'If you want to find the best way of getting out and staying out, I am here to advise and help you', or 'If you want to find the best way of getting around, with or without an artificial leg, I am here to advise and help you'. It may be thought that it comes to the same thing. But the point is that in one case the doctor presents himself as the agent of society and makes a threat to the patient, whereas in the other he presents himself as the patient's doctor and offers to help him choose a course which will be for the best in the circumstances in which he is placed—placed by society, not by the doctor, and rightly so placed because of what he will do to others if he is not. This way of putting it has the advantage that the compulsion involved is not imposed by the doctor, and can be clearly seen not to be imposed by him; it is society which confines the prisoner, and the doctor who is trying to get him out if he chooses what the doctor thinks is a possible way.

But such treatments (if they exist) ought not to be imposed without the prisoner's consent, if he is competent to give it; nor ought they to be imposed as a punishment, nor indeed for any other reason than the interest of the patient. For a prison psychiatrist to do otherwise would undermine the whole basis of the doctor–patient relationship; and on the maintenance of this all therapy depends, so that, if therapy is in the interest of patients, the relationship has to be maintained.

4.8 What then of the difference between offenders confined in prisons and mental patients confined in hospitals? To begin with, the psychiatrist treating the latter lacks certain means which psychiatrists in prisons have. The psychiatrist in a prison has a patient who is suffering a punishment imposed by the court in accordance with the law, involving loss of liberty and various rigours which free persons do not have to put up with. If the psychiatrist is allowed to use the remission of some of these rigours as a reinforcer, that increases his armament. I see no harm in this; but I do see harm, for the reasons I gave earlier, in the imposition *by the psychiatrist* of additional rigours simply in order that their possible removal may be used as a reinforcer. It is for the legislature and the courts to fix the maximum severity of the penalty to which the offender is to be subjected.

The psychiatrist treating in a mental institution someone who has broken no law does not have, and should not have, this weapon, because the possession of it would imply that the people in these institutions were being punished, which they are not. It is very much in the general interest not to blur the distinction between criminals and non-criminals. In the interests of the patients conditions in mental institutions should be as comfortable as the competing interests of those who pay for those institutions will allow. Given a reasonably generous policy on the part of these latter, and sensible rules about the extent to which patients can be required to work for their keep (and why should they not, like the rest of us?), the base-line above which the incentives of the psychiatrist start to operate will be higher than it is in a prison. But he, like the prison psychiatrist, can offer earlier release as an incentive to undergo the treatment.

I agree with Wexler (1975) that the use of the promise of release in order to secure the co-operation of the patient in the treatment does not invalidate consent. All our choices are between alternatives presented to us by the situations in which we find ourselves; and it is usually the case that many of the features of the situations are the results of the actions of others. My contract to buy a house is not invalidated by the fact that the vendor said he would not sell it for less than £100,000, and that I therefore had to choose between agreeing to pay that price and not getting the house. The prisoner, or for that matter the mental patient in a non-penal institution, is in a certain situation. The first is in it because of his own unwisdom in breaking the law; the second is in it because of his misfortune in having a mental condition which made his confinement necessary for his own or the public's safety. The psychiatrist did not impose the situation on the prisoner; he may have imposed it on the mental patient, but he had, let us hope, adequate reasons for imposing it (subject to legal restrictions), which did *not* include the intention of using the promise of release as an incentive to the patient to undergo therapy. Anyway, the patient is in both cases in a given situation, and the psychiatrist says to him that if he submits to a certain treatment it may make it possible to ameliorate the situation. This no more invalidates the consent than a promise of marriage is invalidated because the girl said to the boy that she would not go to bed with him unless he promised to marry her. The boy was in the unfortunate position of being overcome with unrequited love for the girl, and she said that she would ameliorate his situation only if he co-operated by making the promise; but we do not say that the promise was therefore made under duress and therefore invalid.

4.9 The last question I shall have room to deal with is that raised by Wexler (1975), of whether the regulation of psychiatric practice in prisons and mental institutions should be done by the courts or administratively. I think I agree with Wexler in the suggestions he makes, and with his reasons for them. These suggestions really amount to a division of the roles of courts and administrators along the lines that I have been following in this paper. The law, as Aristotle said, speaks generally (1137^{b}20); and courts are suited to enforcing general rules laid down by the legislature or established by precedent, and unfitted to adapt specific therapeutic measures to particular cases. They are also unable to act quickly, or to modify treatment in the light of changed circumstances. The individual psychiatrist, on the other hand, can act quickly and flexibly according to the needs of the individual patient, but, as shown by the cases we started with, needs general guidance and control. There is therefore a place, in between the rigidity of court procedures and the specificity of individual treatments, for an administrative system which will regulate the latter while keeping within the rule of law enforced by the former (to which, of course, there has to be an appeal in cases of abuse).

I will end by summing up the method of this paper, to show how its conclusions have been reached. We started from a formal ethical theory about the right method of moral reasoning, drawn from my other writings and indirectly from Kant and the utilitarians. From this theory we elicited a system of moral reasoning requiring us to give equal weight to the equal interests of all parties affected. We then saw that for the implementation of such reasoning in practice it was necessary to have general and firmly held principles, themselves selected by thought at a higher level and of a more specific sort, in order impartially to safeguard, to the greatest degree possible, the interests of all. We saw that these principles will be of different kinds; two of these kinds are, respectively, those which impose on doctors the duty of looking after their patients, and those which impose on courts the preservation of justice and order. We noticed that our present problem arises out of the difficulty of disentangling these roles when dealing with individual patients or prisoners, and of resolving conflicts between the two sorts of principles. By carefully considering various distinctions between cases, we tried to effect such a resolution. Our conclusions are all based on the attempt to serve impartially the interests or ends of the parties affected, treating equal interests as of equal weight, as the logic of the moral concepts requires us to do.

5

Possible People

5.1 Can we have duties to people who will never actually exist? That the answer is 'No' has seemed obvious to many writers. I shall be arguing to the contrary that, where we have a choice between bringing someone into existence and not doing so, the interests of that possible person have to be considered. The question has an obvious relevance to such topics as abortion, embryo experimentation, and above all population policy, which will be the main subject of this paper. I discuss the other two topics on similar lines elsewhere in this volume.

It is clear that, for a utilitarian of the older sort who puts his theory in terms of maximizing happiness, the interests of possible people have to be considered; for, other things being equal, to bring into being such people, given that they will be happy, increases the sum of happiness. It is not so clear that the same is true for a version of the sort that is nowadays more commonly favoured, which interprets the utility that has to be maximized as the satisfaction of preferences. For it might be held that if the people in question do not yet exist, they have no preferences yet which we could have a duty to satisfy. I do not myself accept this view, for reasons which will become apparent when I have shown how the contrary view follows from the deeper theory about moral reasoning that I have advocated in *MT*. And whether or not this theory be accepted, it certainly looks as if, by bringing into being people who, when in being, will have preferences which are satisfied, we do increase preference-satisfaction (6.1 ff., 7.9, 8.6, 10.4, 11.3).

Nor is this a problem only for utilitarians. Derek Parfit (1986), from whom I have obviously learnt so much, argues, not on a utilitarian basis, but on the basis of intuitions which many people have. As we shall see in a moment when I outline his argument, it could be taken in two ways. If we accept the intuitions, it could be used to support his 'Repugnant Conclusion'. But it could be used, instead, as a *reductio ad absurdum* of the intuitions themselves.

In any case, the view for which I shall be arguing is not directly contrary to his. For the basis of his argument is only that, for any given population with a given quality of life, it is possible to *conceive* of a higher population with a lower quality of life that is compensated for by the increased numbers enjoying it. By pursuing this line of thought, we can *conceive* of a population vastly increased in size, but with a quality of life for all barely above the level at which life is just worth living. This huge population, by the same sort of compensation, would be as a whole better off than the smaller population we started with.

I do not wish to dispute this. I shall be arguing, rather, that *in practice* enough disutilities would be created by the transition to this end-state, and by the circumstances that would then obtain, to cancel the balance of advantage. The conclusion which most people find repugnant is one about what we ought now to do in our actual situation. To distinguish this conclusion from Parfit's, I shall call it 'the Counter-intuitive Conclusion (CC)'. It is, that we ought now to take steps to increase the population until the end-state, which I have just agreed is conceivable, is actually realized. And when the question is what we ought to do, the distinction between what is conceivable and what is practicable is of the highest importance.

The kind of utilitarianism that I have advocated provides a defensible answer to this practical problem about population policy, as to so many others. But I shall have room only to hint at it, and to show at least that the problem creates in principle no difficulty for a properly formulated utilitarianism. So the first thing to do will be to distinguish various versions of the utilitarian doctrine, and see how the problem is supposed to arise. One way of dividing up kinds of utilitarianism is according to the class of people, or beings, whose utility is to be considered. This may be held to include all sentient beings, or all humans, or all of some more limited class of humans, such as those capable of having a concept of their own self-interest. The distinction I have in mind is of this general sort. It divides up versions of utilitarianism into those which take into account the utility of all people or sentient beings, whether or not they have or will have actual existence, and those which take into account only that of those people or sentient beings who do or will have actual existence. For short, let us call the first class 'all possible people' and the second class 'all actual people'. The class of those who are or will be possible but not actual let us call 'merely possible people'.

To give an example of what this means: suppose that my wife and I are trying to decide whether to have another child: any child that we might have has no actual existence now, nor will it ever have if we decide not to have any more children: it will then be, or have been, a merely possible person. As is well known, the kind of utilitarianism called *total* utilitarianism bids us take into account the utility of this possible person in making our decision, because any utility which it has will add to the total, and therefore the failure to produce this child may make the total less. On the other hand, the kind of utilitarianism called *average* utilitarianism bids us take into account utilities to possible people only to the extent that they would affect the average utility per life lived. So if the addition of this child to the population, although the child itself gets some positive utility, diminishes the average utility because its utility is less than the pre-existing average, we have a duty not to produce it, according to average utilitarianism (10.7, H 1973: 244 ff. = 1989*e*: 166).

It is also generally accepted that there is a difference in the prescriptions generated by average and total utilitarianism only in cases where the prescriptions are about bringing into being, or not bringing into being, new persons who would not otherwise have existed. There has been a lot of discussion of this dispute. People have argued for average and against total utilitarianism on the ground that total utilitarianism would give us a duty to increase population to an enormous extent—one which our intuitions do indeed find repugnant. It is easy to understand why people who enjoy a relatively high standard of living should find this counter-intuitive, if it required them to increase the world population until everyone was reduced to the standard of living of the average Indian villager, provided only that the increased numbers of people who enjoyed this decreased average utility were enough to make the total utility greater than it is now.

5.2 I shall go into this problem in greater detail later, and shall try to relate it to our actual circumstances in this world as it is, and not to deal with it in terms of abstract population diagrams as is sometimes done. As we shall see, this may lead us to solutions which escape those who view it only in abstract terms. But first I want to shed more light on the argument by saying why I, in particular, think myself committed by my ethical theory (see *MT*) to the total version of utilitarianism. I am going to explain this, not in terms of utility at all, because that is a difficult concept to handle, but in terms of the underlying ethical theory which bids us ask what universal prescriptions we are prepared to assent to, or in other words what we prefer should happen universally, not giving particular attention to the role that we ourselves are actually to play in the resulting course of events. I hope to show that this Kantian method, like the version of utilitarianism that I have based on it (15.2 and refs., H 1993*a*), constrains us to give equal weight to the equal preferences of all possible people, whether they are actual or merely possible. Am I then faced with the allegedly counter-intuitive consequences which allegedly follow?

I will start with some points which I also discuss briefly in 6.2, 10.4 ff., and 11.4. But I will put the points entirely in terms of preferences and prescriptions. First, let me ask whether I prefer being, myself, in existence to not being in existence. In other words, given the power to prescribe existence or non-existence for myself, which do I prescribe? Here there is a danger to be avoided. We shall confuse the issue if we allow into it any thought of the 'fear of death' which we all have. This fear is something which we have had built into us by evolution: genes producing a normal amount of this fear had a greater chance of survival than either genes eliminating it altogether or genes imparting such disproportionate amounts of it that their bearers would not on occasion sacrifice their lives to save several carriers of the same gene.

All this, however, is irrelevant to our question, because the so-called 'fear of death' is a fear of *dying*, or, usually, of *being killed*. By contrast, what I am asking is, not whether I prefer remaining alive to dying or being killed, but whether I prefer existing now to never having existed. Since if I had never existed I could not die, the fear of death does not enter into the question, though it is extremely hard to prevent ourselves being irrelevantly influenced by it.

Some people argue that, once this irrelevancy is put aside, the question itself vanishes. Their reason for saying this is that, since it is impossible for me to *compare* my existence with my non-existence (for I do not know what it is like not to exist), I cannot form any preference between them. Though this argument has been popular, it goes too far (10.8, 11.4). Most of us are thankful for our existence; and what one can be thankful for must surely be something which one prefers to its absence. I am not suggesting that existence is *in itself* a benefit, but only that it is, for those who enjoy life, beneficial as a necessary condition of this.

Suppose that we dramatize the argument by imagining that we can timelessly prescribe to our fathers and mothers, or to God, whether to bring us (or to have brought us) into existence (6.2, 10.4, 11.4). My claim is that, if we have greater than zero happiness (if our lives are at least just worth living) we shall all so prescribe. Here a difficulty arises about the notion of timeless prescription. It is analogous to the notion, which has been thought to create difficulty for my theory, of past-tense prescriptions. I cannot avoid either difficulty, because I want to say that moral judgements are *universal* prescriptions, and time-references, such as a restriction to present and future times, cannot occur in universal sentences as I define 'universal'. Any universal prescription will have some past-tense implicates or logical consequences; and this is indeed in accordance with our ordinary use of words like 'ought' and 'wrong': we say that someone ought *to have* done something, and that what he actually did *was* wrong. If my theory could not deal with such locutions, it would not be a starter.

I must say that this problem does not cause me any loss of sleep (see *LM* 187 ff., H 1979*b*). I have never claimed that moral judgements are just like ordinary imperatives, which are confined to the future tense. In extending the range of moral prescriptions to cover present and past times, we are merely saying that, if certain things are or were being done, they are or were breaches of the prescription; and I have no difficulty in understanding this. But I shall not have room to go into this here. Assuming for the sake of argument that there can be universal (and therefore tenseless) and past-tense prescriptions, shall we not most of us (that is, those who are glad that we exist) prescribe that God or our fathers and mothers should have brought us into existence? In other words, do we not *prefer* that they should have?

The universalizability of moral judgements, to which I am committed, requires us to extend this prescription to all similar cases. If, therefore, we are looking for universal prescriptions to cover all procreation-decisions, we shall have to disregard entirely the fact that we ourselves occupy the roles that we do. The principles we adopt will have to cover the procreation of anybody. Can we restrict this by saying that they have to cover only the procreation of people who are actually procreated (that is of actual people)? I think not, for reasons which I have given in *MT* 114 f. Actuality is a property which cannot be defined without bringing in references to individuals, and therefore no such restriction can occur in a properly universal prescription. Or, to use an alternative argument (ibid.), any attempt to discriminate morally between actual and possible cases when making moral judgements will run counter to our linguistic intuitions, which allow no such discrimination. If one makes a moral judgement about an actual case, one is committed to making the same judgement about a possible case having the same universal properties.

I have been trying to show why my theory commits me to the view that there can be duties to merely possible people; I shall be defending this view later. Note that I am not required by my theory to accept duties to all possible people whatever their characteristics, or whatever the world is like. I am not, for example, required, when discussing what I ought to do in actual situations, to ask how my actions would affect a possible person who had skin so light-sensitive that drawing back the curtains would be torment to him. I only have to consider the effects of my actions on people who would thereby be affected (including people who would come into existence) in the world as it is. In other words, I have to consider what the consequences of my actions actually would be; but these consequences might include the bringing into existence of a person who otherwise would not exist; and this I have to consider.

It seems to me to follow from all this that, in considering

whether to bring a new person into existence, I have to look at the question as if I were going to be that person, or as if that person were going to be myself. So it would be relevant what, for that person, it would be like to exist; and, of course, what, for him, it would be like not to exist. Granted, I can form no idea of what the second state of affairs would be like *for him.* For it would not be like anything for him. The nearest comparison, perhaps, is with being totally unconscious. But if the first state of affairs—that is to say, his existence—would be moderately agreeable for him, then it seems to me that I am constrained by universalizability to treat this fact as just as relevant to my moral thinking as a similar fact about my own actual existence; and we have seen that most of us have reason to be thankful for our own actual existence.

If, when seeking to maximize preference-satisfactions, I give equal weight to the preferences of such possible people, am I then forced to embrace CC? I am going in what follows to use the word 'utility' instead of the more cumbrous 'satisfaction of preferences'; but it is to be understood in the light of what I have been saying. The argument for CC goes as follows. Let us imagine a world population of a given size (call it *x* people), enjoying an average utility *a*; and call this world the *A* world. If *a* is substantially above the level at which life is just worth living, it will always be possible to imagine another world *B* in which the *average* utility is *b* (where *b* is less than *a*), but in which the *total* utility is greater, because the population (call it *y*) has increased to compensate. So it is *theoretically* always possible to increase total utility by increasing total population sufficiently, even if the effect is to reduce average utility to near zero, provided only that it is positive (i.e. to produce a state in which on average the members of the population only just prefer existence to non-existence). Each of them may have extremely little to be thankful for, but between them they have more to be thankful for than the inhabitants of world *A*. According to CC we have a duty to try to bring about this state (call it *Z*) by increasing the population vastly (6.3, 10.7, 11.8).

5·3 I have several arguments against CC. Most of them depend on asking how, in practice, one could get from world *A* to world *Z* without thereby introducing more disutility than

would be compensated for by the increased utility. But first let
me suggest an argument which does not depend, or not so
much, on practical considerations. Let us imagine we are actually living in the lap of luxury (as, relatively speaking, I and
most of my readers are). Even so, it will be open to us, if we
want to resist CC, to do so by claiming that on average even
our life is only just above the critical point at which we stop
preferring to exist. This claim will appear at first sight absurd;
but I hope to deepen our understanding of what is valuable
and not valuable in life by asking what truth there is in it, and
by how much our life would have to deteriorate before the
claim became not absurd at all.

In Britain one of our greatest blessings is abundance of
space to move around in. Americans, Australians, and many
other peoples are, indeed, more fortunate still; and so, in *this*
respect if not in many others, are the inhabitants of the
Sahara. I myself do value tremendously my liberty to walk in
the English countryside on public footpaths, or in the national
and other parks when in America.

Now it might come to be the case, and probably will, that
by intensive methods, not of animal husbandry (for I do not
mind in the least going without meat—see 15.1 ff.) but of crop-
production, the countryside can be dispensed with; all our food
can be grown in factories in a very small space. Then an enormous increase in population will become possible within a
given area. I have heard it said that, allowing one square
metre ground area per person, the entire present population of
the world could be accommodated within the state of
Delaware. At such a density, America or Australia, or even
Britain, could hold an astronomical population, by becoming
one vast city with people living in tower blocks so designed
and placed as to give them just sufficient light and air for their
physical health (a series of huge *Unités-d'Habitation*). It is open
to us to say that, if that happened, existence would not be
worth having. And there are other things that make us value
space; one is the ability to get away from our neighbours.
Even in the case of seagulls, who cram themselves into an
available habitat, an increase in numbers beyond a certain
point leads to outbreaks of aggression; and there are mechanisms, genetically implanted, which prevent this happening,

mostly to do with the preservation by each mating pair of its own territory. The same sort of thing happens with many species, and I suspect that it happens with humans.

So, if a proponent of CC is going to topple the opposition, he will have to get the opposition to accept that life really will be worth living in world Z. And it is difficult to see how he is going to do this. What makes our life worth living is a very difficult thing to decide, and something that everyone has to decide for himself. I will give examples from my own experience. The times at which I have been unhappiest were not times at which I was materially ill-provided for—quite the reverse. They were times at which I had been bereaved, or at which one or other of my children was doing things I was sure they would regret. At such times I even got near wishing that I did not exist.

But, more to the point, when I was a prisoner of war in the Far East (15.1), the conditions under which we lived could be divided into two phases. In one of them we lived in camps in Singapore, having malaria from time to time, and so little to eat that when I got out I put on 30 pounds in a month to get back to my pre-war normal weight of 150 pounds. Our calorie intake was well below the internationally accepted minimum. But we did grow vegetables (otherwise we should have actually starved), and had interesting and pleasant talk with one another; indeed, we got on very well with one another in the group I was lucky to belong to. The Japanese left us more or less to ourselves and the climate was ideal. So, although I would *prefer*, if I had to live by subsistence horticulture, to be a smallholder in, say, Malaya or Jamaica, I could not possibly claim that our life was not worth living. On the other hand, during the time when we were working as slaves on the Burma Railway, I would claim this, apart from the hope of eventually getting out that sustained us. I think that, faced with the prospect of such an existence prolonged throughout my life, I would prefer not to exist. But it is hard to be sure.

What does this show us? I think it shows that there is a limit below which non-existence becomes preferable, and that it is a highly subjective matter where this limit will lie for any particular person. I am not sure that the proponents of CC will find it easy, if they limit themselves to considering states of life which are concretely possible, to secure agreement that the average level of utility which we have a duty to go down to by increasing the population is so low as to make the conclusion all that counter-intuitive.

To take my own case: if the proponent of CC says that by my own confession I am compelled to agree that we have a duty to increase the population until we are all in the condition of the prisoners in Singapore with our vegetable gardens, but not until we are in that of those on the Burma Railway, I may reply that I do not necessarily find *that* conclusion so repugnant (this is because I have experienced both conditions), but that I cannot speak for other people, who have not had the experience, and perhaps find it impossible even to imagine it, and if they did experience it might react to it very differently from me. I know that many of my fellow-prisoners did react very differently.

To put the point in a somewhat more sophisticated way: everyone has his (or her) own scale of preferences, and it will differ from person to person how great a decline in material conditions is required to bring them to the break-even point above which life is just worth living. This enables a determined opponent of CC to claim that so far as he is concerned they cannot decline very much before he reaches this point, and to claim further that there are enough people like him to soften, at least, its counter-intuitiveness. However, I should not be content with this argument. Its weakness, like that of the original argument which it seeks to refute, is that it looks at things in too static terms. It considers possible *states* of the world, but does not consider the *process of transition* between them, which may have its own disutilities.

5.4 It is true in general that the thing that causes us most distress is the transition from a relatively happy to a relatively unhappy state of life. When I was put into prison, that was terrible, even though it was a relief not to be being shot at any longer in that most unpleasant and demoralizing battle. But once I was in the bag and got used to it, it was not so bad. By contrast, the day on which it became certain that we would be released was one of the happiest days of my life. The proponent of CC has the problem of showing that the *transition* to Z will not introduce disutilities that will more than cancel out the improved total utility in the state itself once achieved. Suppose that one could introduce state Z just by waving a wand, and everybody at once forgot what they had been before, then it would be easier; but history does not operate like that.

It will not do to say, as some do, that, by assuming a sufficiently *gradual* transition, the disutility of the transition itself can be made to vanish. For, since people will still be able to compare their state with that of the Golden Age several generations before, they will regret the transition, and that will cause them pain. And, secondly, the gradualization of the process of transition will have the effect that the achievement of state Z will be postponed into such a remote and unpredictable future as no longer to be a sensible object of policy. This is relevant, if the question facing us is what we ought to be actually doing now.

Still, let us suppose the next best thing. Suppose that we are able, by starting now, to put all our children born from now on into training centres, or even just to treat them rough at home, so that, by continuing this process for the many generations which will in any case be needed to bring population up to the desired level, we shall eventually get our descendants of many generations hence well acclimatized to the new conditions. Even this process may generate some disutilities: we have to find a way, for example, of preventing there being a highly acrimonious generation gap, as the children come to envy the standard of living of their parents which they, the children, are never going to be allowed to reach. Here again, however, I find myself inclined to say that *if* it were possible, and the children were well prepared, I do not find the conclusion necessarily counter-intuitive. People have found happiness in communes and monasteries approximating to the conditions we are envisaging. What most repels me about such a suggestion is something I have not mentioned yet: we should be taking away the possibility of people leading *different* lives from each other (as it was to a large extent taken away from us in Singapore, because we all had to do much the same things in order to survive). If allowance is made for this, perhaps we shall be led, in order to avoid intolerable uniformity in society and make possible the variety of life-styles which is the spice of our existence, to raise the level of the break-even point a bit.

5.5 However, the most powerful argument against CC is yet to come. Consider again world *A*. I said that the *average* utility over the whole of its population was *a*. But how was this utility distributed? I have given reasons elsewhere (14.1, H 1978, *MT* ch. 9) for saying that, with a given population and a given amount of material wealth, the distribution of the wealth that maximized utility would be moderately but not absolutely equal. The reasons why it would be moderately equal had to do with diminishing marginal utility and with the disutility of occasioning envy. The reasons why it would not be absolutely equal were also the usual ones: principally the need for incentives to get people to give of their best; and also the value to society of having some people who are well enough off to turn around and do things which benefit society in general, like practising and supporting the arts, but which could not be done by everybody in a society unless it were pretty affluent.

It is of course going to be irrelevant to the present argument to say that if the society *were* affluent enough, everybody in it could equally be in a position to perform this function, and so wealth could be distributed equally. It will be irrelevant, because we are precisely discussing a change to a very much less affluent society in which this will not be so. The first effect of the change from the world *A* to world *Z* would be to destroy this possibility of equally distributed affluence, and impose on us the necessity of either allowing some privileges or else forgoing the flowers of civilization. Whatever may happen in the future, neither Renaissance Italy nor fifth-century Athens would have been possible without gross inequalities.

Let us suppose, then, leaving this irrelevant consideration on one side, that in world *A* wealth (and therefore utility, though the two have of course to be distinguished) is, to some moderate, though not enormous, extent, unequally distributed. Let us then examine the transition to world *Z*. It can come about in two ways. In world *Z* average utility *z* is just enough to make life worth living. But this says nothing about the distribution of the utility. So it is possible either (1) to have an equal distribution in world *Z*, or (2) to have an unequal distribution. In the latter case a lot of people's lives will not be worth living. Let us consider this possibility first. What is going to be the effect on society of containing these submerged members?

If they are rational and overcome the fear of death, they will all commit suicide. But this will be bad for the proponent of CC, because it will reduce the population again, just when he has been at such pains to increase it. He increased it to increase utility; but a side-effect was to produce a lot of people who had so much disutility in their lives that they chose to opt out: so the level of utility was only restored by undoing his work. In practice, no doubt, the disutility of the suicide process would be considerable, involving as it would overcoming the fear of death. So he would have done better not to produce these people in the first place. But if he resolves not to produce them, then he has the problem of how to raise the population to the optimum, at the cost of decreasing average utility to the minimum level that just makes life worth living, without thereby producing a lot of people who are below this level.

More probably the people below the line will rebel if they are able. That will land us in a civil war, whose disutility will take away all our gains. If the war results in the institution of an absolutely equal society, that will be a reversion to case (1), which we shall be looking at in a moment. If, as is more likely, it merely results in a redistribution of inequalities, so that again our society has a submerged portion (only with different people in it) which is below the level at which life is just worth living, we shall be back at square one, and the process will begin all over again. If the better off manage to institute repressive measures to prevent those below the line from rebelling, the disutility of the measures both to the repressed and to their oppressors will be great; we shall in fact have a slave society, the disutility of which I hope I have demonstrated in H 1979*a*. Note that, even independently of the present argument, the juxtaposition of penury and wealth is going to create great disutilities from various kinds of disaffection; so that the length to which we can take CC is again greatly reduced.

The upshot is that any attempt to increase utility by increasing population to the point at which the average life is just worth living will founder, unless the distribution of utility in the new society is absolutely equal; if it is not, those who fall below the break-even point will cause enough trouble, one way or another, to cancel out the gains. So the possibility of actually realizing the utopia of CC will depend on creating a society in which everybody has an absolutely equal share of the utility, at the minimal level just above the break-even point. Extreme egalitarians will be pleased with this result; but that is not the point at issue. Before they become too pleased, I want to show that this outcome is of no use to the proponent of CC.

Forgetting for a moment about population increases, consider first a population of fixed size. There must be a distribution, whether equal or more or less unequal, at which utility is maximized (I neglect for simplicity the possibility of alternative maxima). Any attempt to make the distribution more equal than this will lessen average, and also total, utility (assuming, as we are, a fixed population). Suppose that in our world *A* this ideal distribution has been realized, and that we then go on to consider the further question of whether the population should be increased in order to increase total utility, in the way that CC prescribes. But if the distribution was optimal before the increase in population, this cannot be done by having greater equality. It can only be done by lowering the average but retaining the existing more or less unequal distribution. So, if we go on increasing the population by steps, at the same time decreasing the average utility but increasing the total utility, the point will eventually be reached at which the lowest segment of the population has lives not worth living. This is the limit to the process, because, as we saw, the existence of any substantial number of people in this condition will produce disutilities (mass suicide, rebellion, or slavery) which will cancel out the gains.

I have no wish to suggest that this limit will be reached at anywhere near present standards of affluence. The proponents of CC could well insist that, given greater equality than we have at the moment, the population could be increased substantially without producing these dire results. It is true that the other obstacles in the way of CC that I mentioned earlier will have to be taken account of, and their effect will be to raise the level that we shall reach, in our process of increasing population and decreasing average utility, before we get to the point at which disutilities start to cancel out the gains. But, leaving that aside, how are we to calculate this limit? I am no mathematician, so I cannot do it in detail and exactly; and in any case it depends on many imponderable factors about people's preferences. But I should guess that, given that the inequalities which are inevitable in any viable economy are quite large (no Eastern European country, nor even Maoist China, has got anywhere near absolute equality), and given the other factors I have mentioned, the conclusion we reach is not going to be nearly so counter-intuitive as has been thought.

5.6 What it comes to, in the simplest terms, is this. If we start off with a society which is unequal and affluent and has a small population, we ought, according to my version of utilitarianism, first to get an optimal (i.e. utility-maximizing) distribution among the existing population of the utility which either exists or can be generated by that population. After we have done that, we have to increase the population, thereby diminishing the average but increasing the total utility, without altering its proportionate distribution, except in so far as the optimal distribution becomes different with a different average. We should go on doing this until we reach the point at which the lowest segment of the population comes below the break-even point at which life is just worth living. Then we shall have to stop. Given the inequalities which remain, this will leave the rest of the society's members above this point, and no doubt in many cases well above.

But now we come to the crunch. Consider our existing society in Britain or America or Australia. It is, needless to say, still pretty unequal. There are probably good utilitarian arguments for reducing inequalities further. How much further is a point on which there will be political disagreements, with extreme right-wingers saying that we have gone far enough, or even too far, and extreme left-wingers saying that we have hardly begun. Into these disputes I shall not enter. But if we take a middle-of-the-road position on this, is it not bound, even with our present affluence, to leave quite a lot of people who, whether from poverty or from some other cause, have lives barely worth living? I have suggested already that poverty is not the chief cause of misery. There are certainly many such people at the moment; attempts to help them by welfare state methods have not been very successful; I do not myself believe that those or any other methods will cause there no longer to be such a segment of our population. It is a most intractable

problem. Their existence is a great disutility not only to themselves but also to society as a whole, which has to do its best to
look after them. Might it not be argued, therefore, that we
have reached the limit already: if we increase the population
and decrease the average affluence, we shall inevitably be
increasing the proportion of our population which is below the
line?

That is probably too extreme a view. I could envisage some,
perhaps a considerable, increase of population in Britain or
America or Australia which would not create an intolerable
problem of poverty for some, because the distribution in those
societies remains very unequal, and if inequalities were
reduced a bit, the numbers could with advantage go up. But
once that had been done, the scope for increased population
would probably be rather small, and CC would not after all be
so counter-intuitive. It would be simply what any moderate
egalitarian who wanted to make best use of the available
resources would wish us to do.

In conclusion, I must add that for the sake of brevity I have
made two gross oversimplifications. First, I have been confining myself to the position in Britain, America, and Australia.
Obviously any thorough examination of the problem would
have to look at the world as a whole. But then we should have
to go into the extremely intractable problem of the just distribution of wealth between nations, about which I said a very
little, but not enough, in *MT* ch. 11. Secondly, although at the
beginning I spoke of sentient creatures, I have thereafter considered only the population of humans. A defensible population policy would have to take account of the interests of
sentient non-human animals. But to formulate this, we should
have to make very difficult judgements about the relative quality of life of humans and other animals in the circumstances
that alternative policies would produce. This problem I
thought too intractable for brief discussion in this paper (15.6,
H 1987*b*). It could be that leaving room for the right numbers
of animals in each species, whatever those are, would reduce
the amount of land available for humans. I have no wish to
make light of these difficulties; but I think that my treatment
of the problem within the limits of single countries and of the
human species has done something to show that CC, as an

argument against total utilitarianism, is not very powerful. And, since CC and similar arguments are often used in discussions of our duties to foetuses and embryos, it is helpful to show that utilitarian approaches to those issues are not successfully impugned by it.

6

When does Potentiality Count?

6.1 This paper started life as a comment on a highly original, provocative and clear paper by Michael Lockwood (1988). In it, he addressed the question, raised by the reports of the Warnock and of several other committees (7.7 ff., 8.4), of what it is morally legitimate to do, or to allow to be done, to embryos. After some criticism of other views, he gave his own solution. This is to find a point, or at least rough boundary in time, after which it becomes possible to say that the embryo or the foetus has interests, and therefore rights, and that therefore we have duties towards it. He finds this point at the stage at which the embryo develops an at least rudimentary brain. His argument can be summarized, I hope not too unfairly, as follows.

(a) 'Moral claims and rights are . . . grounded in individual *interests*' (1988: 199). But

(b) 'A potential for X generates an interest only where there is some individual for whom the development of the potential for X constitutes a *benefit*?' (ibid.). So

(c) 'Faced with a fourteen-day-old human embryo, with the potential for developing into a human person, the question we must ask is: Does there now exist any individual for whom the development of this potential would constitute a direct benefit?' (1988: 200).

Lockwood answers, in the case of an early embryo, that there does not. His reason turns on a claim that such an embryo is not *identical* with the person who will be born if the embryo survives, and who will normally enjoy the benefits which existence makes possible.

He supports this claim of non-identity with a highly sophisti-cated metaphysical argument which boils down to this: a con-dition of identity between persons is possession of the same brain:

(d) '. . . considerations of identity firmly favour the view that before the brain has matured to the point of being able to sustain psychological functions, a human life has yet to begin . . . If this is right, then the potential of a human embryo for developing into a Person does not confer on it any right to protection. For it has no brain at all. Consequently, that which would stand to benefit by the development of this potential *does not yet exist* . . . Briefly put, it is potential plus identity that normally counts for something, here. Bare potential counts for nothing, except perhaps in impersonal terms—as an opportunity for worthwhile life. It generates no moral claims or rights' (1988: 207 f.; all italics are Lockwood's).

In scrutinizing this argument, it will be clearest to start with two apparently simple but actually fundamental logical points about tenses and moods. Between (b) and (c) above there are two important changes which Lockwood does not appear to have noticed: from 'there is' to 'Does there now exist?' and from 'constitutes' to 'would constitute'. The second of these is clearly correct, for two reasons. First, if what we are speaking of is potential, it cannot be the case that the development of the potential constitutes a benefit *now*. If the benefit were present now, it would be actual not potential; the potential is the possibility (*potentia* is derived from *posse*) that its development will, or would under favourable conditions, occur in the future (on potentiality, see also 5.1 and refs.).

Secondly, the benefits that Lockwood is thinking of are those referred to in the preceding paragraph, and listed on his p. 197: 'the ability to converse, self-reflective awareness, the power of rational deliberation and so forth'. These, he says, 'give normal human life its special worth'. To them we could add some benefits that are not specifically human, such as companionship with others, a vigorous and active life, and so on. Embryos cannot *now* have these benefits, as Lockwood would no doubt agree; they are benefits that the person into whom the embryo would under favourable conditions turn would have (11.4). But it is important to notice that what I have just said about the embryo could also be truly said about the foetus or even the neonate. None of these entities can have any of these benefits now, even if equipped with a brain. This creates difficulties for Lockwood's solution. For that consists in making a distinction between embryos on the one hand and foetuses with brains and infants on the other. The former, he says, cannot have interests, but the latter can. But if the first passage cited is taken as it stands, none of them can have interests.

So we have at least to recast Lockwood's sentence (b) cited above to read:

(b') A potential for X generates an interest only where there is some individual for whom the development of the potential *would constitute* a benefit.

But we have next to ask whether the step is legitimate from 'there is' to 'Does there now exist?'. 'There is' is often tense-less, like the 'There is an *x* such that' of quantificational logic. In expressions like 'There is an *x* such that F*x*', the 'F*x*' may or may not contain a tense, but the 'There is an *x* such that' does not have to contain one as well. This is evident in ordinary language too: it is perfectly natural to say (in August) 'There are three dates in October on which it will be possible for you to give your talk'. To say 'There will be three dates . . .' would be incorrect, because it would imply that at some future time unspecified there will *still* be three dates, which is not the meaning intended. The timetable may fill up.

We have to ask, therefore, whether in the first passage cited the 'there is' is tensed or tenseless. It would seem that in order to make the statement true it has to be tenseless. For it is pos-sible for there to be an individual who *would* benefit, even though that individual (the individual who will enjoy the benefits listed by Lockwood and the ones we have added to his list) does not now exist. Let us suppose that we are talking about this individual even before there is the corresponding embryo—say when it is only a gleam in its parents' eyes. Sup-pose that they are rich and have no child, and (having read the parable of the rich fool in St Luke 12) are worried about who will benefit from their wealth after they are dead. They may still comfort themselves by saying 'But there is someone who would benefit, namely the child that we hope to have'.

6.2 This point appears to have escaped the attention of many who write on this subject, and so it will be worth rub-bing in. The potentiality of the embryo to develop into someone who can enjoy the listed benefits (let us say for short 'into a grown person') is important just because, if it does, that grown person will benefit. The benefit is not to the embryo. Nor is it to the foetus or even the neonate. The preservation of embryos, foetuses, and neonates is important just because if they are preserved they will turn into grown people who will benefit from existing (not indeed because bare existence in itself is a benefit, but because in normal circumstances those who exist can have *other* benefits like those listed).

This is clear if we consider cases where the possibility of development into such a grown person is removed. Lockwood himself mentions some of these in relation to the embryo (chromosomal abnormality, or no womb available—1988: 191). But foetuses and infants too can be in this predicament for the first of these reasons or others. I do not believe that Lockwood thinks we have a duty to preserve inevitably doomed foetuses and infants, for example anencephalic ones (8.6, 10.4, 11.3). He must surely therefore agree that where the possibility of development into a grown person is removed the duty to preserve, which arises just because of this possibility, is removed too. What such examples show is that in all these cases it is in the main (I shall discuss other factors below) the interest of the possible future grown person into whom they might turn that imposes on us, in normal cases, a duty to preserve them.

Some will now object that merely possible people cannot have interests. I have answered this objection in 5.2, 10.4 ff., 11.4, and 15.6, so here I can be brief. The answer can be put dramatically by asking Lockwood to suppose that he is a presently existing human adult (as he is), but one who came into being through *in vitro* fertilization (as actually he did not). Suppose also that, at some stage in the medical procedures, the surgeons were faced with the question, 'Shall we implant this embryo or that other embryo?'—an embryo which would have turned, not into Lockwood, but into someone else.

On these suppositions, Lockwood can certainly be glad and grateful that they implanted the embryo that turned into him, and not the other one, assuming that they could not implant both (see his p. 202). When they were making the decision, both embryos had the potential to turn, given a favourable environment, into adult humans; but only one of them had any potential to turn into this individual, namely Michael Lockwood. Although, if the other had been implanted and come to birth, that neonate too might have been *called* 'Michael Lockwood', it would have been a different Michael Lockwood. The present existing Michael Lockwood has every reason to be thankful that the surgeons implanted the embryo that turned into him, instead of experimenting on it. So the choice that they made undoubtedly conferred a benefit on him.

So if at that time they asked, 'Is there (tenseless) an individual for whom the development of this potential would constitute a direct benefit?', they could truly answer 'Yes'. And the important point is that the answer would still, at the time they asked the question, have been 'Yes' even if, later, they had decided not to implant the embryo but to experiment on it. For even so, it was the case that they could truly say to each other 'There is (tenseless) an individual for whom the development of this potential would constitute a direct benefit'. For here, now, we have supposed, is the existing individual Michael Lockwood, large as life, talking to us; and *ab esse in posse valet illatio*. That he now exists shows that it was at that time possible that he should now exist. Even if they had later removed that possibility by starting an experiment on him, it was still true *before* the experiment started that he *could* exist. The embryo still had the potential; and this potential, it might be argued, imposed on them a duty at least to consider the interest of the person whom they *could* bring into existence.

6.3 People find it hard to accept this point, because they are confused by some objections which I must now consider. Some of them are answered elswhere in this volume.

(1) It is alleged that only existing people can have interests. This is plainly false, as the example just given shows. It *was* in Lockwood's interest that they should implant the embryo that turned into him, although *he* did not at that time exist.

(2) It is also alleged that people who cannot be identified cannot have interests. This would mean that very few people in the future after at most a few years can have interests, because which identifiable individuals are born depends on actions which are not yet decided on, including actions of procreating those individuals. Which individuals are born depends

on when we copulate, and that is still a matter of choice; and so, indeed, is whether we copulate at all (Parfit 1984: 351 ff.). But the allegation is in any case false. The person who will occupy my carrel at the library next may be now unidentifiable, but it is in his interest that I should leave it tidy (10.8).

(3) It is also claimed that if people who might be born have interests (in particular an interest in being procreated) this could impose on us a duty to procreate all the people we possibly *could* procreate, and this is held to be absurd. But the argument is fallacious. All procreation is choice (even if the choice is random), because procreating one person entails not procreating another (5.1 ff., 10.7, 11.8).

Even if they worked at it as hard as they could, a single couple could not (allowing for a few twins) produce many more children on average than one every nine months; but there are many other children they could alternatively have had if they had copulated on different nights. And even the interests of the maximum number of children they could have do not impose on them a duty to have them all. For if they had them all, they might all starve, and that would not be in their interests. The maximum duty that is imposed is to do the best impartially for all the possible people there might be; and this can only be done by having an optimal family planning or population policy, which in turn means excluding some possible people (if only by abstinence). The best policy will be the one which produces that set of people, of all the possible sets, which will have in sum the best life. I have discussed in 5.3 ff. in more detail how we should address the problem of balancing quality of life against quantity. Quality of life is also discussed in 15.6.

(4) It is also objected that if the interests of possible people have to be considered when deciding what we may do to embryos, the same will be true of gametes, certainly in pairs, but perhaps even singly. For, after all, the now existing individual Michael Lockwood has reason to be glad that, and has benefited from the fact that, the gametes which led to his production were not destroyed either singly or conjointly. For if they had been, he would not have existed. This conclusion also is held to be absurd (cf. Lockwood 1988: 197 f.).

But it is not. From the present point of view, contraception and abortion really are on a par, though there may be other reasons for preferring contraception (10.6, 11.8). Both are wrong, though defeasibly so, in that they involve the prevention of somebody coming into existence in whose interest it almost certainly was to exist. But, given that parents cannot have a duty to produce all the children they could produce, they have to choose when to copulate, and how often to do so without contraception; and this choice results in the production of some of these people and the exclusion of others.

It is true that Lockwood has reason to be glad that the gametes which produced him were not destroyed. But *some* gametes (innumerably many indeed) are inevitably destroyed, and whichever are destroyed *might* have survived if others had not. If some other sperm had succeeded in fertilizing the ovum, to the exclusion of the sperm which contributed the genes for Lockwood, then somebody else would have had as much reason, *ceteris paribus*, to be glad to exist as Lockwood has now. Lockwood's parents did not have a duty to secure that he in particular was born; at the most they had a duty to secure that some child was—and perhaps not even that, if enough children are being born anyway to produce the optimum size of population. The same is true of the surgeons deciding which embryo to implant. Given that they have more embryos than they can implant, they have at the most a duty (given the consent of the parents) to implant as many as can, after developing into children, find a place in a family of optimum size. And what that size is, is a question on which the present discussion has little bearing.

The upshot of the discussion is that contraception, abstinence, the destruction of embryos, abortion, and even infanticide ought to be controlled, not by the interests of gametes, embryos, foetuses, or infants, but by the interests of possible future developed people who there might otherwise be, and that the number of these ought to be decided by finding the right population and family planning policy. Gametes and embryos do not as such have interests. The developed people they might turn into, or be instrumental in producing, do indeed have interests, and these have to be balanced against one another within the limits of what we can do; but the mere existence of the present gamete or embryo or foetus or even neonate provides no reason why it should have precedence over the others, beyond two relatively weak reasons which I shall be considering in a moment.

6.4   (5) Lockwood says (1988: 198 f.) that it strikes him as preposterous to suggest that there is 'nothing intrinsically wrong with ending the life of a perfectly normal healthy new-born infant, or that infanticide is intrinsically no worse than deliberately preventing conception'. It is not clear what he means by 'intrinsically'; but whatever he means, the 'preposterous' conclusion does not follow from the position I have been maintaining. I have just said that both infanticide and contraception are *pro tanto* wrong ('intrinsically wrong' if Lockwood wishes). They are wrong because they prevent the existence of a grown person who has an interest in existing. And, though from this point of view contraception and infanticide may be equally wrong, their wrongness is, as I said, defeasible: and there are in most cases reasons why contraception is less wrong.

Lockwood himself alludes to one of these reasons (1988: 199): 'fertilized egg, embryo, foetus and newborn baby are as it were, successively further down the track towards realizing their potential for worthwhile life' (cf. 11.8). Another, which Lockwood does not mention, is that infants, unlike ova (whether fertilized or unfertilized) and sperms, are normally already objects of affection, and killing them inflicts grief on those who have come to love them (even if they have decided that all things considered their child, say because of some severe defect, ought to be allowed to die or even killed in order that another may take its place). I argue in 12.2 ff. that in such cases the interest of the possible future healthy child ought to take precedence over that of the existing severely handicapped child. A third reason is that, in spite of what some writers have claimed, infants, unlike gametes or even embryos, almost certainly do have some pleasures and desires (for example, in or for their mothers' milk); and infanticide frustrates these. These desires cannot weigh much in the balance against the desires of a grown person that might come into existence if the infant did not; but they are something that the infant has and gametes and embryos do not have.

The considerations I have mentioned may account for the

intuition to which, in any case, Lockwood says he is not going to appeal (1988: 199). The dilemma in which he seeks to place us (1988: 197), only in order to extricate us from it by his preferred solution, might not arise at all if we realized that intuitions are not a secure guide in out-of-the-way cases. As I have argued in 1.7, 2.3, and 10.6, there are at least two different levels of moral thinking which need to be distinguished, the intuitive and the critical. The intuitive level, at which we apply learnt moral responses, is, if we have learnt good ones, adequate for the ordinary run of cases (which, indeed, is why they are good ones). But cases in which infanticide or experimentation on embryos are in question are never ordinary ones, and in them our intuitions cannot be relied on to give the right answer.

Probably the best intuitions to have are ones which forbid infanticide but allow contraception. The stages in between are not catered for by these, and therefore we have to think about them more critically. That the intuition which forbids infanticide ought to be overridden in cases like that which I have described does not entail that it is not the best intuition to have for all but the most abnormal cases. So it is perfectly possible for someone to have both these good intuitions, but to say that infanticide is in abnormal cases justified, and contraception in abnormal cases unjustified (say where the human race is in danger of extinction).

The reason why these are the best intuitions to have for the ordinary run of cases are not hard to find. It would nearly always be wrong to kill infants, and people would be badly educated morally if they could even contemplate it without horror. If we had been brought up that way, a lot of grown people would not come into existence who would have been glad to exist, and this would be a very bad thing. On the other hand, an intuition which in general permits contraception is probably better than the one it has recently replaced, which forbade it, because on the whole people who limit their families by contraception have good reasons (even good *moral* reasons) for doing so; it would be worse if they were prevented from limiting them.

True, we *could* have had (like some other cultures) an intuition that allowed infanticide as a means of family limitation.

But our own culture sets a great deal of store by the loving care we give to infants (rightly, because infants treated in that way are much more likely when they grow up to be glad to be alive); and we cannot simultaneously cultivate this loving attitude and be ready to kill infants whenever we find it convenient. Only in extreme cases such as I have described are the two attitudes compatible; cases, that is, where the child is so handicapped that parents think it would be better to give the love to another future and more fortunate child, if one is not going to have them both to love. The reasons for thinking contraception less wrong than infanticide are therefore, though in general good reasons, defeasible, as many people already recognize. Some people may still disagree with the opinion that infanticide in rare cases is justified; but it is certainly not 'preposterous'.

I do not understand what Lockwood means by saying that the first of the reasons that, following him, I have for preferring contraception to infanticide 'is not . . . a reason which speaks to the individual possessor of potential'. Certainly the grown person Michael Lockwood, who is nearer to realization at the stage of the embryo than at the stage of the gametes, is an individual; and we hope he still has potential for further development. The gametes, the embryo, the foetus and the infant are all individual gametes etc., and they all have, as they get 'further down the track', the potential for either producing or turning into the individual Michael Lockwood.

6.5 Lockwood has been misled by the ways in which the problem has so often been posed. If what I have said so far is correct, what makes the moral difference is what the consequences of different treatments of embryos will be for the people into whom they might turn. Once we see this, it becomes clear that writers on this topic have been on a wild goose chase when they have disputed at such length the question of the stage at which individual human life or personhood, or the like, begins. On this point I agree with Mary Warnock (7.9 and refs.). For *whenever* my life as the individual Richard Hare began, anything that would have interfered with my developing into the grown person that I now am would have been against my interest, and therefore *pro tanto* wrong, though possibly right given certain other assumptions. It would have made no difference at all whether the interference took place before or after I became that human individual; so we need not waste any more ink on the question of when this was.

Nor is this a question that need concern legislators. They need to concern themselves, rather, as legislators always should, with the consequences of their legislation. And on these the contentions I have been making shed a great deal of light (8.4 f.). For if the legislators want to do what they ought through their legislation—that is, bring about the consequences that they ought to bring about—they have to concern themselves with the interests of those whom their legislation will affect. And the chief of these are the people that will come into existence if one kind of law is passed, but will not if another kind is passed. And the more restrictive the legislation is, the less IVF embryos there will in practice be, and therefore the less grown people there will be that those embryos turn into.

This is for three main reasons. The first is that IVF could not have been invented, and cannot now be improved, without experiments on embryos, and therefore, just as in the past, if there had been a complete legal ban on experimentation, at least all the people who have been produced by IVF would not have existed, so those in the future whose existence improved methods might make possible will not exist if a ban prevents the improvement. And even with a less restrictive law, the restrictions would impede research and therefore prevent some of them coming into existence.

Secondly, the many grown people who fail to come into existence because of chromosomal abnormalities, but who might come into existence if ways were discovered by research on embryos of detecting and even correcting these abnormalities, will have their existence precluded by a ban. It is of course possible to take the view that detection is enough, and that defective embryos or foetuses or infants should be allowed to die or even be killed, so that people can be born who do not have the defects. But the people who take such a view are not the same people as are most vocal in favour of a ban on experimentation.

Thirdly, the reduction in the number of people produced would not be compensated for by any increase in the number of embryos saved from the experimenter. For if it were illegal to do the experiments, those embryos would not be produced in the first place. A ban on the production of 'spare' embryos would have the same effect. But if spare embryos *are* produced in the course of infertility treatment by IVF, in order to insure against the loss of some, those spare embryos would not, it is true, be experimented on if the law prevented it; but they would (if they were really spare) perish all the same, so that the law would make no difference to the people they would otherwise have turned into. All this I argue in greater detail in 8.5 ff.

6.6   From the point of view of securing the existence of grown people, it is not necessary to put any ban on embryo experimentation. If we ask, what the law on embryo experimentation ought to be, the answer will be found by asking, first, how the law should limit experiments on humans in general (and for that matter on other animals) so that those which ought not to be done are not done. This is a question of balancing the expectation of good through the advancement of research against the expectation of harm to the experimental subject. But in practice firm guidelines and firm intuitions (see above) need to be developed to guide those (for example, ethics committees) deciding individual cases.

Such guidelines should no doubt be restrictive when they are dealing with ordinary adults, and even more so in the case of children who can give consent only by proxy (see Nicholson 1986 and 8.1 ff.). When it comes to foetuses, embryos, and gametes, however, the harm to be expected from destructive experimentation diminishes successively to vanishing point. This is because (assuming that any possible suffering can be avoided by anaesthesia if necessary) no harm is in these cases done to the subject as such by destroying it, but only to the person that it might turn into; and this may be compensated for by the bringing into being of some other person. Experimentation not involving destruction but only damage is of course another matter; that should be strictly regulated and even banned, in the interests of the person who might survive to be born damaged.

This is most evident in the case of gametes; to destroy a sperm in an experiment makes in practice no difference at all to the number of people that there are going to be, except in very contrived cases. To destroy an ovum is a little more likely to make a difference, but not much. To destroy an embryo *in vitro*, again, makes little difference, for the reasons I have given; but an embryo *in vivo* is another matter. When we come to the foetus and, even more, the infant, which is 'further down the track', much more harm is done if it is destroyed, because it takes a lot of time and effort to get to the same stage again (to say nothing of the other reasons I gave earlier).

The best law, therefore, would, it seems to me, grade the harms done by experimentation from zero in the case of sperms to a very high figure in the case of viable infants (one that would forbid all but negligible harm), and balance these against the good expected from experiments. Lockwood is quite wrong to say that 'From a purely practical standpoint . . . one cannot apply different cut-off points to different lines of research' (1988: 190). This is exactly what all ethics committees do, or ought to; they ask how much good the research is likely to do, and balance this against the expected harm to the subject, rejecting the research proposal if this is more than negligible. Some harm may be done by experiments at any stage except possibly the sperm; and ethics committees should estimate its magnitude and probability.

In any case, it does not look as if the cut-off point suggested by Lockwood (the point at which the embryo gets a brain) has much to recommend it. Harm may be done if the embryos or gametes are destroyed even before this point, but in general less harm, the earlier in development the experiment occurs. There are exceptions, already mentioned: one would not, for example, be doing *any* harm by experimenting, at any stage in its development, on an embryo that was doomed in any case by chromosomal abnormalities.

But Lockwood is wrong to look for a cut-off point at all; he does so only because he (like the Tate Committee (1986), and many others apparently) thinks that the potential that should protect the embryo is something that in some mystical way inheres in it right now (like the soul?); whereas, properly understood, its potential lies in the fact that if it prospers there will, in consequence, in the future, be an ordinary grown human person who can enjoy all the blessings that Lockwood lists. It is this fact on which the morality of experimentation, and of legislation about it, depends. The duties of surgeons, experimenters, and lawmakers derive from the fact that their actions may further, or may impede, the coming into being of these people.

7

In Vitro Fertilization and the Warnock Report

7.1 The philosophical contribution to discussions like that about *in vitro* fertilization (IVF) and related problems should be to help sort out the good from the bad arguments that are used. One has only to read the many pronouncements on this subject in the newspapers to realize that what is needed above all is a sound and generally accepted method of argumentation, armed with which those who start with different views can discuss them with one another in the light of the medical facts and possibilities, and in the end, we hope, reach agreement. It is adherence to a sound method of argument that will bring this about; in default of it the discussions can go on inconclusively for ever. Since nearly all the questions involved are moral or ethical, it is the moral philosopher, the specialist in ethics in the narrow philosophical sense, who should, if he is good at his trade, be able to help here. The help consists not in handing down conclusions but in enabling others to reach them by sound arguments.

Moral philosophers differ from one another about their subject; there is not just one accepted theory in moral philosophy any more than there is in any other field. I have to try to say what I think is correct, and at the same time not to stray too far from what would be generally accepted by those in my profession who understand the issues.

Let me now draw attention to some features of the problems raised by IVF, and to one in particular. This is that they are quite new problems. Until a few years ago hardly anybody envisaged as possibilities what are now actualities; and this makes us take very seriously the problems presented by what are now only informed speculations about what might become possible. The danger is that these possibilities might be realized

From *Ethics, Reproduction and Genetic Control*, ed. R. Chadwick (Routledge, 1987).

before our moral thinking was ready for them. This is indeed what has already happened. Since the problems are new, we ought to be cautious in applying old precepts to them. These precepts got generally accepted when things were very different from what they are now or may become.

7.2 I will start, just to illustrate this point, with a fairly simple example, before I go on to some more contentious ones. There is a generally accepted condemnation of adultery. I say 'generally accepted', not 'universally accepted', because many *avant-garde* people have come to think that there is nothing wrong in it. But let us leave them on one side and just consider the position of those who still think that adultery is wrong. There is an argument that could be, and is, addressed to such people, which goes like this. Adultery is wrong, as we all agree. But adultery is *defined* as the union of the sperm of a man with an ovum of a woman when they are not married, and one of them is married to someone else. That is what adultery essentially consists in; the means adopted is not essential. Hitherto only one means has been available, namely sexual intercourse. But if new means, such as artificial insemination by donor (AID) or some forms of IVF, become available, they do not alter the essence of the act; it is still adultery and therefore, as we all agree, wrong.

There is more than one fault in this argument. One obvious objection that is likely to be made is that that is not what adultery is: a necessary element in it is sexual intercourse. If that objection is accepted, the argument that AID or IVF by donor is adultery and therefore wrong collapses; for they do not involve sexual intercourse. So the union of sperm and ovum is not a *sufficient* condition of adultery. But it is not a *necessary* condition either. A sexual act would be adulterous even if a method of contraception were used which ensured that there was no union of sperm and ovum.

But a less obvious, yet more fundamental, fault in the argument is that it gives no *reason* for the ban on adultery. If a reason were given for it (as I think it can be given), it might turn out that the reason had its basis in circumstances and conditions which used to hold universally but now no longer hold. And if the conditions no longer hold in a certain kind of novel case, it *may* be, or may not be (we cannot say without further discussion) that the reason does not hold any longer either. We can only settle this question by a closer examination of the reasons why adultery has hitherto been thought wrong.

My own reason for condemning adultery would be this. I am firmly convinced, unlike some of the *avant-garde* people I mentioned just now, that marriage is a valuable institution for the happiness of the partners and their children. Though it sometimes goes wrong, I am convinced that in our human situation no other system for the procreation, nurture, and upbringing of children is likely to do nearly so well. I emphasize that on this point my views are completely orthodox and conventional. So they are on the next point, that adultery is one of the greatest dangers to the stability of marriages, and therefore to the happiness of the partners and their success in bringing up their children happily and well. I will not here enquire why it is a danger. The sociobiologists will perhaps tell us that there are genetic reasons why in humans the marriage bond is normally a firm one. That is why anything that endangers it is commonly the subject of severe condemnation. Adultery, because it diminishes trust and for other reasons, does so endanger the marriage bond. Let us, anyway, suppose that this condemnation is justified by the evil consequences that adultery normally has in weakening the marriage bond, not only for the particular partners, but in general.

So far I am in agreement with the general condemnation of adultery. Why then do I not accept the argument I have just outlined, which starts from this condemnation as a premiss, adds nothing but a definition of adultery, plus some medical facts about AID and IVF which are not in dispute, and ends with the conclusion that AID and IVF by donor are adultery and therefore wrong?

The answer is that, even if we conceded that AID came within the definition of adultery, in such a case the reasons which made adultery wrong in the ordinary case would not apply. The ban on adultery was a general rule, a very valuable and important one, whose firm acceptance and hence almost universal observance did the best for people's well-being in nearly all ordinary cases. It could be, even before the invention of AID and IVF, that cases arose in which adultery would be the best way of furthering the purposes of marriage. There have been societies in which, if a man was infertile, his brother or some near relative was expected to secure children for his wife—children who would be members of his family—by begetting them for him. The service done for Abraham by Hagar provides a somewhat similar example (Genesis 16). If this was done with the knowledge and approval of all, I can see nothing wrong in such a custom, as a good means of securing the ends which marriage serves—among them those so beautifully set out in the Prayer Book marriage service: 'for the procreation of children, to be brought up in the fear and nurture of the Lord, and to the praise of his holy Name'.

What AID and IVF can do is to make such solutions readily available to an infertile couple, without any sexual intercourse (such as might be thought objectionable) by any but them. If there is agreement between the partners, this may be a way of cementing the marriage by providing children for them. Therefore the reasons, which I said I accepted, for the general condemnation of adultery do not apply in this special case. We can go on accepting the general condemnation, but say nevertheless that it applies only *in general*, not universally, and that AID and IVF cases, with mutual consent, can be treated as exceptions to it, because in those cases the reasons for the general condemnation are absent, and there are good reasons for making the exceptions.

7.3 It may now be suggested that it is dangerous to allow exceptions to the general ban on adultery, because that will weaken it, and so lead to a widespread relaxation of moral standards in relation to marriage as an institution. Note that this is a practical argument, and needs to be answered on practical grounds. It belongs to a type of argument commonly known as the slippery slope, or the thin end of the wedge (10.6, 11.7). It is certainly true that there are many good rules of conduct which we treat as inviolable or at least very sacred, and are alarmed by anything which tends to weaken their hold on people. Examples are rules of honesty and rules forbidding violence. If a few people start cheating other people, and are not condemned and brought to book, there is likely to be a general collapse of honesty and nobody will be able to trust anybody else. If a few people who feel like it, and are strong enough, violently assault their neighbours in pursuit of some advantage for themselves, and get away with it, others will soon copy them and anarchy will be the result.

I must stress again that this is a practical argument. For it to succeed, it is necessary not merely to show that *in theory*, if the fraud or the violence were condoned in a particular case, widespread fraud or violence in other kinds of case could ensue. It is necessary to show that, as the world is, it is *likely* to ensue. There are cases in which the principles forbidding fraud and violence are with general consent relaxed. The most notable of these is where the police use force or deceit, in ways permitted by the law, in order to catch criminals; nobody says they must not, because if *that* fraud or violence is allowed, fraud and violence will spread in society. What should be permitted to the police in the way of force or deceit can be, and is, disputed; but nobody thinks that they should be forbidden altogether.

It is perfectly practicable to have exceptions to well-established principles, provided that the cases in which the exceptions are allowed are well demarcated and easily recognizable. I want to suggest that the use of AID and IVF to secure children for a childless couple might be such a case. We might allow it, on clearly specified conditions, without in any way weakening the prohibition on adultery in general. There are two ways in which we might describe this exception to the general rule, and it is important to be clear that, though I shall give a reason for preferring one of these ways, we could choose either without making any substantial difference to the argument. We could say either that, though the definition of 'adultery' remains the same, and AID is adultery, it is allowable when it is without intercourse and with the consent of the other spouse in order to secure a family; or we could say that in such a case the union of sperm and ovum is not adultery. Similarly, in the case of the police, we could say that the use of force within the law is not violence (it is *vis* but not *violentia*), or that it is justified violence. And we could say either that the use of deceit to catch criminals is not fraud, or that it is justified fraud. It does not matter.

I mention this point because in the discussion of such questions there is a danger that a lot of time will be wasted in disputes about whether such and such an act is really adultery, or really murder, just as it has been on disputes on whether the embryo or the foetus is really a human being. What matters is whether a certain act, about whose nature we are quite well enough informed, is right or wrong, not what we are to call it. Philosophers are, among other things, concerned with the use of words: they should use such skill as they may have acquired to *prevent* our wasting time on disputes about words, not to bog us down more deeply in them.

The reason why people get bogged down in such verbal disputes is that they have some general principle, the reasons for which they cannot give, and want to hang on to it at all costs: 'Always keep a-hold of Nurse for fear of finding something worse' (Belloc 1908: 110). From this unreasoned point of view, there is an incentive to persuade oneself that AID is not really adultery; one can then go on holding the principle that all adultery is wrong, and still allow AID when it seems right to do so. If by contrast one's original principle was a reasoned one, one can, without any detriment to it, say that, although AID is, strictly speaking, adultery, the *reasons* for condemning adultery in general do not apply in this particular case. This second way of speaking has the disadvantage that 'adultery' has become fairly well accepted in our language as a word implying condemnation, as Aristotle noticed (1107^a11); and therefore, if we called the donor an adulterer, it would be difficult to avoid giving the impression that we were somehow condemning him, which, if we approve of what he has done, we do not mean to do. But all the same the verbal question is not important enough to detain us for long.

7.4   I want now to sum up the lessons to be drawn from this relatively easy case for our understanding of the right method of argument about such questions. We may then be able to handle more difficult questions with greater hope of settling them. The method I advocate goes in the following steps:

(1) Where a new practice looks as if it might be a breach of an old principle, but otherwise seems to have a lot to recommend it, first ask what were the reasons for the old principle. They will be found to consist in certain good consequences that come from the general acceptance of the principle, and certain evils that would ensue on its general abandonment.

(2) Ask, next, whether in the new case these same reasons still hold. If they do not, there is the beginning of an argument for relaxing the principle in such a case.

(3) Ask, then, whether such a relaxation is likely to lead *in practice* to a general weakening of the hold that the good old principle has on people's attitudes and behaviour. This may depend on whether the type of case in which we want to relax it can be easily recognized and demarcated from the cases in which we want to keep the prohibition.

(4) If the answers to the last two questions are favourable— if, that is to say, the reasons for the old principle do not hold in the new case and the making of an exception will not in practice put us on to any slippery slope—then we can make an exception of the new case, if the situation resulting from the acceptance of the principle with the exception written into it is better than that resulting if we retain the old principle unmodified.

I have been speaking throughout in terms of moral principles; but the same will hold if we are talking about laws. In the AID case and the analogous IVF case the question was one of adultery, and adultery has in Britain not usually been treated as a crime (though it often has in America and in Muslim countries, and has had consequences in civil law even in Britain, for example in divorce cases). That was why I dealt with it as a moral, not a legal matter. Nevertheless, even the cases I have so far considered can become, and have become, matters for proposed legislation; and the same applies *a fortiori* to some other uses of IVF.

However, I need not say anything more about laws over and above what I have said about morality. This is not because law and morality are the same thing—far from it—but because in this area the reasons for, and the arguments for, changes in the law are closely analogous to the reasons for changes in our moral attitudes. Not all sins should be crimes; but if we are wondering whether to make some new practice into a crime, the questions we should ask ourselves are rather like those which should guide us if we are thinking of treating it as a sin. There are differences into which I shall not have room to go. But in general the question we have to ask ourselves in both cases is, 'If we changed our law or our moral attitudes, would the new state of affairs be preferable to the old, from the point of view of all those affected?'

7.5 The approach which I have been recommending has been, broadly speaking, a utilitarian one, such as I have defended in *MT* and elsewhere in this volume. I have adopted it because it is the only approach which seems to me to yield clear answers to questions like these, and because the answers which it gives are, I am sure, those that would commend themselves to anybody who had a firm understanding of the questions he was asking and of the facts. Utilitarianism is, however, not a universally accepted doctrine among philosophers, and it sometimes arouses the hostility of theologians. I wish to try to mollify anti-utilitarian philosophers and theologians by showing that all the same things can be said in their different languages.

Some such anti-utilitarians may wish to say that the good old principles, like that forbidding adultery, should be sacrosanct; we ought not to question them. Intuitionist philosophers will say that we know them by intuition. Theologians may say that we know them by revelation either in scripture, or to the Church or its members by the Holy Spirit. I will take each of these contentions in turn and show that, properly understood, I do not need to maintain anything substantially different from them.

As regards moral intuitions, a place can easily be found for them within a utilitarian system such as has been guiding me. It is certainly a good thing that we have them, and do not normally question them—that we are very firmly convinced that some kinds of act, like adultery in the ordinary case, are wrong. The same applies to the *feelings* on which Lady Warnock lays so much stress in her thinking. It *is* important that we have feelings of outrage and shock, as Sir Stuart Hampshire (1972) calls them, or intolerance, indignation, and disgust, to use Lord Devlin's expression (1965).

But there are two different reasons, one good and one bad, why these reactions might be thought important, which it is crucial to distinguish, as I think the Warnock Report (1984) does not. The first is that it is one of the facts of life that certain things shock people. Legislators have to take account of such facts. If a lot of people are shocked by what happens as a result of some piece of legislation, then there may be adverse consequences for society. Devlin was quite right about that; and it is obvious that *if*, as was not the case, the consequence of liberalizing the laws about homosexuality had been a breakdown of public morals and of respect for the law, Devlin would have had a good *utilitarian* reason for deploring such a reform (and he does, generally speaking, argue on such utilitarian grounds).

The other, bad, reason for thinking such reactions important is the thought that they might have some value as premisses in our moral reasoning. I mean that the *opinions* might have value, not the fact that they are current. On this view, we are to argue, not from the premiss that a lot of people *think* homosexuality wrong but from the premiss that it *is* wrong. But the fact that those feelings exist does very little to establish that. The most that it establishes is, if people have been thinking about the matter for generations, and are well informed and not muddle-headed, that they may have by trial and error come to some sensible opinions. I have at least *some* confidence in the wisdom of the ages. But it may be doubted whether the old prejudices about homosexuality have this standing. And when we are arguing about wholly new problems like surrogacy by IVF, this is manifestly not the case. To judge by the rapidity with which people changed even their inveterate opinions about homosexuality that Devlin took so much for granted, it would be most unsafe to rely on the Clapham commuter as a moral guide. It would only be safe if she had been thinking deeply about the matter and was well informed. It is very important to have moral reactions, but still more important to have the ones we ought to have.

To come back to my first example: the difference between an intuitionist and a utilitarian does not consist in the first holding that adultery is wrong and the second holding that it is not wrong. It consists, rather, in the first being unable or unwilling to give any cogent reasons for his conviction that it is wrong, whereas the second is able to show why it is a good thing that we should have this conviction and seek to cultivate it in others, including the children that we bring up. The reason is that the state of affairs in which adultery is condemned is better than that in which it is condoned or encouraged. Naturally I think that a philosopher who is able to give cogent reasons for his convictions is superior to one who is unable or unwilling to do so; but, although they disagree about method, they need not disagree on any point of substance.

7.6 In facing the theologians I am more anxious, because I am not at all well versed in their arcane disciplines. But all the same I think that my utilitarian approach can be amply justified in religious terms. I take as my starting point the Golden Rule, common to all the great religions, that we should do to others as we wish that they should do to us (that is to say, in identical circumstances, 'identical' being taken to include the mental states and dispositions of those affected, so that someone is not required to go round whipping people because he himself likes being whipped). The Golden Rule has the same effect as the injunction to love one's neighbour as oneself. Both of these are really consequences of the other great commandment to love God. If we believe that God himself loves his creatures, and therefore wills their good impartially, we shall think that to show our love of God is to strive to do his will by loving our neighbours as ourselves, seeking their good as we do our own, and treating their good as of equal weight to ours, and therefore to each other's; and that is the utilitarian doctrine.

However, in our human condition of ignorance, lack of time for thought, proneness to self-deception, and sheer confusion of mind it is impossible for us to determine reliably, on particular occasions, what is God's will—that is, what would do the best for all our neighbours, showing equal love to them all as God loves them all equally. So, inescapably, we have to be ruled by more particular commandments, since we cannot apply the great commandment directly. These above all are the content of what is called 'conscience'.

One of the wisest of the English philosopher-divines, Bishop Butler, expressed extremely well the relation, about which it is easy to be confused, between the great commandment of love and the particular commandments, for example the commandment not to commit adultery. He said:

From hence it is manifest that the common virtues and the common vices of mankind, may be traced up to benevolence, or the want of it. And this entitles the precept, *Thou shalt love thy neighbour as thyself*, to the pre-eminence given it, and is a justification of the Apostle's assertion, that all other commandments are comprehended in it; whatever cautions and restrictions there are, which might require to be considered, if we were able to state particularly and at length, what is virtue and right behaviour in mankind. For instance [he adds in a footnote], as we are not competent judges, what is upon the whole for the good of the world; there may be other immediate ends appointed to us to pursue, besides that one of doing good, or producing happiness. Though the good of creation be the only end of the Author of it, yet he may have laid us under particular obligations, which we may discern and feel ourselves under, quite distinct from a perception, that the observance or violation of them is for the happiness or misery of our fellow-creatures. (Butler 1726)

Note the appeal to St Paul (Romans 13: 9); he supplies the authority both of scripture and of the Church that I said earlier might be relied on by those who do not wish, or do not feel able, to think rationally for themselves. There is more about this in Butler's *Dissertation on Virtue* (1736), which should be read by all who are interested in the relation between benevolence and the particular virtues and obligations. These latter, Butler thought, are revealed to us by our consciences.

But this leaves a gap in our thinking which theologians do not do enough to fill. The *content* of what our consciences tell us (like the intuitions which are the same thing under another name) is not constant from one person to another. It is partly the result of their different upbringings. We bring up our children to (as it is sometimes put) 'know the difference between right and wrong'; but what they think right and what they think wrong may be influenced by what in particular we teach them. So, especially when we are thinking about novel questions like the present one, we sometimes do not know what to teach them, or what to think ourselves, and conscience gives us no clear guidance. We enquire (as best we may, and I am not pretending that it is easy), 'What would a being, who could do this kind of thinking better than we can, be likely to want us to think? What ought our moral convictions to be?' And we shall have to decide this question, as best we may, in the light of what we think God's purposes are. We can take it that he wishes good to all impartially, so we can only ask ourselves, what will secure this. And so we find ourselves asking, as the utilitarians also bid us ask, what moral attitudes, convictions, and the like will best serve the purpose of doing good to all those affected, treating them all as equally objects of our love. So I do not think that there ought to be any conflict on this matter between the best theology and the best philosophy (see H 1992: pp. 60 ff.).

7.7 I have illustrated the questions before us, and the method we should adopt in settling them, by taking one of the easiest. If we could grasp the right method in relation to this relatively easy question, we might then be able to go on to handle more difficult ones. I mean questions like 'Is it wrong, and is it murder, to propagate human embryos by IVF and then use them for purposes of experimentation or transplants?' and 'Ought we to allow women to bear other women's children for payment?'. I have opinions on all these questions, arrived at by the same method as I have been describing; but I shall not discuss them directly now, because I want to go on first to apply what I have said about methods of argument about these matters to an assessment of the Warnock Report. In the course of it I shall refer to two of these questions, but shall not have room to defend my opinions about them. Actually my opinions about surrogacy are not in general very different from those of Peter Singer and Deane Wells in their excellent book on this subject (1984); so I can refer to it for a defence of them. The views of the two dissenters in the Warnock Report are quite similar.

I suppose that there are two obvious alternative lines that philosophers in a committee like Mary Warnock's can take. One is to try to get the committee to clarify the issues before it, bringing into the light of day the arguments on both sides, assessing them and then making clear the reasons which have led the committee to its own conclusions. But Mary Warnock seems to have abjured any such ambitions. She was content with a second-best alternative, which was perhaps all she could manage. This was to find some conclusions which the members of the committee, or as large a majority of them as possible, would sign, and not bother too much about finding defensible reasons for them. Since the members were fairly typical in their moral attitudes or prejudices, it might be hoped that conclusions to which they could agree would also be acceptable to the public, and that government policy would duly conform. It is in such matters easier to get people to agree about conclusions than about the reasons for them.

On most of the matters the committee discussed, this policy on the part of Mary Warnock proved, from the purely political point of view, absolutely sound. The committee had a very good press; initially its recommendations seemed to be welcomed by the government and the public, and legislation to implement them was in the offing. There was, however, more dispute about two of the main recommendations: to permit some experimentation on embryos up to two weeks; and to forbid professional or administrative assistance, whether commercial or non-commercial, for surrogate motherhood, and make contracts for surrogacy unenforceable in the courts, but not to ban it altogether.

I should like to observe in passing that the consequences of forbidding professional assistance for surrogacy are illustrated by an actual case recently reported in the papers: two people who did not in the least want to go to bed with one another had to do so in order to achieve a surrogate pregnancy, and this would have been quite legal under the Warnock recommendations, since nobody arranged it but the people involved. And, as is argued and illustrated at length in Singer and Wells's book, nearly all the troubles with surrogacy as it is beginning to be practised in America would be overcome by having a *public* (state or licensed) agency to manage it, somewhat as is done for adoption in many countries.

The public, in a field that it had not yet thought much about, was in general inclined to accept the judgement of the good and great on the committee; but these two recommendations about surrogacy and embryo research seem to have aroused more unease. The result was the Enoch Powell Bill, which was a great deal less liberal than the Warnock recommendations, and, supported by Cardinal Basil Hume (1985), very nearly got through Parliament, where it commanded a large majority and was only stopped by a procedural manœuvre. But in the end Parliament, after some vacillations, and without much in the way of good argument, reached a reasonable compromise, which it is to be hoped may last. The Warnock Report contributed something to this compromise.

What this showed was that Members of Parliament, like the public, had not thought nearly enough about these difficult and novel problems, which had only emerged in very recent years, and which nobody had studied enough to clarify the issues even to those working in the field, let alone make the public clear about them. It may seem too severe to say so, but *this was what the Warnock Committee should have been doing*. What was missing in the public discussions was any understanding of the arguments on one side or the other of these questions. In default of reasons, people fell back on their prejudices.

Why was the Warnock Committee unable to do much about this? There are of course the difficulties I have mentioned already; to get members of the committee to study, and even agree in the clear statement of, the arguments on both sides, a lot of hard *philosophical* work would have been required; and, according to Michael Lockwood (1985: 1 f.), Mary Warnock has said that this proved unpalatable to the committee. But I do not think it should have been impossible to do better. We have, in the Report of Bernard Williams's Committee on Obscenity and Film Censorship (1980), a very good example of what can be done by a philosopher who is determined to get such a committee to think rationally. It would be hard to better the chapter in that report called 'Harms?', in which the costs and benefits of restrictive and permissive legislation about various kinds of pornography are very well discussed. It must be admitted that, perhaps *because* it was so enlightened, the Williams Committee did not get nearly such a good press as the Warnock Committee, and its recommendations were not taken up. But it may have in the end a more lasting influence, because, although with changes in the pornography scene the Williams Report may go out of date in some respects, the reasons are all there and will eventually be absorbed.

If we want a *successful* example of a more ambitious approach, we have only to look at the Wolfenden Committee's Report on homosexuality (1957). This was published many years ago when prejudice against homosexuals was pretty strong; but the report succeeded in actually influencing public opinion, or at least crystallizing it in a way which made a very sweeping reform of the law a possibility, so that now we have

what is on the whole a fairly satisfactory law on adult homosexuality. This was what Devlin was protesting against; and
perhaps Lady Warnock's committee, like Lord Devlin, will
prove to have been voicing, on the questions of surrogacy and
embryo research, opinions typical of her own generation,
which may in the twenty-first century come to seem archaic.

Why were the Williams and the Wolfenden Committees
able to give reasons for their recommendations, whereas on
these controversial questions the Warnock Committee gives
hardly any, and certainly few that will stand up to any sustained attack? The explanation is a philosophical one. Both
Wolfenden and Williams (surprisingly, in the light of his well-
known anti-utilitarian views) argued in a consistently utilitarian
way. The chapter in the Williams Report called 'Harms?' is, as
I said, a careful and extremely well worked out cost-benefit
analysis of various legislative proposals. The procedure of the
Wolfenden Committee was similar. It seriously tried to discover what would actually happen if various policies were followed, and what impact this would have on the interests of the
various parties affected, including members of the public.
These were the reasons it gave.

The Glover Report to the European Commission (Glover
1989) later did a similar job for the questions discussed by
Warnock, though it has sadly not had much influence in
Britain, perhaps because it appeared too late, after Warnock
had captured the attention of the press and the public. There
is hardly any argument of this quality in the Warnock Report.
We are simply told how the committee feels, and how other
people feel, about surrogacy and embryo research. The reason
why the committee was not able to help in giving very solid
reasons for these feelings is that its chairman is not a utilitarian, and all the reasons that in the end will hold water are utilitarian ones. Her committee ought to have been asking what
would happen if, for example, embryo research was forbidden
or allowed, or surrogacy was permitted under various restrictions. I mean, what would happen to those affected: the people
who would be helped by the research; even the animals who
would otherwise have to be sacrificed in alternative research;
the potential people into whom the embryos would turn if it
were possible to implant them (6.2 ff.); and so on. But instead,

they were content on the whole with recording their own reactions to various proposals, which, no doubt, they hoped the public would share. This was intuitionism in action. The committee was moved by its feelings of 'outrage and shock', 'indignation and disgust'.

It may be that most of what shocked it shocks me too, so I can accept many of its recommendations. But when it turned out that some things shocked Enoch Powell and a large number of Members of Parliament which did not shock the committee, what could she say? She wrote a piece in *The Times* (1985) condemning the 'absolutism' of Powell and his supporters. But the absolutism was not the real source of the trouble. It is, admittedly, important to distinguish between two sorts of intuitionists: those whose intuitions support absolute prohibitions couched in very simple and general terms, and those whose intuitions allow them to qualify their moral view almost *ad libitum* according to how they feel about particular matters (on absolutists see 1.3). But because neither of these parties is able to give any reasons for its views beyond deploying more intuitions, the 'absolutists' are in a much stronger position than the other kind of intuitionists like Mary Warnock, at any rate when it comes to the propaganda battle. They can claim to be defending simple sound principles against erosion; and indeed the principles often are sound ones, though only in general. However, as I think Mary Warnock sees, the whole issue in this area is whether, in view of the differences between the ordinary circumstances for which the sound principles were framed and the extraordinary and novel possibilities with which these new techniques confront us, we ought to make exceptions to the principles. I have already illustrated this with regard to IVF and adultery.

So, if intuitions are all that are allowed to count, the absolutists are likely to have a big advantage. What are needed to counter the rhetoric of the absolutists are much more detailed arguments giving the pros and cons of exceptions to the general principles. But the Warnock Committee is extremely cursory in doing this, and the 'reasons' it gives are often no more than expressions of moral conviction without any support. The support would take the form of predictions of actual harms that would come from the introduction of the practices condemned. If the committee just does not *like* the idea of the practices, what force has that?

7.8   On surrogacy, for example, some arguments are given against allowing it. They are larded with such expressions as 'inconsistent with human dignity', 'treat [the uterus] as an incubator' (is it not always an incubator, if you choose to use that word?), and 'the child will have been bought for money'. Then some arguments are given on the other side, using such expressions as 'a deliberate and thoughtful act of generosity'; but also usefully countering some of the excesses of the first lot of arguments. And the main benefit from allowing surrogacy is mentioned: it 'offers to some couples their only chance of having a child genetically related to one or both of them. In particular, it may be the only way that the husband of an infertile couple can have a child' (see *Report*, paras. 8 ff.).

When the committee comes to its own recommendations, one would expect it to have assessed these various arguments and said which of them were good ones, as I am sure the last one was. But what it actually says is:

The moral and social objections to surrogacy have weighed heavily with us. In the first place, we are all agreed that surrogacy for convenience alone, that is where a woman is physically capable of bearing a child but does not wish to undergo pregnancy, is totally ethically unacceptable [well, maybe, but no reason is given]. Even in compelling medical circumstances the danger of exploitation [a highly emotive word used in contentions which have already been rebutted in the preceding argument] of one human being by another appears to the majority of us to outweigh the potential benefit. That people should treat others as a means to their own ends, however desirable the consequences, must always be liable to moral objection. Such treatment of one person by another becomes positively exploitative when financial interests are involved.

So, in the end, the committee comes down on one side without giving any but the most sketchy reasons. If the risk to the surrogate mother is a reason, does that make it equally exploitative to employ steeplejacks if one pays them well? What differentiates surrogate motherhood from other forms of personal service? Maybe something does, but we have not been told what it is. Why am I not 'treating others as means to my own ends' whenever I employ anybody? In case Lady

Warnock should invoke Kant here, I must point out that (as is well known) what Kant said was not that one must never treat people as a means—he never said *that* was always open to moral objection, and he would have been absurd if he had—but that one must 'always treat humanity . . . never *simply* as a means, but always at the same time as an end' (1785: BA67 = 429). If I employ a steeplejack I am using him as a means, but also as an end, because I enable him, by paying him a high wage, to realize his own end of having good money to live on. It may be that surrogacy is different, but we are not told in what respect.

7.9 I have no room even to sketch my difficulties with what the Warnock Committee says about embryo research as briefly as I have in the matter of surrogacy. I deal with it more fully in 8.4 ff. The committee makes one extremely important and valuable philosophical move, thus locating itself in the centre of the moral problem instead of remaining on the periphery as so many do (1.2, 8.7, 10.3, 11.1). This is where it says:

Although the questions of when life or personhood begin appear to be questions of fact susceptible of straightforward answers, we hold that the answers to such questions in fact are complex amalgams of factual and moral judgments. Instead of trying to answer these questions directly we have therefore gone straight to the question of how it is right to treat the human embryo. We have considered what status ought to be accorded to the human embryo, and the answer we give must necessarily be in terms of ethical or moral principles.

To have got *that* into a public document is, I think, Mary Warnock's chief claim to a place in the philosophical Hall of Fame. However, when the committee comes to discuss *what* moral principles, we are again left without any but the thinnest of reasons for adopting one principle rather than another; and this is, as before, because the committee, relying on its intuitions, is in no position to give any. For example, it says 'Everyone agrees that it is completely unacceptable to make use of a child or an adult as the subject of a research procedure which may cause harm or death', and it is then asked whether this applies to embryos. But I should be surprised if many people do in fact agree with this sweeping condemnation of research on humans (see 9.1 ff.). Taking a blood sample by finger-pricking *may*, in very exceptional circumstances, cause harm or even death, but, given informed or even, in the case of children, proxy consent, it is a common and accepted experimental procedure in research (e.g. on atmospheric lead pollution, to determine how much lead is getting into people's blood). One of the unofficial working parties I have sat on has produced a report on the question of when experimentation on human children is allowable and when not, with reasons given (see Nicholson 1986).

The committee mentions the argument that the embryo is not a potential person because, unless it implants, it 'has no potential for development'. But if we are in a position to implant it, as normally we are if we really want to and are prepared to find a recipient mother, the embryo *does* have the potential and *is* a potential person. The whole question of what moral bearing this potentiality has, has been extensively discussed in the literature following the denial by Michael Tooley (1972) that potentiality has moral relevance; the treatment by the committee is most inadequate. My own view is that potentiality is morally relevant (see 5.1 and refs.), but that, as is argued by Singer and Wells, it is equally relevant in the case of as yet uncombined gametes; and that, since there is an almost infinite potentiality for producing human beings *ad libitum*, we cannot have a duty to produce one from any particular pair of gametes or embryo (10.7, 11.8).

In general, the committee gives no cogent reasons for its recommendation that experimentation on embryos should be allowed up to two weeks but not thereafter. What was needed was a thorough examination of the consequences for all those affected. These include, besides parents and possible parents, the potential person into whom an embryo might if implanted turn, and the potential people that might be brought into being if other embryos were implanted, or *other* pairs of gametes turned into embryos. And we must remember that research on embryos might make this possible in cases where it is not now possible. In short, they should have enquired into the good and harm that would come from allowing or forbidding such research. But this, perhaps, they were not ready to do, because Mary Warnock had abjured utilitarianism and consequentialism (which is the only rational and sensible way of handling these questions), and persuaded them to keep off such topics so far as they decently could. So we have in the report some enquiry into consequences, but it is not nearly far reaching enough; and instead we have plenty of appeals to intuitions, i.e. prejudices. This did little to help the public become clearer on the arguments.

Mary Warnock is a far better politician than I am, and therefore a better judge of the art of the possible; and legislative developments since this paper was first published have to some extent vindicated her political judgement. It may be that she *could not*, in the circumstances of her committee, do any better. If so, she is not to be blamed. But Wolfenden did, and got the law changed, and Williams did, though he failed at that time to get the law changed. I still have a lingering doubt as to whether, if Mary Warnock's *philosophical* views had been more as I think they should be, she might not have produced a more cogent, and therefore more effective, report.

8

Embryo Experimentation
Public Policy in a Pluralist Society

8.1   What is the proper relation between the moral principles that should govern public policy, including legislation, and moral principles which may be held—often passionately—by individuals, including individual legislators? The adherents of such 'personal' principles often object that proposed laws would allow people, or even compel them, to transgress the principles. Obvious examples are homosexuality and abortion law reform. People who think homosexuality an abominable sin object to the repeal of laws that make it a crime; and those who think that abortion is as wrong as murder of grown people object that a law permitting abortion in certain cases might make it permissible for other people to—as they would say—murder unborn children, or even, if they are nurses and want to keep their jobs, compel them to do so themselves.

So the question we have to consider is really this: What weight ought to be given to the objections of these people when framing and debating legislation and policy? We live in a pluralist society, which means that the moral principles held sacred among different sections of society are divergent and often conflicting; and we live in a democratic society, in which, therefore, policy and legislation have to be decided on by procedures involving voting by all of us or by our representatives; so the question becomes: What attention should we pay, whether we are legislators in parliaments or simply voters in a constituency, to the personal moral opinions of other people, or even to our own? In short, how ought people's moral convictions to affect the actions done by them or by others which influence public policy?

But we cannot address this question until we have answered a prior one, namely: What consideration ought in general to

From *Embryo Experimentation*, ed. H. Kuhse and P. Singer (Cambridge UP, 1992).

be given to moral principles of any kind when framing legislation and policy? There are three positions on this which I wish
to distinguish. The first two seem to me unacceptable, for reasons which I shall give. I will call the first the *Realist* or 'Keep
morality out of politics' position. It holds that the function of
policy and of legislation is to preserve the interests, which may
be purely selfish interests, of the governed; if moral considerations seem to conflict with this function, they should be
ignored. Politicians have a moral duty to subordinate, in their
political actions, all *other* moral duties to that of preserving the
interests of the governed. This position leaves them with just
one moral duty; it treats the situation of a government in
power as analogous to that of an agent (say a lawyer who
might be thought by some to have a duty to preserve the
interests of his client even at the cost of ignoring some other
supposed moral duties).

The difficulty with this position is that no reason is given by
its advocates why that should be the politician's supreme and
only duty. When a moral question is in dispute, as this one
certainly is, we need some method, other than appeals to the
convictions of those who maintain the position, of deciding
whether to believe them or not. I shall therefore postpone discussion of this position until we are in possession of such a
method, which will be after we have examined the third position.

8.2 The second position goes to the opposite extreme
from the first. It holds that morality does apply to political
actions and to legislation (very much so). The way it applies is
this: there are perfect laws (laid up in Heaven as it were), to
which all human laws ought morally to be made to conform.
There are various versions of this position, which I shall call
generically the *Natural Law* position, although that expression
also has other different uses. One version says that there is a
moral law, and that the function of ordinary positive laws is to
copy this and add appropriate penalties and sanctions. Thus
murder is wrong according to the moral law, and the function
of positive law and the duty of the legislators is to make it illegal and impose a penalty.

According to this version all sins ought to be made crimes.
But there is a less extreme version according to which not all

ought to be: there are some actions which are morally wrong but which the law ought not to intervene to punish. For example, in many societies adultery is held to be wrong but is not a criminal offence. And it may be further added that not all crimes have to be sins. If the law requires people always to carry an identity card, I may be subject to penalties if I do not, but many people would not want to say that I am *morally* at fault. But it does not follow from my not being morally at fault if I break the law that the legislators were morally at fault when they made the law. They might have had very good reasons—even good moral reasons—for making the law (for example, that it would facilitate the apprehension of criminals). A distinction is thus made between what are called *mala in se* (acts wrong in themselves) and *mala prohibita* (acts wrong only because they have been made illegal).

The trouble with this position is very similar to that with the first and extreme opposite position. No way has been given of telling what is in the natural law, nor of telling what sins ought to be made crimes, and which crimes are also sins. That is why, when appeal is made to the natural law, or to a moral law to which positive laws morally ought to be made to conform, people disagree so radically about what in particular this requires legislators to do. To quote the great Danish jurist Alf Ross, 'Like a harlot, the natural law is at the disposal of everyone' (1958: 261). Here again we shall have to postpone discussion until we have a safe method of handling such questions as 'How do we decide rationally, and not merely by appeal to prejudices dignified by the name of "deep moral convictions", what legislators morally ought to do?'.

There is another, more serious, thing wrong with the second or Natural Law position. It assumes without argument that the only moral reason for passing laws is that they conform to the natural law. But there can be many reasons other than this why laws ought to be passed. If, for example, it is being debated whether the speed limit on motorways ought to be raised or lowered, the argument is not about whether it is in accordance with the moral or natural law that people should drive no faster than a certain speed. There may, certainly, be moral reasons, irrespective of any law, why people ought not to drive faster than, or slower than, a certain speed on certain roads at certain times and under certain traffic and weather conditions. But that is not what legislators talk about. They talk about what the *consequences* of having a certain law would be. For example, they ask what effect a lower limit would have on the overall consumption or conservation of fuel; what the effect would be in total on the accident figures; whether a higher limit would make it necessary to adopt a higher and therefore more costly specification for the design of motorways; whether a lower limit would lead to widespread disregard of and perhaps contempt for the law; and so on. What they are asking, as responsible legislators, is not whether 70 or 80 m.p.h. conforms to the natural law, but what they would be doing, i.e. bringing about, if they passed a certain law.

And this requirement to consider what one is doing does not apply only to the decisions of legislators. What I have said responsible legislators do is what all responsible agents have to do if they are to act morally. To act is to do something, and the morality of the act depends on what one is doing. And what one is doing is bringing about certain changes in the events that would otherwise have taken place—altering the history of the universe in a certain respect. For example, if in pulling the trigger I would be causing someone's death, that is a different act from what it would be if I pointed my gun at the ground; and the difference is morally relevant. The difference in the morality of the acts is due to a difference in what I would be causing to happen if I tightened my finger on the trigger. This does not imply that I am responsible for *all* the consequences of my bodily movements. There are well-canvassed exceptions (accident, mistake, unavoidable ignorance, etc.), and there are many consequences of my bodily movements that I cannot know of and should not try to, such as the displacement of particular molecules of air. Only some, not all, of the consequences are morally relevant (see *MT* 62 ff. and refs.). But when allowance has been made for all this, what I am judged on morally is what I bring about.

It is sometimes held that we are only condemned for doing something when we *intend* to do it. This is right, properly understood. If we are judging the moral character of an agent, only what he does intentionally is relevant. But it is wrong to think that we can circumscribe intentions too narrowly for this purpose. There is a distinction, important for some purposes, between direct and oblique intentions (see Bentham 1789: ch. 8, sect. 6; Hart 1967). To intend some consequence directly one has to desire it. To intend it obliquely one has only to foresee it. But in the present context it is important that oblique intentions as well as direct intentions are relevant to the morality of actions. We have the duty to avoid bringing about consequences that we ought not to bring about, and are to blame even if we do not desire those consequences in themselves, provided only that we know that they will be consequences. I am to blame if I knowingly bring about someone's death in the course of some plan of mine, even if I do not desire his death in itself—that is, even if I intend the death only obliquely and not directly. As we shall see, this is very relevant to the decisions of legislators (many of whose intentions are oblique), in that they have a duty to consider consequences of their legislation that they can foresee, and not merely those that they desire.

8.3 The legislators are to be judged morally on what they are doing (i.e. bringing about) by passing their laws. They will be condemned morally, in the speed limit example, if they make the limit so high that the accident rate goes up significantly, or so low that it is universally disregarded and unenforceable and, as a result, the law is brought into disrespect. And this brings me to my third possible position on the question of how morality applies to law-making. I will call it the *Consequentialist* position. It says that legislators, if they want to make their acts as legislators conform to morality (that is, to pass the laws they morally ought to pass and not those they ought not), they should look at what they would be doing if they passed them or threw them out. And this means, what changes in society or in its environment they would be bringing about.

What legislators are doing, or trying to do, is to bring about a certain state of society rather than some other, so far as the law can effect this—that is, a state of society in which certain sorts of things happen. The legislators are not going themselves to be doing any of these things directly, though, as I have been maintaining, they will be bringing it about intentionally that the things happen, and the bringing about is an act of theirs.

There is a school of casuistry which holds that we are not to be held responsible for things which other people do as a result of what we do. I do not think that this school can have anything to say about the question we are considering. For *everything* that happens as a result of the laws that the legislators pass is something that other people do. In the narrow sense in which these casuists use the word 'do' the legislators do nothing except pass the laws. So on this view the legislators are simply not to be held responsible for anything that happens in society; so far as morality goes they can do as they please. I shall therefore say no more about this school of casuistry.

Consequentialism as a theory in moral philosophy, which I have been advocating, has received a lot of hostile criticism in recent years. This is because people have not understood what the consequentialist position is. I do not see how anybody could deny the position I have just outlined, because to deny it is to deny that what we are judged morally for (what we are responsible for) is our actions, i.e. what we bring about. What makes people look askance at what they call consequentialism is the thought that it might lead people to seek good consequences at the cost of doing what is morally wrong—as it is said, to do evil that good may come. But this is a misunderstanding. It would indeed be possible to bring about *certain* desirable consequences at the cost of bringing about certain *other* consequences which we ought not to bring about. But if the whole of the consequences of our actions (what in sum we do) were what we ought to do, then we must have acted rightly, all things considered.

There is also a further misconception. People sometimes speak as if there were a line to be drawn between an action in itself, and the consequences of the action. I am not saying that according to some ways of speaking such a line cannot be drawn; but only that it is not going to divide the morally relevant from the morally irrelevant. In the 'gun' example, nobody would wish to say that my victim's death, which is an intended consequence of my pulling the trigger, is irrelevant to the morality of my act, and that only the movement of my finger is relevant. I intend both, and, as I have said, what I intend obliquely is relevant to the morality of the act as well as what I intend directly. There are a lot of questions, interesting to philosophers of action, which could be gone into here; but I have said enough for the purposes of the present argument.

8.4   It is now time to look again at the first two positions I distinguished. What is wrong with both of them is that they ignore what the third position rightly takes into account, namely the consequences of legislation and policy, that is, what the legislators and policy-makers are *doing* by their actions. In short, both these positions encourage irresponsibility in governments. The first position, indeed, does impose on governments a moral duty of responsibility so far as the interests of their subjects go. But what about the effects of their actions on the rest of the world? Ought the British government not to have thought about the interests of Australians when it arranged its notorious atomic tests at Maralinga? Ought it not now to think about acid rain in Norway when regulating power station emissions? Hitler, perhaps, was a good disciple of this position when he thought just about the interests of Germans and said 'Damn the rest'. If we are speaking of moral duties, surely governments have duties to people in other countries. What these duties are, and how they are to be reconciled with duties to the governments' own citizens, is a subject that is fortunately outside the scope of this paper. I shall consider only what duties governments and legislators have in relation to the states of their own societies which they are by their actions bringing about.

What I have called the Natural Law position is even more open to the charge of irresponsibility. It says that there are model laws laid up in heaven, and that the legislators have a duty to write these into the positive law of the land no matter what the consequences may be for those who have to live under them. This might not be so bad if we had any way of knowing what was in the model code. But we have not; all we have is a diversity of moral convictions, differing wildly from one another, without any reasons being given by those who hold them why we should agree with them. That is one of the facts of life in a pluralist society. So what happens in practice is that people set up pressure groups (churches are ready-made pressure groups, and there are others on both sides of most disputes), and produce rhetoric and propaganda in attempts to bounce the legislators into adopting their point of view. It cannot be denied that in the course of this exercise useful argu-

ments may be produced on both sides. But when the legislators come to their own task, which is to decide what they
morally ought to do, we could wish that they had more to go
on than a lot of conflicting propaganda. There ought to be a
way in which they can think about such matters rationally,
and decide for themselves what they really ought to do. This is
especially to be hoped for when they are deciding about
embryo experimentation.

Commissions and committees that are set up to help governments decide such questions are often no help at all. If, like
the Glover working party (1989), they examine and assess the
arguments on both sides and clarify the issues between them,
they can be of great help. If, on the other hand, like the
Warnock Committee (1984), they simply repeat the intuitions
that are current, without going carefully into the arguments
that might support them, they will not much enlighten the
public discussions (7.7 ff.). It is plain that the latter procedure
will not do as a means of arriving at rational guidance for governments on moral questions affecting policy. Suppose we were
to try this method in a committee in, say, South Africa. A lot
of people in South Africa think it is immoral for blacks to
swim even in the same private pool, let alone on the same
public beach, as whites. So, if a lot of such people found themselves on a government committee about racial policy with
somebody of Mary Warnock's philosophical views presiding,
the committee would certainly and unanimously recommend
the retention of 'whites only' beaches, and would not think it
necessary to give any but the most perfunctory reasons. This is
simply a recipe for the perpetuation of prejudices without having to justify them. And it is what has happened frequently on
committees about IVF, surrogacy, embryo experimentation,
and the like.

All who handle or advise on such questions ought to be
looking for arguments and testing them. So the next thing we
need to ask is: What makes an argument on this sort of topic a
good one? The answer has been anticipated in what I have
said already. Reasoning about moral questions should start
by asking what we would be doing if we followed a certain
proposal. And what we would be doing is bringing about
certain consequences. So what we have to ask first is: what

consequences would we be bringing about if we followed it? That is what any responsible government, and any responsible committee advising a government, has to ask first.

It is not, of course, the last thing that they have to ask. They have then to go on to ask which of these consequences are ones that they morally ought to be trying to bring about and which not. But at least they will have made a good start if they have tried to find out what the consequences would be. The question of embryo experimentation illustrates this very well. Suppose that Australian legislators are persuaded by one of the pressure groups in this field, or by the Tate Committee (1986), that they ought to ban all embryo experimentation, and proceed to do so. One consequence is likely to be that the advance of technology in this field will be retarded by the cessation of such experiments, at least in Australia. Perhaps the scientists will get jobs elsewhere in order to continue their experiments; but perhaps, if other governments are taking or likely to take the same line, they will find it difficult to do so. So there will be the further result that the benefits that could come from the research (for example, help to infertile couples to have children, or the elimination of some crippling hereditary diseases) will not be realized.

8.5 I have given the strongest arguments on one side. What are those on the other (6.5)? We might start by thinking that a further consequence of the legislation will be that a lot of embryos will survive which otherwise would not have survived (assuming for simplicity that, as is probably the case, nearly all experiments on embryos using present techniques involve the subsequent death of the embryo). But actually that is wrong: the consequence will not be that embryos survive— at least not in all cases. Whether it is will depend on whether the embryos in question are so-called 'spare' embryos, or embryos created specially for experimentation. If they are spare embryos, indeed, the consequence of the legislation will be that they will survive *the threat of experimentation*. But if we ask what will happen to them if they survive this threat, the answer will be that either a home will be found for them and they will be implanted (perhaps after a period in the freezer) or they will perish, because there is nothing else that can be done with them. In the first case they were not really *spare* embryos. But if we assume that there are going to be at least some embryos which really are spare, and for which, therefore, no home can be found, the result of the legislation will not be different from what it would have been if there had been no legislation: they will perish just the same.

Suppose, however, that, faced with this argument, the legislators were to tighten up the law and say that *no* embryos were to be allowed, or caused, to perish. The consequence of this would be that no embryos would be produced artificially except those for which it was certain that a home could be found. For under such a law nobody is going to produce embryos knowing that no homes can be found for them, and that therefore he (or she) will end up in court. So the consequence of this tighter law will be that those embryos will not be produced in the first place.

The same is true of embryos produced especially for research. The result of a ban on such research will be that embryos for whom a home is in prospect will be produced and implanted, but that those (whether spare or specially created for experimentation) for whom there is no hope of implantation will simply not be produced at all. The legislators, in making the decision whether to impose such a ban on experimentation or not, are in effect deciding whether to make it the case that these embryos perish, or to make it the case that they never come into existence at all.

It is not in point here to argue whether the intentions of the experimenter (to kill or to let die, or not to produce in the first place, for example) make a difference to the morality of *his* (or her) actions, or to our assessment of his moral character. That is not what we are talking about. We are talking about the morality of the *legislators'* actions, and possibly also about *their* moral character (though it is not clear whether the latter should concern us—the fact that the moral character of some legislators is past praying for does not affect the morality of the legislation they vote for). We are talking about the morality of the actions of the legislator, not of the experimenter, and it is the consequences (the intended consequences) of the legislation that affect this. And since it is the consequences to the embryo and to the grown person that the embryo might turn into which are thought to be relevant here, and the legislation makes no significant difference to these, I shall be arguing that such considerations provide no argument for banning the experimentation: no argument to set against the arguments for allowing it that I have already mentioned (see also 6.5).

8.6 Suppose, then, that we try to look at the question from the embryo's point of view (though actually, as we shall see, the embryo does not *have* a point of view, and this is important). The alternatives for the embryo are two: never to have existed, and to perish. I cannot see that, if we take the liberty of allowing the embryo a point of view, the embryo will find anything to choose between these two alternatives, because in any case embryos know nothing about what happens to them. So the legislation makes no difference to the embryo. For an ordinary grown human being, by contrast, there is a big difference between never having existed and perishing, because perishing is usually an unpleasant and often a painful process, and frustrates desires for what we might have done if we had not perished. But for the embryo it is not unpleasant to perish, and it has no desires.

I conclude that from the point of view of these embryos (namely those for whom the alternatives are as I have described) the legislation makes no difference. But now what about the point of view of the grown person that the embryo might develop into if it were implanted? That grown person certainly would have a point of view; he (or she) would have desires and would not want to perish now that he was grown up. But is there any difference, for this grown person, between not having been produced as an embryo in the first place and, after having been produced, perishing before achieving sentience? I cannot see any; so it is hard to avoid the conclusion that the legislation makes no difference to the grown person either.

The Tate Committee, rightly in my opinion, attached great importance to the *potential* that the embryo has of becoming a grown person (1986: 8, 25, and see 5.1 and refs.). But it drew what seems to me the wrong conclusion from this potential. What makes the potential of the embryo important is that if it is not realized, or is frustrated, there will not be that grown person. But if, as in the cases we are considering, there will not be that grown person anyway, how is the potential important? Indeed, *is* there really any potential? That is, if what is important is the possibility (this word is to be preferred to 'potential') of producing that grown person, and there is no such possibility (because the legislators have a choice between either doing something that will result in the embryo that would develop into that grown person not existing, or doing something that will result in it perishing), it looks as if the legislators can forget about this reason for imposing a ban on experimentation. For a possible explanation of why the Tate Committee was led into this false move, see Buckle 1988.

It seems, therefore, as if the reason we have been considering in favour of a ban, namely that it is necessary in order to save the lives of embryos, falls down; for this is only a reason if thereby the possibility of there being those grown people is preserved, and in these cases this is not so. They are analogous to a case in which the embryo has a defect because of which it is sure to perish before it develops into a baby; in *that* case is there any moral reason for preserving it (6.2, 10.4, 11.3)? They are also analogous to the case where because of 'cleavage arrest' (see Dawson 1988) there is no hope of the embryo ever becoming a child; such embryos just stop developing, and in the present state of *in vitro* technology nothing can be done to start development up again. It is hard to see what is lost if such embryos with no potentiality for turning into babies are destroyed, since they will perish anyway; and it is just as hard to see why the same does not apply to other embryos with no hope of survival.

But the preservation of the embryo is the main—indeed, the only significant—reason given for imposing a ban; and since, so far as I can see, the reasons given on the opposite side, also concerned with the consequences of imposing it, are much more cogent, and affect many more lives much more powerfully (the lives of those who will be given children if the experiment leads to advances in techniques, the lives of those children themselves, and the lives of those who will otherwise suffer from genetic defects which research could help eliminate), I conclude that rational and responsible legislators would not impose a ban, and that clear-headed committees who could tell the difference between a good and a bad argument would not recommend it. I give this as an illustration of how those concerned with such questions should reason about them. The same method works for other questions in this field, such as surrogacy and IVF by donor (7.2 ff., 7.8), and indeed for the whole question of whether *all* artificial methods of reproduction should be banned, as the Vatican (1987) seems to think. But I have had to be content with an illustration.

8.7 To put the matter bluntly: we should stop wasting our breath on the question of when human life begins (7.9 and refs.). Even if we grant for the sake of argument that it begins at fertilization (however that is defined)—even if we grant that there is a continuity of individual human existence from that time, so that I can answer Professor Anscombe's strikingly phrased question 'Were you a zygote?' in the affirmative (1985)—it is going to make no difference to the moral question of what the law ought to be on embryo experimentation. For imagine that I am a grown person who was once a zygote produced by IVF. In that case, I am certainly very glad that I was produced, and that nobody destroyed me, or for that matter the gametes that turned into me. But if you ask me whether I wish there had been a law at that time forbidding embryo experimentation, I answer that I am glad there was no such law. For if there had been, then very likely the IVF procedure which produced me would never have been invented. And such a law could not, in principle, have done anything for me. For though, if I had come into existence, it would have prevented my being destroyed, it would also have made false the antecedent of this hypothetical: I never would have come into existence in the first place.

I have spoken generally throughout of the embryo and the grown person, and not mentioned much the stages in between, such as the foetus, the neonate, and the child. This is because the point I have been trying to make can be made clearly for the two extreme cases. What implications all this has for neonates and foetuses—and for that matter for pairs of gametes before fertilization—requires further discussion (see papers 10, 11, and 12 in this volume). But it is a big step towards clarity if we can see that at any rate in the case of the embryo it simply does not matter morally whether, or at what point in time, it became an individual human being. What matters is what we are doing to the person, in the ordinary sense of 'person', that the embryo will or may turn into.

9

Little Human Guinea-Pigs?

9.1 There is, or at least should be, a close relation between ethical theory and the discussion of practical moral issues. The benefit is mutual. If an understanding of ethical theory (that is, of how to tell good from bad arguments about moral questions) is lacking, our arguments will be reduced to the bandying of one unsupported opinion against another, and victory will go to the side that can command the biggest *claque*. On the other hand, the ethical theorist who neglects to try out his proposals on moral issues of importance is often left maintaining views which would not remain attractive if submitted to this test.

It is very easy, however, to mistake the nature of the test. Some ethical theorists, of an intuitionist and deontological persuasion (those who base morality on duties which are grasped a priori by intuition), think that they only have to bring their opponents into conflict, on a practical issue, with some commonly held opinion to put them out of court. They would not use such arguments if they reflected that many moral views that are now abhorrent to us have been in some societies almost universally held: for example, that cruelty to animals, or even to blacks, does not matter. The appeal to received opinion in support of ethical theory has to be more subtle and more indirect than this. If, at a certain point in history, we find some opinion widely shared, what does this prove? Not that it is correct, as the example just given shows. It indicates, rather, that the reasoning processes used by people in that society lead naturally to such an opinion.

The reasoning processes may be at fault. They may be based on ignorance or neglect of relevant facts, and on muddled thinking or the rationalization of self-interested motives. But if there has been much public discussion of the questions

From *Moral Dilemmas in Modern Medicine*, ed. M. Lockwood (Oxford UP, 1985).

at issue, conducted in the language (*moral* language) that the parties to the discussion have in common, the fact that they have come to this conclusion shows something about the rules of this language, which are the rules of argument employing the concepts of the language. If we make the charitable assumption that people do not get their facts wrong all the time, and sometimes think clearly and disinterestedly about moral questions, it is reasonable to hazard the guess that the conclusions they reach are such as can be justified by argument in accordance with these rules, provided that there are no obvious logical muddles or factual mistakes or special pleadings that we can detect. Thus the fact that, when these faults are excluded or allowed for, we can explain the opinions that many thoughtful people come to, and explain them by the hypothesis that they have been arguing, however implicitly or inarticulately, in accordance with certain rules of argument that they accept, shows us something about the rules that they do accept, and thus about the nature of the concepts they are employing; that is, about ethical theory.

So it is always likely to be helpful to the ethical theorist to join in practical moral discussions; and if in return he can help clarify the discussions and expose bad arguments, that is an added incentive. Recently I took part in a working party on the ethics of research on children, which had as its members some distinguished medical people, as well as lawyers, theologians, and philosophers (for our report, see Nicholson 1986, from which I have drawn many ideas and examples). In the course of preparation for this work, I prepared the list of arguments used for and against particular experiments that is the basis of this paper. I present it as an example of how ethical theory can help moral discussion and vice versa.

It is indeed extremely useful, when faced with a general moral problem of this kind, to draw up such a list. If we put down all the arguments on both sides that we can think of or hear of from others, we have at least some assurance that we have not left out anything that could bear on the question. I drew up the list for the working party, and added to it as new arguments were produced. I then asked myself, in the case of each argument in turn, what sort of argument it was. Was it, for example, an appeal to rights: or was it an appeal to utility?

Or was it both—that is to say, was it an appeal to rights, the preservation of which could itself be justified by the utility of preserving them? When all the arguments which seemed in the least acceptable had been included in the list, were there any of them that could not be validated in terms of such a utilitarian theory of rights? It will, I hope, be obvious how enormously helpful such an exercise can be in sorting out the dispute between the utilitarians and their opponents. And it helps even more if it is done before a court of practical people who produce real cases in all their specificity, and not before an audience of philosophers who think they can prove points by trotting out fantastic examples with many important details left out.

Before I start on my list of arguments, I must make it clear that I know of no evidence that any clearly objectionable experiments on children are being done in Britain. There was a disturbing case in America some time ago in which children had been deliberately infected in an experiment (Nicholson 1986: 29); but that is not the sort of thing I shall be mainly talking about. There are procedures being used in Britain (for example, the taking of blood samples by finger-pricking from children, not for diagnostic purposes) to which, I suppose, nobody would at first sight object, but which *might* be thought to infringe the rights of the child and might also, in extremely rare cases, put the child at some small risk. It is difficult, obviously, to draw a sharp line between this and hypothetical cases in which the risk would not be so negligible, such as a renal biopsy in the course of an operation for some other purpose (where the child, perhaps while having its appendix removed, has a tiny piece of one kidney removed as well, for use in kidney research unrelated to the child's condition—see Nicholson 1986: 10). I can well understand the medical profession's desire to have some guidelines in this area.

9.2 So let us start by listing some arguments which might be used *for* a particular piece of research of this kind, or for research on child subjects in general. We have to distinguish between (1) research that is incidental to, and helpful for, the treatment of the particular condition from which the child is suffering (an obvious example being the trying out on the child of a treatment which is still not proved to be a cure for the child's condition, but which may cure him: this is done all the time to both children and adults, and often to their advantage), and (2) research which is not intended in any way to help the patient recover from his condition. An example of this would be the renal biopsy in the case I have just mentioned, where the child had nothing wrong with its kidneys.

The first of these two kinds of research is often called *therapeutic research* and the second *non-therapeutic research*. Some people have thought the distinction between these so important that they have made it the basis of proposed restrictions, saying that non-therapeutic research on children should be banned absolutely. The distinction is not entirely clear, however. Therapy as such—I mean the cure of the individual patient—is never the purpose of research. The two aims are distinct though often combined. If, therefore, we ask for reasons for engaging in research of any kind, the cure of the individual patient cannot be given as one of them. We may hope to learn more about the disease and thus become able to cure *other* patients; but the results of the research, except in extremely rare cases, will not be known until it is too late to use them to help *this* patient.

The key to understanding the distinction between therapeutic and non-therapeutic research is to notice that both research and therapy are marked out as such by their aims, which are different from each other. Research aims at the advancement of knowledge, therapy at the cure of a patient. Therapeutic research cannot be research which is therapy or therapy which is research (that is impossible); it is, rather, an activity which has *both* aims. In the purest case, the very same intervention on a patient may be intended both to cure and to discover something. In less pure cases interventions may take place which have a therapeutic intention but which are modified in some way as an aid to research (for example, a few extra millilitres of blood are taken when doing a diagnostic sample, so that the additional blood can be used for research). Therapeutic research is thus an activity which has both aims; non-therapeutic research is an activity which has only a research and not a therapeutic aim.

9.3 Why do we carry out research on children, as contrasted with therapy? It is done on humans in general when tests on animals are insufficient to give us the information we need, usually because animals have different physiologies from humans. I must mention in passing that there is of course a very big question about the justification for using animals in experiments; I am not taking up a position on that in this paper, and shall put the question on one side for the present. Granted, however, that it is all right to use human adults, with their consent, in certain experiments, why use children?

One reason for experimenting on human beings is to test new types of treatment. Now, there are some treatments that are applicable only to children, usually because the conditions that they are treatments for only afflict children. Or it may be that a treatment which is suitable and safe for adults is not for children. An example would be if, as is normal, the safe maximum dose for an adult of a certain drug would not be safe for a young child. Or it might be that a much smaller dose was effective for a child; for instance, because the child himself is smaller and therefore the blood-concentration produced by a given dose is larger.

If, therefore, we are to test either the effectiveness or the safety of drugs to be given to children, we may have to try them out on children. There are more and less rigorous ways of trying out new treatments. All those with any claim to rigour use control groups; a drug, for example, is given to one group and not given to another, and the results compared statistically. In the most rigorous procedure, neither the patients nor those observing the effects of the drug know which patients have had it. In a less rigorous procedure the researchers know but the patients do not. In a still less rigorous procedure everybody knows. The reason for withholding knowledge is to guard against the danger that patients or their doctors may think, or persuade themselves, that they are being helped by a treatment when they are not, or may even be being helped, but only by the so-called 'placebo effect': they think the treatment will help them so they get better, even if the treatment is only doses of coloured water—as happens fre-
·quently enough to vitiate tests of drugs if the more rigorous precautions are not observed.

As we shall see, the necessity, in rigorous testing, for these blind and double-blind trials, and the necessity for controls at all, provides one argument against experimentation on humans. If some are given just coloured water and no drug, this is depriving them of something which might have helped them. This argument is less strong when one drug is being compared with another (usually a new with an established one); but even here objections can be raised. I should like to mention one example, on the other side, of a case where the omission of controlled tests led to immense harm. At one time paediatricians used to administer oxygen quite freely to newborn babies for various disorders; it helped the disorders and was assumed to be harmless. Only after many years was it discovered that oxygen given in these quantities to neonates can result in their developing a disease of the eyes called retrolental fibroplasia, which is a cause of blindness. If controlled tests had been used from the beginning, this side-effect of the treatment would have been discovered much earlier and a lot of children would not have lost their sight. When it was first suspected that this harmful side-effect was occurring, a controlled trial was done; and this in itself presents ethical problems, because it involved giving the oxygen to some children even though it endangered their sight (Nicholson 1986: 54). I suspect that the same findings could have been achieved statistically by examining past records. A controlled trial at the beginning would not have raised this problem, because then nobody knew, nor was there even any reason to suspect, that oxygen was harmful, and also because, by carefully monitoring its effects, the trial could have been terminated as soon as any adverse ones became apparent. Thus at no time would the researchers have been administering a treatment which they knew, or even had reason to suspect, was other than wholly beneficial. However, this question of the ethics of controlled trials is a subject for a paper by itself, and I shall not pursue it here. Michael Lockwood has written an interesting and provocative paper on the issue (1983).

The other main use of research on children (as on adults) is entirely non-therapeutic; it is where, in order to study certain abnormalities properly (for example, deficiency diseases like · rickets), we have to know what is the normal value of a certain variable—what, say, is the normal amount of a certain substance in the blood of children in a given population. Only then can we know what variations are departures from the normal, and which are significant. One could not combat rickets in a population of children safely and effectively without this information. More generally, the acquisition of new knowledge in medicine is bound to require the doing of various things to human bodies; and some of these things cannot be done without interventions which, if made without consent and outside the medical context, would count as assaults. Some of these are quite trivial like the taking of blood samples and the testing of kneejerks; others, like the renal biopsies I mentioned, are more serious. If, however, we think the advance of medical knowledge to be on the whole in the general interest, and agree that it would be to some degree hampered if such interventions were forbidden, this may make us ready to allow them in at least some cases.

9.4   So far I have been talking of the reasons that could be given for using children as subjects which arise from the advance of the research itself. Next we must consider some benefits which the children themselves may get out of the research. I am not speaking of benefits to other children who may be cured as a result of the development of the treatment; that has already been covered. But the child himself who is the subject may, as a result, get a new drug which may cure him, when the drug, because it has not yet been fully tested or because it is not yet mass-produced, is not generally available. We have only to think of the great efforts that some cancer patients have made to obtain interferon, even though it was not yet known to be effective against cancer of any sort. There are certainly conditions under which I would allow myself to become a research subject for that reason; and I would also allow my child to be, at least if the child were dying.

Then there are certain quite extraneous reasons why one might wish to become a subject—reasons which a child also might acknowledge, if he were able to understand what was going on. First, suppose that some handsome payment is given for a quite trivial intervention. There are obvious dangers in hiring children as research subjects; it puts temptation in the way of their parents. But I do not think that these dangers should altogether rule out the practice. Other incentives, such as giving badges to children who surrender their baby teeth when they fall out so that the teeth can be used for research, seem relatively harmless. This is perhaps the place to mention what we might call the moral inducement: we might say that we all, including children, have a duty to help our fellow humans, and one way we can do this is by furthering the progress of medical research. So if I allow myself to be used as a research subject, I am adopting one way of fulfilling this duty. If an older child did this voluntarily knowing what he was doing, then it would be one up to the child; we should think of him as we do of voluntary blood donors. This inducement is not applicable to young children; but it has been suggested (not by me) that it is not unreasonable to expect them to do their duty by the community if there is something which they alone can do, and at very small cost to themselves.

The last category of pro-arguments that I shall consider will raise eyebrows; but I include it for the sake of completeness. Both the researcher and his institution get benefits from the research if successful (and sometimes even if not). His knowledge and skill is improved; so is the reputation of the institution. This may produce financial advantages by advancing the career of the researcher or the attractiveness of the institution to funding bodies. Though there are obvious dangers in these motives, and they have led to research of all sorts being carried out which ought not to have been, the motives are not in themselves bad. They need some measure of control; but in the absence of counter-arguments they would be perfectly respectable.

9.5   That, then, is the end of my list of pro-arguments. It may not be complete. But what are the considerations on the other side? First, it can be said that almost any intervention in somebody's body carries a risk, however trivial, of discomfort, or danger to health, or even to life. This applies even to things like taking blood samples. Using anybody as a research subject therefore needs justification. This is seen most easily in the case of non-therapeutic research, where there is no intended benefit to the subject's condition. It may be that the benefits to society through the advance of research will outweigh the danger, but this needs to be shown.

Even in the case of therapeutic research, where the patient may benefit through possible cure, there are still difficulties.

First, if the treatment is new, it may have undesirable and unexpected side-effects. Or it may turn out to be less effective than an older treatment, and in research it is not usually possible to give both at once. If, in a controlled trial, a placebo is used for the control group, then, as we saw earlier, the patients in that group are being denied, through their bad luck in being in that group and not in the group which receives the treatment, the chance of benefiting from it. This unfairness is not so apparent where a new treatment is being compared with an old, as is much more common; but even here there is the likelihood that one treatment will turn out to have been better than the other, so that the ones who got the worse treatment were disadvantaged. On the other side, it could be said that, since it was not known in advance which treatment would turn out better, both groups were given an equal *chance* of benefit. This argument could even be used with placebos in cases where there is no alternative treatment: those who get the treatment get a chance of cure and a chance of harm through side-effects; those who get the placebo get neither, but the risks they avoid and the benefits they lose may exactly balance out. However, this is unlikely always to be the case.

It would seem that all these counter-indications apply at least as much to child subjects as to adults, if not more. There are others which apply especially to children. To take the simpler ones first: children are easily frightened, and it is often difficult or impossible to explain to them what is going on. They may find themselves taken in charge by strange people and subjected to procedures whose effects and whose purpose they know nothing about; they may not know from one moment to the next what is going to happen to them. Children usually make a fuss about injections even when attended by loving parents and handled by the most kindly doctors and nurses; great benefits obviously have to be claimed before it becomes justifiable to subject children to these traumas. The same would apply even more forcefully to any procedure which involved separating children from their parents when it was not necessary for their treatment. For all these reasons it may be wrong to do to a child what it would be perfectly all right to do to an adult with his consent (on consent, see 2.7 f. and refs.).

9.6 But it is this question of consent which makes the biggest difference between adults and children. It is generally held, and is held by the law, that children below certain ages cannot give valid consent for certain things to be done to them. This is on several grounds. First, it is held that consent requires full information about what is being consented to; and children do not have this, if they cannot understand what is to be done to them. There is obviously a gradation here: a new-born baby knows absolutely nothing, but a 15-year-old may have a very good idea—perhaps better, if he is intelligent, than some less intelligent adults.

Secondly, consent requires that the consenter is free to refuse; but this can mean two things at least (see 2.8, 13.6, and Aristotle 1109^{b}30 ff.). In one sense a person is not free if you tie him to the operating table, or administer an anaesthetic without his knowledge, and cut him up. In a different sense he is not free if he is subject to threats of some evil or other if he will not consent. For example, his parent may say he will give him a whipping if he will not. I am going to call this 'duress'. It needs to be asked whether children necessarily lack freedom in any of these ways. I think it can be taken for granted that if a child, or anybody else, is ignorant or physically manhandled, he does not consent freely. Duress is more tricky. The illustration I gave is clear enough. But what if the parent is in the habit of giving the child sweets and says the sweets will stop if the child does not consent? What, on the other hand, if the parent is not in the habit of giving the child sweets, but says that he will on this occasion if the child consents? Lawyers can say more about this; but I shall not. If the bride tells the bridegroom that she will not marry him unless he promises that the children of the marriage will be brought up in the Roman Catholic religion, has he consented freely if he so promises? If I am told that I cannot have the car unless I pay £3,000, and consent to pay it, is my consent free?

This is a murky area, but some things can nevertheless be said about it. It seems safe to say that at any rate some children on whom experiments of minor sorts might be performed cannot consent validly to them. This must be the case with new-born babies. Are we to ban such experiments altogether because valid consent cannot be given? The reasons for the inability to give valid consent are the very same reasons that make us protect children by keeping them—so long as and to the extent that these reasons hold—under the tutelage of their parents or guardians. Because children lack knowledge of the effects of their actions and of what is done to them, we to a greater or lesser extent allow parents to decide for them what they may do or what may be done to them; the parents supply the knowledge which the children lack. Similarly with freedom; because children are weak and therefore at the mercy of force and duress, we keep them under the protection of parents, who can prevent unauthorized persons submitting them to such force or duress, but who are themselves allowed to apply force or duress for what they think is the child's own future good.

For these two reasons—the child's lack of knowledge and of freedom—parents normally make and enforce a great many decisions for their children. The question in the present case is whether these decisions may rightly include decisions to let the child be experimented on. In order to answer this question, we have to ask more generally why there should be a right, even of adults, not to have things done to their bodies without their consent. I fancy that it is here that an apparent division will come to the surface between utilitarians and their intuitionist opponents—a division which I hope to have shown elsewhere to be only apparent, because it is fairly easy for a utilitarian to give an account of rights, and of intuitions about them, within his theory (see e.g. *MT* 147 ff., H 1989*b*: 79–120, and Sumner 1987).

9.7   Some people will claim that there just *is* this right; we all know it exists and no reason needs to be given for it. I do not myself belong to this school of thought, because I like to have reasons for what I say—it comes in so handy when others disagree with one. The grounds on which I would defend this right are utilitarian. It seems generally to be the case that normal adults are better judges of their own future good (their own interest) than other people who may think they know better. It is in this belief that we seek to protect people from interference, however well meant, by other people. This protection we give by acknowledging and preserving a right to non-interference, and entrenching it or hedging it about with very strong moral feelings, if ever the right is infringed. So, even if our reasons for according the right are utilitarian, we do want people, ourselves included, to have these intuitions, and normally to act on them without hesitation, rather than sickly them over with the pale cast of thought, which may lead us into all kinds of special pleading (particularly if the experiment is important to our career), and in any case will be based on knowledge which, though it may be greater than the patient's, is a great way from omniscience, and may be quite insufficient for forming a wise opinion. We do better in most cases to stick to our moral convictions, provided that these are in general sound ones.

However, once we see the reason for acknowledging this right, we see also that it is only a right in general, or prima facie; it is, as the lawyers say, defeasible. Even if, for practical reasons, we want, as we should want, to keep our moral principles manageably simple, there may be certain broad classes which we make into exceptions to a principle. For example, we all think killing people is wrong, but most of us think that it is all right to kill somebody if that is the only way of stopping him killing us. The question for us here is 'Given that in general we acknowledge a right not to have one's body interfered with without one's consent, ought the right to be relaxed in the case of some children? Ought, therefore, the well-entrenched general rule to have an exception of some sort written into it, allowing some kinds of research on children without their own consent? And if so, in what sorts of cases, and under what conditions? In particular, if the children cannot give consent, who should be required to give it?'

Since consent is required from adults because that is thought to be in general the best way of securing their interests, we have to ask what is the best alternative way of securing the interests of children who cannot give consent. An extreme way might be to forbid all experiments on children. An only slightly less extreme way would be, as some have suggested, to forbid all non-therapeutic research on them. But this would be in some cases to forgo great benefits to the advance of medicine in order to avoid negligible harms to subjects. Most of us are utilitarians to this extent, that if, by pricking some children's fingers to take blood samples, we could produce crucial evidence which would lead to the elimination of a disease that killed large numbers of children, we would think it reasonable to allow the children's parents to give consent to the experiment on the children's behalf. Such a widespread opinion in itself proves nothing, except that in such a case the utilitarian verdict is not wholly counter-intuitive.

If it were a case of adults, we might reason as follows: the benefits that come from the experiment are likely to be very great; the discomfort and risk to the subjects are extremely small; so, although the adult should have a *right* to withhold consent, it would be wrong of him to exercise that right. In the case of a child who cannot give or withhold consent, the same considerations apply at one remove. For the same reasons as we give to adults a right to refuse consent (namely because we think that that is the safest thing in the interests of adults generally), we give children a right not to be interfered with without the consent of their parents (because that is the safest thing in the interests of children generally). But for the same reason as we say that it would be wrong for an adult to refuse consent in a case like this (because the benefit hoped for is very large and the risk extremely small), we say that it would be wrong for a parent, whose consent is made a condition in order to protect the interest and the right of the child, to refuse it (because, again, the benefit is large and the risk small). This result could easily be reversed if the benefit were smaller or more unlikely, or the risk greater. The whole question is therefore going to turn on the quantification of these risks and benefits. Our working party's report has a whole chapter on risks and their quantification (Nicholson 1986: ch. 5).

9.8 Since there is obviously going to be some quantification of risks and benefits to be done, it will never be sufficient, even in the case of adult subjects, to leave the decision simply to the researcher and the subject between them. For the researcher is an interested party, and the subject, if a layman, may not have, and may not even be able to understand, the information which is required for a rational decision. The same applies to parents making such decisions on behalf of their children. That is one reason, though not the only one, why hospitals and research institutions ought to have ethical committees containing disinterested experts who can look at the details of proposed experiments and see whether the benefits do exceed the risks by a sufficient margin. Since all experiments are different, general guidelines in writing cannot achieve this, necessary as they are. A parent making such a decision ought to have the safeguard of knowing that such a committee has passed the experiment, even if he cannot himself weigh up the benefits and risks as an expert can.

Another reason for having ethical committees is that they can look at these questions continuously over a period of time, and thus gain experience, and so perhaps be able to lay down for themselves and others general guidelines, so that experiments will not even be proposed which the committees would be unlikely to permit. They can also exercise a general surveillance to see that the rights of children and their parents are not being infringed, or, if they are, to make recommendations which, if such abuses turn out to be widespread, may lead to a tightening of the law.

I have said that such committees should contain experts, as obviously they must if they are to understand what they are deciding. Ought they also to contain laymen with special qualifications? The same question applies to any *national* bodies that advise or adjudicate on such questions. Or ought there to be two kinds of committee, one consisting of experts and the other at least partly of laymen? That was the solution proposed in Florida to look after a similar problem—the regulation of the use of behaviour therapy in prisons and mental hospitals (see 4.2 and Wexler 1975). It has been suggested in Britain that there should be, in addition to the General Medical Council, which is an expert body, a different body consisting in part of experts in medicine but in part of practitioners of other relevant disciplines like law, and of others experienced in the problems that arise. Our own working party had, of course, such a composition, and so have many similar *ad hoc* and temporary committees and commissions, some enjoying a more official status than others. The suggestion is that there should be a *permanent* body of this sort for all problems arising in medical ethics and bioethics (Kennedy 1982). Apart from a fear that its proceedings might become too congested if it took on so much, and that it would have to proliferate subcommittees to cope with various specialist fields, I have nothing in principle against the proposal. But I can conceive of some doctors objecting.

Obviously there is a lot more to be said about possible procedures. But the most useful thing our working party did was to discuss questions of principle, illustrating the principles by considering real cases. We were able by this means to display, and even to some extent quantify, the factors that are important in such decisions. This paper has consisted of a list of these factors without any attempt at quantification; but we thought it possible for those engaged in research to give an idea of how important each factor is in a selection of typical cases, and so enable us to devise a set of helpful guidelines. That is what our working party tried to do.

9.9 In conclusion, it will have been noticed that all the pros and cons that I listed were of a broadly utilitarian sort. I tried hard to include every reason, whether utilitarian or not, that anyone could suggest for or against conducting such experiments; but it turned out that all the sustainable reasons were compatible with utilitarianism, even those which had to do with the rights of children and parents.

It is worth while to emphasize this point. Looking at the surviving reasons again, it seems to me that the only ones that are not obviously utilitarian are those concerned with unfairness to control groups who do not get a drug which might have benefited them, and those concerned with a right not to be experimented on without one's consent. I hope I have shown in the latter case that the requirement of consent has a utilitarian justification, as has the allowing of proxy consent, with safeguards, in the case of children. As regards unfairness to control groups, I have not discussed the question fully; but two points can be made. One is that, as I have argued elsewhere, there is an adequate utilitarian justification for our insistence on justice in general and on the particular principles of justice that most of us accept. To put it baldly, things go much better in a society where such principles are respected (*MT* 156 ff.). The other is that in actual cases of research, as opposed to fictional ones, it should be possible to observe these principles without invalidating the research. Certainly there are nearly always both advantages and disadvantages in belonging to the control group, and so it is not treated unfairly. If the same requirement of consent or proxy consent is imposed in controlled experiments as in others, the subjects in the control group can have their interests protected. For the fact that he is taking part in the experiment will be known either to the subject himself or to the proxy consenter (though neither may know which group the subject has been assigned to). So consent can be refused if being a control seems not to be in the subject's best interests. It would be wrong if such a refusal resulted in the withholding of therapy altogether; but I assume that this is not in question.

So I was left at the end of the working party convinced that a carefully constructed utilitarian system of the sort that I advocate can handle an issue like this in a way that does justice to the intuitions and convictions that most of us have, or at least to those which we shall retain when we have reflected sufficiently on the issue.

Abortion and the Golden Rule

10.1 If philosophers are going to apply ethical theory successfully to practical issues, they must first have a theory. This
may seem obvious; but they often proceed as if it were not so.
A philosopher's chief contribution to a practical issue should
be to show us which are good and which are bad arguments;
and to do this he has to have some way of telling one from the
other. Moral philosophy therefore needs a basis in philosophical logic—the logic of the moral concepts. But we find, for
example, Professor Judith Jarvis Thomson, in an article on
abortion (1971) which has been justly praised for the ingenuity
and liveliness of her examples, proceeding as if this were not
necessary at all. She simply parades the examples before us
and asks what we would say about them. But how do we know
whether what we feel inclined to say has any secure ground?
May we not feel inclined to say it just because of the way we
were brought up to think? And was this necessarily the right
way? It is highly diverting to watch the encounter in the same
volume between her and Mr John Finnis (1973), who, being a
devout Roman Catholic, has intuitions which differ from hers
(and mine) in the wildest fashion. I just do not know how to
tell whether Mr Finnis is on safe ground when he claims that
suicide is 'a paradigm case of an action that is always wrong';
nor Professor Thomson when she makes the no doubt more
popular claim that we have a right to decide what happens in
and to our own bodies. How would we choose between these
potentially conflicting intuitions? Is it simply a contest in
rhetoric?

In contrast, a philosopher who wishes to contribute to the
solution of this and similar practical problems should be trying
to develop, on the basis of a study of the moral concepts and
their logical properties, a theory of moral reasoning that will

From *Philosophy and Public Affairs* 4 (1975).

determine which arguments we ought to accept. Professor Thomson might be surprised to see me saying this, because she thinks (1968: 2) that I am an emotivist, in spite of the fact that I devoted two of the very first papers I ever published (H 1949, 1951) to a refutation of emotivism. Her examples are entertaining, and help to show up our prejudices; but they will do no more than that until we have a way of telling which prejudices ought to be abandoned.

10.2 I shall abjure two approaches to the question of abortion which have proved quite unhelpful. The first puts the question in terms of the 'rights' of the foetus or the mother; the second demands, as a necessary condition for solving the problem, an answer to the question, Is the foetus a person? The first is unhelpful unless supplemented by an account of how we might argue conclusively about rights. Rights are the stamping ground of intuitionists, and it would be difficult to find any claim confidently asserted to a right which could not be as confidently countered by a claim to another right, such that both rights cannot simultaneously be complied with. This is plainly true in the present controversy, as it is in the case of rights to property—one man has a right not to starve, another a right to hold on to the money that would buy him food. Professor Thomson evidently believes in property rights, because she curiously bases the right of a woman to decide what happens in and to her own body on her ownership of it. We might ask whether, if this is correct, the property is disposable; could it be held that by the marriage contract a wife and a husband yield up to each other some of their property rights in their own bodies? If so, might we find male chauvinists who were prepared to claim that, if the husband wants to have an heir, the wife cannot claim an absolute liberty to have an abortion? As a question of law, this could be determined by the courts and the legislature; but as a question of morals . . . ?

In the law, cash value can be given to statements about rights by translating them into statements about what it is or is not lawful to do. An analogous translation will have to be effected in morals, with 'right' (adjective), 'wrong', and 'ought' taking the place of 'lawful' and 'unlawful', before the word 'rights' can be a dependable prop for moral arguments. We need a theory of rights which links the concept firmly to those of 'right', 'wrong', and 'ought'—concepts whose logic is even now a little better understood. The simplest such theory would be one which said that A has a right, in one sense of the word, to do X if and only if it is not wrong for A to do X; and that A has a right, in another sense, to do X if and only if it is wrong to prevent A from doing X; and that A has a right to do X in a third sense if and only if it is wrong not to assist A to do X (the extent of the assistance, and the persons from whom it is due, being unspecified and, on many occasions of the use of this ambiguous word 'rights', unspecifiable). It is often unclear, when people claim that women have a right to do what they like with their own bodies, which of these senses is being used. Does it, for example, mean that it is not wrong for them to terminate their own pregnancies, or that it is wrong to stop them doing this, or that it is wrong not to assist them in doing this? For our present purposes it is best to leave these difficulties on one side and say that when a reliable analysis of the various senses of 'rights' in terms of 'wrong' or 'ought' is forthcoming, arguments about rights will be restatable in terms of what it is wrong to do, or what we ought or ought not to do. Till then we shall get the issues in better focus if we discuss them directly in terms of what we ought or ought not to do, or what it would be right or wrong to do, to the foetus or the mother in specified circumstances. I have made a beginning of explaining the concept of rights in terms of other more perspicuous concepts in *MT* ch. 9; see also H 1989*b*: 79–120 and Sumner 1987.

10.3 The other unhelpful approach, that of asking whether the foetus is a person, has been so universally popular that in many of the writings it is assumed that this question is the key to the whole problem. The reason for this is easy to see; if there is a well-established moral principle that the intentional killing of other innocent persons is always murder, and therefore wrong, it looks as if an easy way to determine whether it is wrong to kill foetuses is to determine whether they are persons, and thus settle once for all whether they are subsumable under the principle. But this approach has run into well-known difficulties, the basic reason for which is the following. If a normative or evaluative principle is framed in terms of a predicate which has fuzzy edges (as nearly all predicates in practice have), then we are not going to be able to use the principle to decide cases on the borderline without doing some more normation or evaluation. If we make a law forbidding the use of wheeled vehicles in the park, and somebody thinks he can go in the park on roller skates, no amount of cerebration, and no amount of inspection of roller skates, are going to settle for us the question of whether roller skates are wheeled vehicles 'within the meaning of the Act', if the Act has not specified whether they are; the judge has to decide whether they are to be counted as such (Hart 1961: 123). And this is a further determination of the law. The judge may have very good reasons of public interest or morals for his decision; but he cannot make it by any physical or metaphysical investigation of roller skates to see whether they are really wheeled vehicles. If he had not led too sheltered a life, he knew all he needed to know about roller skates before the case ever came into court.

In the same way the decision to say that the foetus becomes a person at conception, or at quickening, or at birth, or whenever takes your fancy, and that thereafter, because it is a person, destruction of it is murder, is inescapably a moral decision, for which we have to have moral reasons. It is not necessary, in order to make this point, to insist that the word 'person' is a moral word; though in many contexts there is much to be said for taking this line. It is necessary only to notice that 'person', even if descriptive, is not a fully determinate concept; it is loose at the edges, as the abortion controversy only too clearly shows. Therefore, if we decide that, 'within the meaning of' the principle about murder, a foetus becomes a person as soon as it is conceived, we are deciding a moral question, and ought to have a moral reason for our decision (7.9, 8.7, 11.1 f.). It is no use looking more closely at the foetus to satisfy ourselves that it is really a person (as the people do who make so much of the fact that it has arms and legs); we already have all the information that we need about the foetus. What is needed is thought about the moral question, 'How ought this creature, about whose properties, circumstances, and probable future we are quite adequately informed, to be treated?' If, in our desire to get out of addressing ourselves to this moral question—to get it settled for us without any moral thought on our part—we go first to the physicians for information about whether the foetus is really a person, and then, when they have told us all they can, to the metaphysicians, we are only indulging in the well-known vice of philosophers (which my fellow linguistic philosophers, at any rate, ought to be on their guard against, because that is the mainstay of our training)—the vice of trying to settle substantial questions by verbal manœuvres.

I am not saying that physiological research on the foetus has no bearing on moral questions about abortion. If it brought to light, for example, that foetuses really do suffer on the same scale as adults do, then that would be a good moral reason for not causing them to suffer (11.3). It will not do to show that they wriggle when pricked; for so do earthworms, and I do not think that the upholders of the rights of unborn children wish to extend these rights to earthworms. Encephalograms are better; but there are enormous theoretical and practical difficulties in the argument from encephalograms to conscious experiences. In default of these latter, which would have to be of such a sort as to distinguish foetuses radically from other creatures which the anti-abortionists would not lift a finger to protect, the main weight of the anti-abortionist argument is likely to rest, not on the sufferings of the foetus, but on harms done to the interests of the person into whom the foetus would normally develop. These will be the subject of most of the rest of this paper and the next.

Approaching our moral question in the most general way, let us ask whether there is anything about the foetus or about the person it may turn into that should make us say that we ought not to kill it. If, instead of asking this question, somebody wants to go on asking, indirectly, whether the foetus is a person, and whether, therefore, killing it is wrong, he is at liberty to do so; but I must point out that the reasons he will have to give for saying that it is a person, and that, therefore, killing it is wrong (or that it is not a person and, therefore, killing it is not wrong) will be the very same moral reasons as I shall be giving for the answer to my more direct question. Whichever way one takes it, one cannot avoid giving a reasoned answer to this moral question; so why not take it the simplest way? To say that the foetus is (or is not) a person gives by itself no moral reason for or against killing it; it merely encapsulates any reasons we may have for including the foetus within a certain category of creatures that it is, or is not, wrong to kill (i.e. persons or non-persons). The word 'person' is doing no work here (other than that of bemusing us).

10.4 Is there, then, anything about the foetus which raises moral problems about the legitimacy of killing it? At this point I must declare that I have no axe to grind—I am not a fervent abortionist nor a fervent anti-abortionist—I just want fervently to get to the root of the matter. It will be seen, as the argument goes on, that the first move I shall make is one which will give cheer to the anti-abortionists; but, before they have had time to celebrate, it will appear that this move brings with it, inescapably, another move which should encourage the other side. We shall end up somewhere in between, but perhaps with a clearer idea of how, in principle, to set about answering questions about particular abortions.

The single, or at least the main, thing about the foetus that raises the moral question is that, if not terminated, the pregnancy is highly likely to result in the birth and growth to maturity of a person just like the rest of us. The word 'person' here re-enters the argument, but in a context and with a meaning that does not give rise to the old troubles; for it is clear at least that we ordinary adults are persons. If we knew beyond a peradventure that a foetus was going to miscarry anyway, then little would remain of the moral problem beyond the probably minimal sufferings caused to the mother and just possibly the foetus by terminating the pregnancy now—though these might be less than those caused by a miscarriage (6.2, 8.6, 11.3). If, on the other hand, we knew (to use Professor Tooley's science-fiction example (1972: 60)) that an embryo kitten would, if not aborted but given a wonder drug, turn into a being with a human mind like ours, then that too would raise a moral problem. Perhaps Tooley thinks not; but we shall see. It is, to use his useful expression, the 'potentiality' that the foetus has of becoming a person in the full ordinary sense that creates the problem (see 5.1 and refs.). It is because Tooley thinks that, once the 'potentiality principle' (see below) is admitted, the conservatives or extreme anti-abortionists will win the case hands down, that he seeks reasons for rejecting it; but, again, we shall see.

We can explain why the potentiality of the foetus for becoming a person raises a moral problem if we appeal to a type of argument which, in one guise or another, has been the formal basis of almost all theories of moral reasoning that have contributed much that is worth while to our understanding of it. I am alluding to the Christian (and indeed pre-Christian) 'Golden Rule', the Kantian Categorical Imperative, the ideal observer theory, the rational contractor theory, various kinds of utilitarianism, and my own universal prescriptivism (see 1.6, 15.2 and refs., and *MT*). I would claim that the last of these gives the greatest promise of putting what is common to all these theories in a perspicuous way, and so revealing their justification in logic; but it is not the purpose of this paper to give this justification. Instead, since the problem of abortion is discussed as often as not from a Christian standpoint, and since I hope thereby to find a provisional starting point for the argument on which many would agree, I shall use that form of the argument which rests on the Golden Rule that we should do to others as we wish them to do to us (Matt. 7: 12). It is a logical extension of this form of argument to say that we should do to others what we are glad was done to us (1.6, 7.6, 11.5 f.). Two (surely readily admissible) changes are involved here. The first is a mere difference in the two tenses which cannot be morally relevant. Instead of saying that we should do to others as we wish them (in the future) to do to us, we say that we should do to others as we wish that they had done to us (in the past). The second is a change from the hypothetical to the actual: instead of saying that we should do to others as we wish that they had done to us, we say that we should do to others as we are glad that they did do to us. I cannot see that this could make any difference to the spirit of the injunction, and logical grounds could in any case be given, based on the universal prescriptivist thesis, for extending the Golden Rule in this way (5.2, 6.2, 11.4).

The application of this injunction to the problem of abortion is obvious. If we are glad that nobody terminated the pregnancy that resulted in our birth, then we are enjoined not, *ceteris paribus*, to terminate any pregnancy which will result in the birth of a person having a life like ours. Close attention obviously needs to be paid to the '*ceteris paribus*' clause, and also to the expression 'like ours'. The 'universalizability' of moral judgements, which is one of the logical bases of the Golden Rule, requires us to make the same moral judgement about qualitatively identical cases, and about cases which are relevantly similar. Since no cases in this area are going to be qualitatively identical, we shall have to rely on relevant similarity. Without raising a very large topic in moral philosophy (see *MT* 62), we can perhaps avoid the difficulty by pointing out that the relevant respects here are going to be those things about our life which make us glad that we were born. These can be stated in a general enough way to cover all those persons who are, or who are going to be or would be, glad that they were born. Those who are not glad they were born will still have a reason for not aborting those who would be glad; for even the former wish that, if they had been going to be glad that they were born, nobody should have aborted them. So, although I have, for the sake of simplicity, put the injunction in a way that makes it apply only to the abortion of people who will have a life just like that of the aborter, it is generalizable to cover the abortion of any foetus which will, if not aborted, turn into someone who will be glad to be alive.

I now come back to Professor Tooley's wonder kitten. He says that, if it became possible, by administering a wonder drug to an embryo kitten, to cause it to turn into a being with a human mind like ours, we should still not feel under any obligation either to administer the drug to kittens or to refrain from aborting kittens to whom the drug had been administered by others. He uses this as an argument against the 'potentiality principle', which says that if there are any properties which are possessed by adult human beings and which endow any organisms possessing them with a serious right to life, then 'at least one of those properties will be such that any organism potentially possessing that property has a serious right to life even now, simply by virtue of that potentiality, where an organism possesses a property potentially if it will come to have that property in the normal course of its development' (Tooley 1972: 55 f.). Putting this more briefly and in terms of 'wrong' instead of 'rights', the potentiality principle says that if it would be wrong to kill an adult human being because he has a certain property, it is wrong to kill an organism (e.g. a foetus) which will come to have that property if it develops normally.

There is one minor objection to what Tooley says which we can pass over quickly. The administration of wonder drugs is not normal development, so Tooley ought not to have used the words 'in the normal course of its development'; they spoil his 'kitten' example. But let us amend our summary of his principle by omitting the words 'if it develops normally' and substituting 'if we do not kill it'. I do not think that this substitution makes Tooley's argument any weaker than it is already.

Now suppose that I discovered that I myself was the result of the administration of the wonder drug to a kitten embryo. To make this extension of the example work, we have to suppose that the drug is even more wonderful and can make kitten embryos grow into beings with human bodies as well as minds; but it is hard to see how this could make any moral difference, especially for Tooley, who rests none of his argument on bodily shape. If this happened, it would not make my reasons for being glad that I was not aborted cease to apply. I certainly prescribe that they should not have aborted an embryo kitten which the wonder drug was going to turn into me. And so, by the Golden Rule, I must say that I should not abort an embryo kitten to whom the wonder drug had been administered and which therefore was going to turn into a creature just like me. And, for what it is worth, that is what I would say. The fact that I confidently assert this, whereas Tooley confidently asserts the opposite—so confidently, in fact, that he thinks that this single example is enough to establish his entire case against the potentiality principle, and produces no other—just shows how inadequate intuitions are as a guide to moral conclusions. The fantastic nature of his example (like that of some of Professor Thomson's) makes it even more difficult to be certain that we are saying what we ought to say about it. Our intuitions are the result of our upbringings, and we were not brought up on cases where kittens can be turned into beings with human minds, or where people get kidnapped and have distinguished violinists with kidney failure plugged into their bloodstreams, as in Professor Thomson's example.

The problem becomes more difficult if we ask whether the same argument could be used to establish that it would be wrong, if this wonder drug were invented, not to administer it to all the embryo kittens one could get hold of. I shall postpone discussion of this problem until we have discussed the similar problem of whether the potentiality principle, once established, will not force upon us an extreme conservative position not only about abortion but also about contraception, and even forbid chastity. If we allow the potentiality of procreating human beings to place upon us obligations to procreate them, shall we not have a duty to procreate all the human beings that we can, and will not even monks and nuns have to obey King Lear's injunction (Act IV, sc. vi) to 'let copulation thrive'? To the general problem which this raises I shall return (10.7 and refs.). We shall see that it is simply the familiar problem about the right population policy, which has to be faced whatever view we take of the present question.

10.5   I propose to take it as established that the potentiality principle is not refuted by Tooley's one example, and that it therefore holds the field until somebody produces a better argument against it—which I do not expect to happen, because the potentiality principle itself can be based on the Golden Rule, as the examples already considered show, and the Golden Rule has a secure logical foundation which I have already mentioned, though I have not had room to expound it.

Why does Tooley think that, if the potentiality principle is once granted, the extreme conservative position on abortion becomes impregnable? Obviously because he has neglected to consider some other potential beings. Take, to start with, the next child that this mother will have if this pregnancy is terminated but will not have if this pregnancy is allowed to continue. Why will she not have it? For a number of alternative reasons. The most knockdown reason would be that the mother would die or be rendered sterile if this pregnancy were allowed to continue. Another would be that the parents had simply decided, perhaps for morally adequate reasons, that their family would be large enough if and when this present foetus was born. I shall be discussing later the morality of family limitation; for the moment I shall assume for the sake of argument that it is morally all right for parents to decide, after they have had, say, fifteen children, not to have any more, and to achieve this modest limitation of their family by remaining completely chaste.

In all these cases there is, in effect, a choice between having this child now and having another child later (12.1 ff.). Most people who oppose abortion make a great deal of the wrongness of stopping the birth of this child but say nothing about the morality of stopping the birth of the later child. My own intuition (on which I am by no means going to rely) is that they are wrong to make so big a distinction. The basis of the distinction is supposed to be that the foetus already exists as a single living entity all in one place, whereas the possible future child is at the moment represented only by an unfertilized ovum and a sperm which may or may not yet exist in the father's testes. But will this basis support so weighty a distinction?

First, why is it supposed to make a difference that the genetic material which causes the production of the future child and adult is in two different places? If I have a duty to open a certain door, and two keys are required to unlock it, it does not seem to me to make any difference to my duty that one key is already in the lock and the other in my trousers. This, so far, is an intuition, and I place no reliance on it; I introduce the parallel only to remove some prejudices. The real argument is this: when I am glad that I was born (the basis, it will be remembered, of the argument that the Golden Rule therefore places upon me an obligation not to stop others being born), I do not confine this gladness to gladness that they did not abort me. I am glad, also, that my parents copulated in the first place, without contraception. So from my gladness, in conjunction with the extended Golden Rule, I derive not only a duty not to abort, but also a duty not to abstain from procreation. In the choice-situation that I have imagined, in which it is either this child or the next one but not both, I cannot perform both these duties. So, in the words of a wayside pulpit reported to me by Mr Anthony Kenny, 'if you have conflicting duties, one of them isn't your duty' (cf. *MT* 26). But which?

I do not think that any general answer can be given to this question. If the present foetus is going to be miserably handicapped if it grows into an adult, perhaps because the mother had rubella, but there is every reason to suppose that the next child will be completely normal and as happy as most people, there would be reason to abort this foetus and proceed to bring to birth the next child, in that the next child will be much gladder to be alive than will this one. The Golden Rule does not directly guide us in cases where we cannot help failing to do to some others what we wish were done to us, because if we did it to some, we should thereby prevent ourselves from doing it to others. But it can guide us indirectly, if further extended by a simple manœuvre, to cover what I have elsewhere called 'multilateral' situations (*MT* 110). We are to do to the others affected, taken together, what we wish were done to us if we had to be all of them by turns in random order (*FR* 123, *MT* 129, Lewis 1946: 547, Haslett 1974: ch. 3). In this case, by terminating this pregnancy, I get, on this scenario, no life at all in one of my incarnations and a happy life in the other; but by not terminating it, I get a miserable life in one and no life at all in the other. So I should choose to terminate. In order to reach this conclusion it is not necessary to assume, as we did, that the present foetus will turn into a person who will be positively miserable; only that that person's expectation of happiness is so much less than the expectation of the later possible person that the other factors (to be mentioned in a moment) are outweighed.

In most cases the probability that there will be another child to replace this one is far lower than the probability that this foetus will turn into a living child. The latter probability is said in normal cases to be about 80 per cent; the probability of the next child being born may be much lower (the parents may separate; one of them may die or become sterile; or they may just change their minds about having children). If I do not terminate in such a normal case, there will be, on the same scenario, an 80 per cent chance of a normal happy life in one incarnation and no chance at all of any life in the other; but if I do terminate, there will be a much lower chance of a normal happy life in the second incarnation and no chance at all in the first. So in this case I should not terminate. By applying this kind of scenario to different cases, we get a way of dramatizing the application of the Golden Rule to them. The cases will all be different, but the relevance of the differences to the moral decision becomes clearer. It is these differences in probabilities of having a life, and of having a happy one, that justify, first of all the presumptive policy, which most people would follow, that abortions in general ought to be avoided, and secondly the exceptions to this policy that many people would now allow—though of course they will differ in their estimation of the probabilities. I conclude, therefore, that the establishment of the potentiality principle by no means renders impregnable the extreme conservative position, as Tooley thinks it does. It merely creates a rebuttable or defeasible presumption against abortion, which is fairly easily rebutted if there are good indications. The interests of the mother may well, in many cases, provide such good indications, although, because hers is not the only interest, we have also to consider the others. Liberals can, however, get from the present form of argument all that they could reasonably demand, since in the kinds of cases in which they would approve of termination, the interests of the mother will usually be predominant enough to tip the balance between those of the others affected, including potential persons.

The effect of this argument is to bring the morality of contraception and that of abortion somewhat closer together. Important differences will remain, however. There is the fact that the foetus has a very good chance of turning into a normal adult if allowed to develop, whereas the chance that a single coitus will have that result is much lower. Further, if a general duty to produce children is recognized (as the view I have suggested requires), to kill a foetus means the non-fulfilment of this duty for a much longer period (the period from its begetting to the begetting of the next child, if any); whereas, if you do not beget a child now, you may five minutes later. Thirdly, parents become attached to the child in the womb (hence the argument, 'We should all think differently if wombs were transparent'), and therefore an abortion may (whatever the compensating good) do some harm to them in addition to that (if any) done to the prospective child that is aborted; this is not so if they merely refrain from procreation. These differences are enough to account for the moral gap between contraception and abortion which will be found in the intuitions of most people; one has to be very extreme in one's views either to consider contraception as sinful as abortion or to think of abortion as just another alternative to contraception.

10.6 We must now consider some possible objections to this view. Some of these rest on supposed conflicts with received opinion. I shall not deal at great length with these, for a number of reasons. The first is that it would be hard at the moment to point to any at all generally received opinion about abortion. But even if we could, it is a difficult question in moral philosophy, which I have discussed at length elsewhere (H 1971*c*, *MT* 11 f. and *passim*), how much attention should be paid to received opinion on moral issues. I shall sum up my view, without defending it (see 2.3 and *MT*). There are two levels of moral thinking. The first or intuitive level consists in the application of learnt principles, which, in order to be learnt, have to be fairly general and simple; the second or critical level consists in the criticism, and possibly the modification, of these general principles in the light of their effect in particular cases, actual and imagined. The purpose of this second, reflective kind of thinking is to select those general principles for use in the first kind of thinking which will lead to the nearest approximation, if generally accepted and inculcated, to the results that would be achieved if we had the time and the information and the freedom from self-deception to make possible the practice of critical thinking in every single case. The intuitions which many moral philosophers regard as the final court of appeal are the result of their upbringings—i.e. of the fact that just these principles were accepted by those who most influenced them. In discussing abortion, we ought to be doing some critical thinking; it is therefore quite futile to appeal to those intuitions that we happen to have acquired. It is a question, not of what our intuitions are, but of what they ought to be—a question which can usefully be dramatized by asking, What opinions about abortion ought we to be teaching to our children?

This may help to answer two objections which often crop up. The first claims that common opinion makes a larger moral distinction between failure to procreate and killing a foetus than the present view would warrant (6.3, 11.8). Sometimes this distinction is said to be founded on the more general one

between omissions and acts. There are strong arguments
against the moral relevance of this last distinction (Tooley
1972: 59, Glover 1977: 94 ff.), and if we are always careful to
compare like with like in our examples, and apply the Golden
Rule to them, we shall not obtain any morally relevant difference between acts and omissions, provided that we are
engaged in critical thinking. However, it may well be that the
intuitive principles which we selected as a result of this thinking would use the distinction between acts and omissions. The
reason for this is that, although this distinction is philosophi-
cally very puzzling and even suspect, it is operable by the ordinary man at the common-sense level; moreover, it serves to
separate from each other classes of cases which a more refined
thinking would also separate, but would do so only as a result
of a very protracted investigation which did not itself make use
of the act–omission distinction. So the act–omission distinction
serves as a useful surrogate for distinctions which really are
morally relevant, although it itself is not.

Thus there may be no morally relevant distinction, so far as
the Golden Rule goes, between killing and failing to keep alive
in otherwise identical cases; but if people have ingrained in
them the principle that it is wrong to kill innocent adults, but
not always so wrong to fail to keep them alive, they are more
likely in practice to do the right thing than if their ingrained
principles made no such distinction. This is because most cases
of killing differ from most cases of failing to keep alive in other
crucial ways, such that the former are very much more likely
to be wrong than the latter. And in the case of abortion and
failure to procreate, it is possible (I do not say that it is so) that
the best intuitive principles for practical use would make bigger distinctions at birth and at conception than a refined critical thinking could possibly support. The reason is that
conception and birth are dividing lines easily discerned by the
ordinary man, and that therefore an intuitive principle which
uses these dividing lines in order to draw the moral line (what
moral line?) may lead in practice to the morally best results.
But if we are arguing (as we are) whether or not this is so,
appeals to the intuitions of the ordinary man are entirely
beside the point.

Secondly, we have the 'thin end of the wedge' or 'slippery-slope' objection (cf. 7.3, 11.7). If we sanction contraception, why not abortion; and if abortion, why not infanticide; and if infanticide, why not the murder of adults? As an argument against the too ready abandonment of accepted general intuitive principles this argument has some force; for, psychologically speaking, if the ordinary man or the ordinary doctor has got hold of some general principles about killing, which serve well enough in the ordinary run, and then somebody tells him that these principles ought not to be followed universally, it may well be that he will come to disregard them in cases where he ought not. The argument can be overplayed—I do not think that many doctors who have come to accept abortion are thereby made any more prone to murder their wives; but at this level the argument has some force, especially if, in the upbringing of the ordinary man and the ordinary doctor, enormous stress has been laid on general principles of great rigidity—such principles are naturally susceptible to thin ends of wedges. But when we are disputing at the critical level about what our intuitive principles ought to be, the argument has little force. For it may be that we could devise other equally simple principles which would be wedge-resistant and would draw lines in different places; it may be that we ought to do this, if the new places were more likely, if generally recognized, to lead most often to the right results in practice. Tooley (1972: 64) recommends such a moral line very shortly *after* birth, and his arguments have a great attraction. If the potentiality principle be granted, the number of permissible infanticides is greatly reduced, though not to nothing (12.1 ff.).

For the present, it is enough to say that if the line proved wedge-resistant and if it separated off, in a workable manner, nearly all the cases that would be pronounced wrong by critical thinking from nearly all those which would be pronounced permissible, then it would be no argument against this proposal that it conflicted with people's intuitions. These intuitions, like earlier ones which made a big distinction at quickening, are the results of attempts to simplify the issues for a laudable practical purpose; they cannot without circularity be used in an appraisal of themselves. As Tooley implies, we have to find real moral reasons for distinguishing cases. If, as is sure to happen, the distinctions that result are very complicated, we have to simplify them for ordinary use as best we can; and there is no reason to assume that the simplifications which will be best are those which have been current hith-erto—certainly not in a context in which circumstances have changed as radically as they have with regard to abortion.

10.7 It might be objected, as we have seen, that the view I have advocated would require unlimited procreation, on the ground that not to produce any single child whom one might have produced lays one open to the charge that one is not doing to that child as one is glad has been done to oneself (viz. causing him to be born). But there are, even on the present view, reasons for limiting the population (5.1 ff., 6.3, 11.8). Let us suppose that fully-grown adults were producible ad lib, not by gestation in human mothers or in the wombs of cats or in test tubes, but instantaneously by waving a wand. We should still have to formulate a population policy for the world as a whole, and for particular societies and families. There would be a point at which the additional member of each of these units imposed burdens on the other members great enough in sum to outweigh the advantage gained by the additional mem-ber. In utilitarian terms, the classical or total utility principle sets a limit to population which, although higher than the average utility principle, is nevertheless a limit (see 5.1 and H 1973: 244 f. = 1989*a*: 166). In terms of the Golden Rule, which is the basis of my present argument, even if the 'others' to whom we are to do what we wish, or what we are glad, to have done to us are to include potential people, good done to them may be outweighed by harm done to other actual or potential people. If we had to submit to all their lives or non-lives in turn, we should have a basis for choosing a population policy which would not differ from that yielded by the classical utility principle. How restrictive this policy would be would depend on assumptions about the threshold effects of certain increases in population size and density (5.3 ff.). I think myself that even if potential people are allowed to be the objects of duties, the policy will be fairly restrictive; but this is obviously not the place to argue for this view.

One big gap in the argument of this paper is my failure to deal with the question of whether, when we are balancing the interests of the potential person into whom this foetus will turn against the interests of other people who might be born, we ought to limit the second class to other members of the same family, or include in it any potential person who might in some sense 'replace' the first-mentioned potential person. This major question would seem to depend for its answer on a further question: To what extent will the birth or non-birth of this person make more or less likely the birth or non-birth of the others? This is a demographic question which at present baffles me; but it would obviously have to be gone into in any exhaustive account of the morality of abortion. I have, however, written (possibly too hastily) as if only other potential members of the same family need be considered. That was enough to illustrate the important principle that I was trying to explain.

10.8 Lastly, a logician might object that these potential people do not exist, and cannot be identified or individuated, and therefore cannot be the objects of duties (6.3). If I had put my own view in terms of rights or interests, the same objection could be expressed by saying that only actual people have these. Two points can be made against this objection at once. The first is a perhaps superficial one: it would be strange if there were an act whose very performance made it impossible for it to be wrong. But if the objection were correct, the act of aborting a possible person would be such an act; by preventing the existence of the object of the wrongdoing, it would remove its wrongness. This seems too easy a way of avoiding crime.

Secondly, there seems to be no objection in principle to condemning hypothetical acts: it would have been wrong for Nixon to stay on any longer in the presidency. And it seems a fairly safe principle that if it makes sense to make value-judgements about an act that was done, it makes equal sense to make opposite judgements about the hypothetical omission to do that act. 'Nixon did right to resign' makes sense; and so, therefore, does 'Nixon would have done wrong not to resign'. But we do commend actions which resulted in our own existence—every Sunday in thousands of churches we give thanks in the General Thanksgiving for our creation as well as for our preservation and all the blessings of this life; and Aristotle says that we ought to show the same gratitude to our earthly fathers as 'causes of our being' (1161^a17, 1163^a6, 1165^a23). So it is at least meaningful to say of God or of our fathers that if they had not caused us to exist, they would not have been doing as well for us as they could. And this is all that my argument requires.

Coming now to the purely logical points, we notice that the non-actuality of the potential person (the supposed object of the duty to procreate or not abort) is a separate issue from his non-identifiability. Unfortunately, 'identifiable' is an ambiguous word; in one sense I can identify the next man to occupy my carrel at the library by describing him thus, but in another sense I cannot identify him because I have no idea who he is (6.3). The person who will be born if these two people start their coitus in precisely five minutes is identified by that description; and so, therefore, is the person who would have been born if they had started it five minutes ago. Moreover (this is an additional point), if we had enough mechanical and other information, we could specify the hair colour and all the other traits of that person, if we wished, with as much precision as we could the result of a lottery done on a computer whose randomizing mechanism we could minutely inspect. In this sense, therefore, the potential person is identifiable. We do not know who he will be, in the sense that we do not know what actually now existing person he will be, because he will not be identical with any actually now existing person. But it is hard to see how his inability to meet this logically unmeetable demand for identifiability with some already existing person affects the argument; he is identifiable in the sense that identifying reference can be made to him. So it cannot be non-identifiability that is the trouble.

Is it then non-actuality? Certainly not present non-actuality. We can do harm to and wrong succeeding generations by using up all the world's resources or by releasing too much radioactive material. But suppose that this not merely made them miserable, but actually stopped them being born (e.g. that the radioactive material made everybody sterile all at once). As before it seems that we can be thankful that our fathers did not do this, thereby stopping us coming into existence; why cannot we say, therefore, that if we behave as well as our fathers, we shall be doing well by our children or grandchildren, or that if we were to behave in this respect worse than our fathers, we would be doing worse by our children or grandchildren. It seems strange to say that if we behaved only a little worse, so that the next generation was half the size it would have been, we had done badly for that generation, but that if we behaved much worse, so that the succeeding generation was reduced to nil, we had not done badly for it at all.

This is obviously a very perplexing matter, and needs much more discussion, which I give it in other papers in this volume. All I can hope to do here is to cast doubt on the assumption that some people accept without question, viz. that one cannot harm a person by preventing him coming into existence. True, he does not exist to be harmed; and he is not deprived of existence, in the sense of having it taken away from him, though he is denied it. But if it would have been a good for him to exist (because this made possible the goods that, once he existed, he was able to enjoy), surely it was a harm to him not to exist, and so not to be able to enjoy these goods. He did not suffer; but there were enjoyments he could have had and did not (6.1 ff.).

10.9 I conclude, then, that a systematic application of the Christian Golden Rule yields the following precepts about abortion. It is prima facie and in general wrong in default of sufficient countervailing reasons. But since the wrongness of it consists, in the main, of stopping a person coming into existence and not in any wrong done to the foetus as such, such countervailing reasons are not too hard to find in many cases. And if the termination of this pregnancy facilitates or renders possible or probable the beginning of another more propitious one, it really does not take much to justify it.

I have not had room to discuss what the law on abortion ought to be (see 11.9). I have been speaking only about the morality of terminating individual pregnancies. I will end as I began by saying that my argument has been based on a developed ethical theory, though I have not had room to expound this theory (see *MT*, H 1976). This theory provides the logical basis of the Golden Rule. Though not *founded on* a utilitarian principle, it also provides the basis for a certain sort of utilitarianism that escapes the vices which have been decried in some other sorts. But I shall not now try to defend these last assertions. If they are challenged, and if the view that I have advanced in this paper is challenged, the issue can only be fought out on the terrain of ethical theory itself. That is why it is such a pity that so many people—even philosophers—think that they can discuss abortion without making up their minds about the fundamental problems of moral philosophy.

A Kantian Approach to Abortion

11.1 The position of somebody wondering whether to have an abortion is usually too wretched for it to be decent for a philosopher to try to make her decision depend on the definitions of words that could in principle have several different definitions. So let us start by putting to rest the question 'Is the foetus a person?', which has occupied so many pages in discussions of this problem. It leads straight to a dead end, and we would best avoid it (7.9, 8.7, 10.3). We know what a foetus is, in the sense that if anybody were to ask whether an object before us or even inside us was a human foetus, there would be no difficulty in principle in determining whether it was. For the same sort of reason, we know how to determine some of the properties the foetus has. We know, for example, that it has the *potentiality* of becoming a human adult—that is, that *if* the pregnancy comes to term, it will have turned into a baby, and if the baby survives it will turn into an adult more or less like us (see below).

There are some things of the same ordinary sort about which we cannot be so certain, but which do not present great problems. For example, we do not know for certain whether foetuses, at any rate at a late stage of pregnancy, may not have some rudimentary conscious experiences, including experiences of suffering. It is fairly certain that at earlier stages, before their nervous systems have become at all developed, they do not have such experiences. So let us avoid this question by supposing, either that the abortion in question would be at such an early stage of pregnancy, or, if later, that it could be done without causing pain to the foetus, for example by anaesthesia (10.4).

As I said, there seems to be no difficulty in principle in

From *Right Conduct*, ed. M. Bayles and K. Henley (Random House, 1988). The passage in square brackets in 11.6 f. is added from the author's reply to R. B. Brandt in *Social Theory and Practice* 15 (1989), where this paper was reprinted.

deciding *these* facts about the foetus. They are facts which may be, and I think are, morally relevant when we are deciding what it is all right to do to the foetus. But what about the question whether the foetus is a *person*? How would we answer that? We have to see that it is not the same kind of question at all as the question 'Will the foetus, if the pregnancy continues and the child survives, turn into a human adult like us, or into, say, a horse?' The reason is that it is uncertain what we *mean* by 'person', whereas it is not uncertain what we mean by 'horse', or 'human adult'. We all know how to tell whether something is a horse or a human adult. But we do not know how to tell whether the foetus is a person. To that extent the term 'person' is unclear.

The main trouble is that 'person', and other words like 'human being' which have been used in this dispute, all have several different meanings. There is a clear sense in which a foetus is *not* a person. It is altogether too different from the things which we instantly recognize as people. If the notice in the elevator says it may not carry more than six persons, a pregnant woman is still allowed to have five adult companions in the elevator.

At the opposite extreme, there is a sense in which it is a necessary condition for something's being called a person that it has the rights which persons have, or that the duties are owed to it which we owe to persons. Obviously, if the foetus were a person in that sense, it would have the rights that other persons have, and to kill it would be murder. But for that very reason, if having the rights is a qualification for being called a person, then we cannot know whether the foetus is a person without *first* deciding whether the foetus has the rights. But that was the question we started with. So it is obviously no use trying to settle that question by asking whether the foetus is a person; we shall not know whether it is, in the required sense, until we have already decided the question about its rights.

There are going to be a lot of senses of 'person' besides these, or in between these, and I shall not have room even to list them all. It should be clear already that most of the disputes about this allegedly crucial question of whether the foetus is a person are going to be a waste of time and can never get anywhere.

11.2 How do people get into this impasse? The cause is this: they have some excellent firm principles about murder and about liberty, and in this difficult case of abortion it looks as if the principles conflict. If one forbids the abortion, one infringes the liberty of the mother; if one allows it, one is allowing murder. So people take sides for one principle or the other, call themselves 'pro-life' or 'pro-choice', and stop thinking. One side even starts bombing the other for want of better philosophy.

We start with these good firm simple principles about life and liberty (though we do not know how to formulate them clearly and explicitly), and then they come into conflict. If we terminate a pregnancy, we are offending against the principle requiring us to preserve life. If we stop women terminating their pregnancies, we are offending against the other principle requiring us to preserve liberty of choice. The right thing to do in this predicament is to think some more and try to formulate the principles exactly and apply them to this case, and see whether we can find forms of them that do *not* conflict with each other. That, indeed, is what people are trying to do when they argue about whether the foetus is a person. For if there were a sense in which the foetus is *not* a person, the conflict might be resolved; in killing the foetus, one would not be committing a murder, because killing is not murder unless it is the killing of people. And so we could observe the principle about liberty by letting the foetus be killed, without breaking the principle about murder.

As we saw, this manœuvre does not do any good, because the word 'person' is indeterminate; taken one way, we can say that it is all right to kill the foetus because it is not a person (in the sense of occupying one person's place in the elevator); but the side that does not think the foetus ought to be killed was not using the word in that sense. It was using it in the sense in which to be a person is to be a possessor of the rights that ordinary persons have. And we are not in a position to say whether the foetus is a person in *that* sense. This is a moral, not a factual question, and we cannot answer it until we have settled the prior question of whether we have the duties to the foetus that we have to ordinary adults, that is, whether the foetus has the same rights as adults have.

So what ought we to do, instead of disputing endlessly about whether the foetus is a person? My advice is that we forget about the word 'person', and ask instead about the properties of the foetus that might be reasons why we ought not to kill it—properties in the ordinary factual sense in which we can *determine* whether or not it has them. It may be that the word 'person' stands for some combination of these properties, or ambiguously for more than one possible set of them. In that case, if we can isolate a set of ordinary properties of the foetus which together constitute a reason why we ought not to let it be killed, we might sum up this set of properties by saying that the foetus is a person. But, for the reasons I have given, we should be able to do this only *after* first answering the moral question. The word 'person' would not have helped in the argument; it would at most be a convenient way of summarizing its conclusion. The real work would have been done in identifying the ordinary properties of the foetus that made us want to say (if that was what we did want to say) that it ought not to be killed. The hard part of the moral thinking is that involved in this identification of the ordinary properties which are the reasons for or against killing the foetus.

11.3 What, then, are these ordinary properties? One is that, if the foetus suffered while being killed, then that would be a reason for not inflicting this suffering on it, though there could be reasons on the other side. But we can ignore this property if we confine ourselves, as I have proposed, to cases where we can be sure it will not suffer (10.4).

What other properties of the foetus, besides its capacity for suffering which we have now discounted, could give us reasons for not killing it? I cannot think of any besides the foetus's potentiality, already mentioned, of turning into someone like us (see 5.1 and refs.). Here is an example that will illustrate why I cannot think of any. Suppose that in the case of a given pregnancy we can be absolutely certain that for reasons beyond anybody's control the foetus will not survive (6.2, 8.6, 10.4). It has, say, some recognizable disease from which foetuses never recover. Let us suppose additionally that, if we did kill the foetus, we could do so painlessly, say by using an anaesthetic. In such a case is there any reason for not killing the foetus, if there are other grounds for killing it (say the health of the mother)? This case illustrates rather well what is wrong with what I shall call the absolutist pro-life position. It also illustrates the difference between foetuses and ordinary human persons. In the case of an ordinary person who you were certain would die in a month, there *would* be reasons for not killing that person. It would disappoint hopes of what he (or she) might have done in the remaining month; the process of killing might cause fear; it might cause sorrow to others; the terminally ill patient might be deprived of the chance of ordering his financial affairs for the benefit of his family, or even reconciling himself and them to his impending death. There could be reasons, all the same, on the other side, such as the suffering he would undergo if his life were prolonged. None of these reasons applies to the foetus. The foetus does not have *now*, at the present moment, properties which are reasons for not killing it, given that it will die in any case before it acquires those properties which ordinary human adults and even children have, and which are our reasons for not killing *them*. A foetus before it has achieved sentience does not *currently* possess any properties that could be morally relevant to its treatment and which are not possessed equally by oysters and earthworms.

If we are to find reasons for not killing the foetus, we must look for some properties which it does not have now, but which it *will* have later if it survives. Philosophers call these 'potential properties', and argue about whether the potentiality that the foetus has of turning into someone like us is morally relevant to what we may or may not do to the foetus now (see 6.1 ff.). The case that I have just described shows that defenders of the foetus, if they are going to make good their defence, have nothing else that they can rely on except the foetus's potentiality. But I shall be arguing in a moment, against the views of many philosophers like Michael Tooley (1972), that potentiality does provide a powerful weapon with which to defend the foetus *in normal cases*.

11.4   In order to set up this argument I shall have to do a little ethical theory, though I will try to make as light work of it as I can. The ethical theory I am going to use is of a more or less Kantian sort. The theory can also be put into a utilitarian form, and I have often so put it. The idea that Kantianism and utilitarianism are irreconcilable is the result of attempts by modern deontologists to borrow Kant's authority for their own intuitionist positions; but they seldom document their claims about Kant, and it could in fact be shown that a properly formulated utilitarianism and a properly formulated Kantianism need not conflict (see 15.2 and refs., H 1993*a*).

I am also going, for reasons which I hope will become clear in a moment, to make a time-switch into the past (5.2, 6.2, 10.4). Suppose that it is not this woman now who is deciding whether or not to have an abortion, but some other woman in the past. Suppose, for example, it was my own mother deciding whether or not to terminate the pregnancy which actually resulted in *me*. In that case, am I going to say that it is morally quite all right for her to have an abortion? Note that the question is *not* 'What *would* I say if I were speaking to her at that time'. Nor is it 'What *would* I say now if I did not exist?'. I have deliberately formulated the question in such a way as to avoid the difficulties with those other questions. The question is, 'What *do* I (a presently existing person) now say about this past situation?'

I will draw attention to an obvious reason why I might not like to say that it was all right for her to have an abortion. It is a reason which might be outweighed by other reasons, but it is at least a reason. The reason is that if she had had an abortion, I would not now have existed. Let us suppose that I am able to reach back in time and give instructions to my mother as to what she should do. Suppose, even, that she is able to ask me questions about what she ought to do. In order to get into a position in which I can communicate with her at that time, I shall have to penetrate some noumenal world outside time (this is really getting very Kantian) and have access to her in that past time. This of course raises deep philosophical problems, into which I am not going to go. But just suppose I can do it. What shall I say to her?

I am sure I shall not say, 'Carry on, have the abortion; it's all the same to me.' Because my existence now is valuable to me, I shall not, other things being equal, will (to use another Kantian term) that she should have the abortion, thereby depriving me of the possibility of existence. I value my existence, not for its own sake, but for the sake of the good things that happen to me, which could not happen if I did not exist (6.1). That we can thank God for our creation (10.8) does not show that mere existence in itself is a good; but it does show that it is a good at least as a means to the other good things that those who exist can have. Therefore, faced with the possibility of either existing now or not existing now, the normally happy person will tell his mother not to have the abortion. And therefore, all things being equal (if, for example, *she* is not going to die if the pregnancy is not terminated), he will say that she ought not to have it.

I put the whole dialogue in the past, because of an argument which is sometimes used by philosophers who write about this question. They say that *potential* people or *merely* possible people do not have any rights, and we cannot have any duties to them. But in the case I described we were talking about an actual person, namely myself. I am asking myself, as an actual person, to prescribe what ought to have been done at a time in the past when my mother was contemplating having an abortion. Potential people do not come into this argument.

11.5 It is a part of ethical theory that is accepted by almost all moral philosophers, however, that if one makes a moral judgement about any case or situation, one must, to be consistent, make the same moral judgement about any other case which resembles it in all its non-moral particulars (1.6, 7.6, 10.4). For example, if it is all right for one person to do something (call him A), it must be all right for anybody else to do the same thing in exactly the same situation. By 'the same situation', I mean the same in all respects, and these include the properties of the people in it. So I am not saying that if it is all right for A to tickle B when B likes being tickled, it must be all right for B to tickle A who hates being tickled. What I am saying is that if the circumstances and all the properties, including the wishes, of the people are the same, the moral judgement has to be the same.

In applying this theoretical doctrine, which, as I said, is accepted by nearly all moral philosophers, at least all who understand what the doctrine is (some have denied it through *not* understanding it), we have to apply it to hypothetical cases as well as to actual ones. If it *was* wrong for my mother to have an abortion, then it *would be* wrong for any other mother to have an abortion in exactly the same circumstances, and therefore would now be wrong for the woman we started with to have an abortion, if the circumstances were the same. And this, in general, is the prima facie case for being against abortion, as most of us are *in general*. By that I mean that most of us, if asked whether it just does not matter in the least whether people have abortions or not, would say that in most cases it does matter; most pregnancies ought to be allowed to continue; those who want to legalize abortion want to do so because that will leave the decision to the individuals concerned in *special* cases where there are strong grounds for termination. Nobody thinks that *no* abortions matter, except those who do not care whether the human race survives or not, or who even want it not to survive.

The reason why most of us think that *all things being equal* pregnancies should not be terminated, is that we think that on the whole they are likely to result in people being born who will in the course of their lives be glad to have been born. There is of course a problem about having too many people: if there were so many people, and the results of over-population made them so unhappy, that they wished they had not been born, that would be different; but I am assuming that this is not the case yet. I shall be returning to this point.

Reverting for a moment, however, to the dialogue between myself in the present and my mother in the past, there is one other thing that I *might* think I could say. We have considered two things I might say, namely 'Do not have the abortion' and 'You ought to have the abortion'. What I said was that I would not say 'You ought to have the abortion', because this would be a prescription to her to have the abortion, and I do not want that. So, if those were the only two things I could say, I would choose the first, 'Do not have the abortion', and rule out the second, 'You ought to have the abortion'. But a third thing I might say is 'I do not say you ought to have an abortion; but I do not claim, either, that you ought not to have it. Of course I want you not to have it, because otherwise I shall not exist; so I still go on saying, so far as I am concerned, "Do not have it". But if you ask me whether it is the case, morally speaking, that you ought not to have it, I would not go so far as that. You will not be doing wrong if you have it, but please do not.'

This possibility, though important, raises difficulties which are really too great for me to deal with here. At least if I am trying to give my mother positive moral guidance, I shall be confined to the two answers, 'You ought' and 'You ought not'; and if this is so, then, because I prefer to be existing now, I shall not say 'You ought', and shall therefore have to say 'You ought not'.

11.6 [In my *MT*: 184 f. there is an argument which I think helps here, and which I will try to apply to the present case. So applied, it goes like this. Assume that we and the mother in question are going to make *some* moral judgements, and not adopt a stance of universal amoralism (a stance which, as I argue in *MT*, ch. 11, there are good prudential reasons for not adopting). Assume, further, that at least some of these moral judgements say that it would be wrong to do some things affecting the interests of people or sentient beings. These moral judgements at least will have to be universalizable. That means that to make them explicit we should have to give (in as specific detail as necessary) the principle on which each rested. But this principle will have to specify not only positively the features the act has which make it wrong, but negatively the features which it lacks, and which if it had them would make it not wrong. This involves *distinguishing* this act from otherwise similar acts which are not wrong, by saying what the differences are that make a moral difference.

Suppose, then, that we are agreed that some acts of harming humans are wrong and have got as far as saying that killing humans is *in general*, though not perhaps universally, wrong. I use the word 'human' without prejudice to include all specimens of the human species including foetuses. We then have to specify the negative features which delimit this principle, as well as the positive—that is, specify the features whose absence is a necessary condition for calling the killing of human beings wrong. Granted that such killing is in general wrong, are there any features of special cases which, in spite of that, would make it not wrong? In other words, does the principle on which we are relying admit of exceptions or does it not? Are there exceptional cases in which killing humans (as thus broadly defined) is after all not wrong? We shall presumably answer that it does admit of exceptions, for example in cases of self-defence; and we could offer reasons for these exceptions. But do these exceptions, or do they not, include any cases in which the human killed is a foetus that would otherwise turn into a normal adult? The judgement that the act of killing a human would be wrong in cases where the victim is an adult, and not in all cases where the victim is a live specimen of the human species at *any* stage of development, pre- or post-natal, is a moral judgement, and therefore has to be universalized. We have to universalize the exceptions we make to our moral judgements as well as the judgements themselves, because, properly understood, moral judgements include their qualifying riders.

This line of argument does not determine what exceptions we can make; it only says that they have to be made in universal terms. Thus, it does not forbid us to say that it is all right to kill foetuses in some cases but not in others, by specifying in universal terms the circumstances in which it is all right. But of any detailed description of an abortion, we have to say whether it falls under the principle forbidding killing, or under one of the exceptions to it. Both possible answers have to be universalizable, because both are qualifications to the moral principle forbidding killing. So the mother is at liberty to say that *no* abortions as so specified (say, cases just like hers in their universal properties) are wrong. What she cannot with logical consistency say is that in her own case abortion is not wrong, but that in other cases, only distinguishable by which individuals have which roles in them, it is wrong. She has to make the same judgement about all cases identical in their universal features, even if it is only a judgement of moral indifference.

In making this judgement, she has to put herself in the places of all those affected—that is, make the same judgement about all identical hypothetical cases in which she is in their situations. I do not think that if she has to do that, she will be so ready as Brandt thinks (1989: 16) to say that anyone in her circumstances who *wants* to have an abortion should have one. She will have to take into account, not just her own preferences and those of mothers in a like situation (though they of

course are relevant and, if very intense, preponderantly so), but
the preferences of all those affected. I shall argue later that
these have to include the preferences of those who will be born
and grow up if abortions are not performed; but for the
moment I must ask the reader to accept this for the sake of
the present discussion.

Note that even if judgements of moral indifference are
allowed her, she will not be able to make one if she universal-
izes and treats all exactly similar cases alike. She cannot say,
about *all* cases, what I said earlier that someone might say
about this case, namely (in effect), 'You would not be doing
wrong, but do not have the abortion.' For if she said that
about all cases *en bloc*, this would be tantamount to accepting a
universal prohibition, which is equivalent to the statement that
it *is* wrong. So she would have contradicted herself. She could
avoid this contradiction by saying in each case that it was not
wrong, but issuing a singular prohibition of it in some cases
but not others. It is hard to see what reasons she could have
for making these distinctions, given that the preferences of the
people in all the cases are the same, except that she is treating
her own preferences as privileged. But then she has become an
amoralist egoist for all the cases like this one. And if she
accepts this argument, arguments of the same form could be
pressed in embarrassingly many other cases.

11.7   We have, then, a typical case of critical thinking, with
its demand for full specification of detail and its verdict based
on the consequences for all affected parties, their preferences
being considered as sympathetically as one's own. It is my
view that such thinking, which I have explained in a rather
Kantian style, will lead to the same conclusions as a properly
formulated act-utilitarianism, which impartially seeks preference-satisfaction—that is, treats everyone as an end by making
his or her ends our own ends, as Kant put it (1785: BA69 =
430, and see 15.2). It seems fairly evident to me that if we were
to consider, by such specific critical thinking, all possible cases
of proposed abortions, taking into account sympathetically the
preferences of all interested parties, we should not say that *no*
abortions were wrong. Nor should we say that they were *all*
wrong. What our critical Kantian-utilitarian thinking would do
for us would be to make us distinguish the cases which were

wrong from those which were not, in universal terms on the basis of their consequences for the affected parties and their preferences or ends.

It seems to me, further, that this critical thinking would lead us to the view that, taking all pregnancies together as a class, abortion would be wrong in the vast majority of them. That was why I said that my argument supported the view that abortion is wrong *in general*. Suppose, then, that we are using our critical thinking, not just to consider specific cases, but, having done this, to pronounce on what reasonably simple prima facie *intuitive* principles it would be best to adopt, cultivate in ourselves and others, including our children, and generally follow. Note that this is a question about *acts* of cultivating principles. These are among the most important acts that we do; and almost all of our acts have this function to some extent. So as an act-utilitarian I can say a great many of the things that rule-utilitarians like Brandt say, and thus avoid the usual vulgar objections against act-utilitarianism. The answer to the question of what principles we should cultivate by our acts is that they would be principles in general forbidding abortion, but allowing it in certain limited cases. This generality allows for exceptions, which have to be justified. In other words, the principle forbidding abortion is defeasible for good reasons. The argument has to be about what limits should be set, how and by whom.]

There is, then, a reason for accepting the general principle which forbids abortions in ordinary cases. The question is whether we ought to allow any exceptions to this principle, and whether they ought to extend further than the exceptions that can be made to the principle that we should not kill adults. Let us ask what are the reasons for having the latter principle. We have looked at some of them already. Nearly all of us want not to be killed, and want not to live in fear of being killed. So, when faced with a choice between a universal prohibition on killing people and a universal licence to kill them, we would choose the former. But most of us do not want to have to choose between these stark alternatives; we want to make *some* exceptions to the principle forbidding killing people, of which killing in self-defence is an obvious one, as we have seen, and killing in war or as a penalty for murder are more controversial. If we are speaking, as we are, of a general principle to be inculcated in children when we bring them up, and protected by the law, the principle has to be fairly simple and cannot contain too many complicated exceptions. So we allow killing in self-defence and perhaps in these other cases, but try to keep the prohibition as simple as we can. This is in the interests of workability.

It is sometimes said that if one allows exceptions to such simple principles one will be inserting the thin end of a wedge, or starting down a slippery slope (7.3, 10.6). This is indeed sometimes the case; but sometimes it is not. Whether it is will depend on whether there is a clear stopping-place on the slope where we can dig in our heels—and sometimes there is. When it was decided in the United States to allow cars to turn right (i.e. to the near side) at a red light after stopping, did anybody say, 'You are starting down a slippery slope: if you let people turn right on a red light, then you will have breached the absolute ban on crossing a red light, and people will soon begin crossing it when they want to go straight ahead or turn left'? People realized that it was quite easy to distinguish the cases in which it was now to be legal to cross the red light from those in which it was still to be forbidden. So the slope was not slippery.

Similarly, nobody says that we ought to forbid killing *even* in self-defence because, if you allow that, people will start killing for other reasons too. In this case, there is a real difficulty in deciding what counts as self-defence, and no doubt there are volumes of cases in the criminal law in which this has had to be sorted out. But, even so (even though, that is, the slope is a little bit slippery), we do allow killing in self-defence, and the slope has not in practice proved *too* slippery.

In principle, we could do the same for abortion. The argument is sometimes used that if we allow the killing of foetuses, people will soon be killing adults ad lib. I cannot see much force in this argument. In many countries the killing of foetuses has been legalized under certain conditions. I know of no evidence that this has led to a greater incidence of ordinary murder.

Although the slope from killing foetuses to killing adults is not slippery, there is a slippery slope from killing foetuses

under certain conditions to killing them under other conditions. This is because it is rather difficult to delimit precisely in
law the conditions under which abortion is allowable. Expressions like 'congenital defect' and 'the health of the mother' are
capable of being stretched. Whether we think it is dangerous
that this slope is slippery, however, will depend on what view
we take about the general question of what abortions should
be allowed, and who should make the decision. For example, *if*
we took the view that abortion should be allowed freely and
the mother should decide, we should not mind the law being
stretched in this way. I do not myself take so extreme a view;
but I do not think it bad that the law has been stretched a bit,
as it has been in different ways in different countries.

But at any rate the slope from killing foetuses to killing
adults is not slippery. So we can reasonably ask whether it
would be all right to allow an exception, in the case of foetuses, to the general ban on killing. How would we decide
such a question? The general ban on killing has a point, as we
saw earlier, namely that people want not to be killed. But does
this point extend to foetuses? *They* do not want not to be
killed.

11.8 I have argued that most people prefer not *to have been*
killed when they were foetuses; and that this gives us a general
reason for having a principle that we ought not to kill foetuses.
But here we have to be rather careful. The general preference
for existence over non-existence does not justify the principle
that we ought to bring into existence all the people we *could*
bring into existence. If we tried to do that, there would obviously be too many people, and perhaps a majority of those
people would wish that we had not brought them into existence, thus destroying the premiss of our argument. So evidently any principle that we are likely to accept is going to
allow some limitation of the population, if only by the use of
the methods approved by the Pope (5.1 ff., 6.3, 10.7).

However we limit the population, it is going to result in
some people not being born who *could* have been born. We
have to ask next, 'Is there any reason for giving precedence to
some of these people over others?' Notice that the argument
used earlier in defence of the foetus does not provide any such
reason. Suppose that if this woman does not have a baby now

she will have one in a year's time, but that she will not have that other baby if she has one now. Each of these people, if born, will, we hope, have reason to be thankful that he or she was born; but, other things being equal, neither will have any *more* reason for being thankful than the other has. So, given that we are going to limit the population, does it make any difference *which* of the possible people is born, and which gets excluded? The argument used so far does not provide any reason for saying that it makes a difference.

There are certainly factors which could make a difference. If, for example, the mother is not at present married but hopes to be soon, this might mean that the present foetus, if born, will not have such a good start in life as the other would. Or, to take a case which points in the opposite direction: if the mother is 35 years old, there is a reason for having a child in the next five years if at all. The reason is that if she postpones having it until she is 40, the chance of the child being born with Down's syndrome is greater. So there can be reasons for choosing to have a child later rather than now, or the reverse. But we have so far not been able to discover any general reason for giving precedence to the child that this foetus would turn into over other possible future children, given that one or another of them is going to be born.

Are there any strong reasons for preferring the child that this foetus would turn into? The feeling many people have that it should have precedence may be due to a false analogy between foetuses and adults. Certainly it would be wrong to kill an adult in order to replace him or her with some other person who might be born. This is because the existing adult has desires (above all the desire to live) which will be frustrated if he is killed. That is the reason why we have a general ban on killing adults. And this applies even to young children. Whether it applies to neonates, who do not have the desire to live, is a controversial question which there is no room to discuss here (12.1). It certainly applies to children from a very early age. But it clearly does not apply to foetuses; so at any rate *that* reason for saying that foetuses ought not to be killed lacks force.

At this point it will be claimed that the argument so far provides no reason for forbidding abortions that does not apply equally to contraception or even to abstinence (6.3, 10.6). I

think that this is right. So far we have no such reason. Perhaps
reasons can be found, but they are relatively weak ones. Abortion is a more tricky procedure medically than contraception.
But there are contraceptive methods which are really abortifacients, because, when used before or during copulation, they
kill the zygote (perhaps by preventing implantation) after it has
been formed. There is no clear reason for distinguishing such
methods from the kind which prevents the formation of
zygotes. Again, the feeling that there is a difference is due to a
false analogy.

There is also the consideration that normally the foetus
attracts feelings of affection on the part of the mother and perhaps others—feelings which do not yet attach to a possible
future child that she might have. To kill the foetus, even if the
mother herself desires this all things considered, is bound to
wound those feelings. She might feel that it would have been
better to have used contraception.

There is also what might be called the 'bird in the hand'
argument. The foetus is *there*, and will turn into an adult if it
survives; future conceptions and births are more problematical
(6.4). Given, however, that there is likely to be a child that will
be born, if not to this family, then to some other family, and
so occupy the place in the demography that this child would
occupy, that does not seem a very strong argument.

11.9 If, as already argued, abortions are in general wrong,
but allowable in particular cases, what such exceptions ought
the law to allow, and who should have the task of deciding
when to perform an abortion? The general principle is that, if
there are interests affected by a decision, then, since we have
to treat people as ends, those interests should be protected
impartially; and this is most likely to happen if those who have
the interests have a say in the decision, or, if they are not in a
position to have a say, are in some way represented, and if the
greater interests have the greater say. This is likely to result in
the maximal and impartial protection of the interests. Those
who like to speak about rights (and I see no harm in that) can
speak equally well of the protection of their rights (4.2, 10.2).
But interests will do for the present argument.

Obviously the mother has a very great interest in the outcome. That is the justification for the claim that the mother

ought to have the only say; and this would indeed be so if there were no other interests affected. But there *are* other interests, and we must consider them. The father has an interest—certainly a smaller one than the mother, but not negligible (10.1). The person into whom the foetus would turn if not aborted has an interest—a very great one. But this interest may be counterbalanced by those of other children who might be born thereafter, if the family is in any case to be limited. Certainly, if it is known that this foetus is seriously defective (the mother, say, had rubella) but she could have a normal child later, the interest of that normal child is much greater than that of the defective child who would be born from this pregnancy. In my view this applies even to defective neonates (12.1 ff.).

There are also the interests of doctors, surgeons, and nurses who may be called upon to perform the abortion. If ever we have an abortifacient pill that can be bought at pharmacies and used at any stage in early pregnancy, that would cut out the doctors; but I think it unlikely that such a pill will be developed soon which could safely be sold without prescription, although an abortion pill is now available on prescription in some countries. So for the moment we have to consider the interest of the doctor who is being asked to act against his conscience—and this *is* an interest, even if the conscience is misguided.

The question of who should decide whether to allow an abortion is the question of how best to be fair to all these interests. The mother's interest is preponderant but not the sole one. What the best procedure is depends on a lot of factors which I am not able to assess with confidence. But I am inclined to think that there are procedures now followed in some countries which have worked well in practice and have done reasonable justice between the interests affected. In any case, that is what we should be aiming at.

The Abnormal Child
Moral Dilemmas of Doctors and Parents

12.1 Like most of the papers in this volume, this is an attempt to apply ethical theory to a particular moral problem. The theory, outlined in 1.6 f. and more fully set out in *MT*, is of a sort that can be described as both Kantian and utilitarian (see 15.2 and refs., H 1993*a*). It asks what are the interests (or as Kant might put it, the rational ends) of the parties affected, and then seeks prescriptions which we are prepared to universalize to all similar cases, and which will maximally satisfy these interests or fulfil these ends. The particular problem to be addressed is that which faces doctors and parents when a grossly defective child is born, or is expected to be born.

I am going therefore, in the hope of shedding some light on the dilemmas of doctors and parents, to ask, first of all, what are the different interests involved in the sort of case we are considering. There is first the interest of the child; but what *is* this? We can perhaps illuminate this question by asking, 'What if it were ourselves in that child's position—what do we prescribe for *that* case?' On the one hand it may be presumed to be in the child's interest to live, if this is possible; but if the life is going to be a severely handicapped one, it is possible that this interest in living may be at least greatly diminished. Then there is the interest of the mother, in whose interest also it is to live, and whose life may be in danger; and it is also in her interest not to have an abnormal child, which might prevent or severely impair the normal development of the rest of the family. The other members of the family have a similar interest. Against this, it is said that good sometimes comes to a

First delivered in 1973 to London Medical Group conference 'Survival of the Weakest' at Royal College of Obstetricians and Gynaecologists; first printed in *Documentation in Medical Ethics* 3 (1974).

family through having to bring up an abnormal child; and I can believe that this is so in some cases.

Then there are the interests (not so great individually but globally very great) of those outside the family: first of all, those of doctors and nurses who are concerned; then those of the rest of the staffs of hospitals, homes, and other services which will be involved in looking after the child and the family. There are also the interests of all those people who *would* be looked after, or looked after better, by all these services if they did not already have too much on their hands; and there are the interests of the taxpayers who pay for it all. And lastly, there is another interest which is commonly ignored in these discussions, and which is so important that it often, I think, ought to tip the balance. But what this other interest is I shall not reveal until I have talked about those I have mentioned so far.

When I said that equal consideration ought to be given to all the interests affected, I did not mean that we should, for example, treat as equal the interest of the mother in continuing to live and that of the doctor in not being got out of bed in the middle of the night. As individuals, these people are entitled to equal consideration; but because life matters more to one than sleep to the other, that makes it right for the doctor to get out of bed and go and look after the mother. If the doctor had a car smash outside the mother's front door and she could save *his* life by getting out of bed in the middle of the night, then by the same principle she should do so. As individuals, they are equipollent; the difference is introduced by the differing importance to each of them of the various outcomes.

The number of those affected can also be important; if a family doctor can save a patient from a sleepless and distressful night by going along in the evening and providing a painkiller, he will often do it, even in these days; but if a pill were not enough, and it were necessary for a whole team of nurses and an ambulance to turn out, he might decide to wait till the morning unless there were a real danger of a grave deterioration in the patient's condition. A very large number of people, each of whom is affected to a small degree, may outweigh one person who is affected to a greater degree. So even the fact that 60 million taxpayers will have to pay an average of 20p extra each a year to improve or extend the Health Service is of some moral, as well as political, importance (14.5). But I agree on the whole with those who ask us not to give too much weight to these economic arguments; although I totally failed recently to get from an economist a straight answer to the question of the order of size of the sums involved in looking after handicapped children, I am prepared to accept for the sake of argument that they are relatively small. So let us leave the taxpayer out of it, and the rival claimants for care, and just consider the interests of the immediate family.

12.2 Here, however, we must notice the other important interest that I mentioned just now—that of the next child in the queue. For some reason that I cannot understand this is seldom considered. But try looking at the problem with hindsight. The example I am going to use is oversimplified, and I am deliberately not specifying any particular medical condition, because if I do I shall get my facts wrong. Suppose the child with the abnormality was not operated on. It had a substantial chance of surviving the operation, and, if it survived, it had a large chance of being severely handicapped. So they did not operate, and what we now have is not that child, but young Andrew who was born two years later, perfectly normal, and leaves school next summer. Though not brilliant, he is going probably to have a reasonably happy life and make a reasonably useful contribution to the happiness of others. The choice facing the doctors and the family was really a choice between (if they did not operate) a very high probability of having Andrew (who would not have been contemplated if they had a paralysed child in the family) and on the other hand (if they did operate) a combination of probabilities depending on the precise prognosis (shall we say a 10 per cent chance of a living normal child, a 40 per cent chance of a living but more or less seriously handicapped child, and a 50 per cent chance of a dead child plus the possibility of Andrew in the future).

If we agree with most people that family planning is right, and that therefore this family is justified in limiting its children to a predetermined number (however large), then that is the kind of choice it will be faced with, and in the situation I have imagined *was* faced with. We should try discussing with Andrew himself whether they made the right choice.

If I have characterized the choice correctly, then nearly everything is going to depend on what the prognosis was, and on our estimates of the value *to the persons concerned* of being alive and normal, and, by contrast, of being alive and defective or handicapped in some specified way. In making these value-judgements I do not see that we can do better than put ourselves imaginatively in the places of those affected, and judge as if it were our own future that was at stake. Since a sensitive doctor is bound constantly, in the course of his practice, to make this sort of imaginative judgement about what is for the best for other people, looking at it from their point of view, I do not think that it can be said that it raises any difficulties of principle; but it obviously raises very great difficulties in practice, which the sensitive and experienced doctor is as likely as anybody to be able to overcome in consultation with parents and others affected.

But the problems mostly arise from the difficulty of prognosis. In principle it might be possible to put a numerical value upon the probabilities of the various outcomes, and having estimated how the various outcomes for the people involved affect their interests, to make a utilitarian calculation and choose the course that gives the best prospect of good and the least prospect of harm for those concerned, all in all. In practice we are bound to rely a lot on guesswork; but when guessing, it is an advantage to have a clear idea of what one is guessing at. I have suggested that what we should be guessing at is what is for the best for all the parties taken together.

The prognosis, however, is always going to be pretty uncertain, and the question therefore arises of *when* the decision should be made. I suppose that it would be agreed that if there is doubt in the very early stages of pregnancy, it might be advisable to wait until the foetus had developed sufficiently to make the prognosis more certain. A hard-headed utilitarian might try to extend this principle and say that in cases of suspected abnormality we should let the child be born, operate if appropriate, and then kill the child if the operation resulted in a very severe handicap, and have another child instead. In this way we should maximize the chances of bringing into the world a human being with a high prospect of happiness. If the medical profession finds this suggestion repugnant, as it almost certainly does, and does not want the law changed, or if it is thought (perhaps rightly) to inflict too much mental suffering on the mother, then we shall have to be content with a far less certain procedure—that of either terminating the pregnancy or, if we do not terminate and the child is born, estimating the chances *before* deciding whether to operate, and (if we do decide to operate) taking the risk, however small, of being left with a dreadfully handicapped child.

12.3 Suppose that we imagine our possible Andrew and his possible brother—the former existing only as a possible combination of sperm and ovum, the latter already existing as a foetus. And suppose that we imagine them carrying out a pre-natal dialogue in some noumenal world (and of course the supposition is just as fantastic in one case as it is in the other) and trying to arrive at a solution which will give them, taken together, the best chance of happy existence. The dialogue might go like this. Andrew points out that if the foetus is not born there is a high probability that he, Andrew, will be born and will have a normal and reasonably happy life. There is of course a possibility that the parents will change their minds about having any more children, or that one of them will die; but let us suppose that this is rather unlikely, and that there is no particular fear that the next child will be abnormal.

To this the foetus might reply, 'At least I have got this far; why not give me a chance?' But a chance of what? They then do the prognosis as best they can and work out the chances of the various outcomes if the present pregnancy is not terminated. It turns out that there is a slim chance, but only a slim chance, that the foetus will, if born and operated on, turn into a normal and, let us hope, happy child; that there is a considerable chance on the other hand that it will perish in spite of the operation; and that there is a far from negligible chance of its surviving severely handicapped. In that case, I think Andrew, the later possible child, can claim that he is the best bet, because the chance of the parents dying or changing their minds before he is born is pretty small, and certainly far less than the chance that the present foetus, if born, will be very seriously handicapped.

In order for the foetus to prevent Andrew winning the argument in this way, there is one move it can make. It can say, 'All right, we'll make a bargain. We will say that I am to be born and operated on, in the hope of restoring me to normality. If the operation is successful, well and good. If it isn't, then I agree that I should be scrapped and make way for Andrew.' This compromise, clearly, gives the best possible chance of having a healthy baby, and at the same time gives the foetus all the chance that it ever had of itself being that baby. But it does this at the cost of abolishing the substantial chance that there was of having this particular child, albeit in a seriously handicapped condition. I call this a cost, because many will argue (though I am not sure that I want to follow them) that life with a severe handicap is preferable, for the person who has it, to no life at all. Of course it depends on the severity of the handicap. And of course this policy involves so much distress for the mother that we might rule it out on that score alone, and terminate instead.

12.4 Perhaps I should end by removing what might be an obstacle to understanding. In order to expound the argument, I suggested that we imagined Andrew and the foetus having a discussion in some timeless noumenal world. This way of dramatizing the argument is perhaps useful though not necessary; and it carries with it one danger. We have to imagine the two possible children conducting this very rational discussion, and therefore we think of them being in a sense already grown up enough to conduct it; and that may lead us to suppose that, for either of them, to be deprived of the possibility of adulthood *after* having had this taste of it would be a very great evil. People (most of them) cling tenaciously to life (though it is a matter for argument, at what age they start to do this); and therefore to deprive a person of life is thought of as *normally* an evil. This certainly does not apply to Andrew, since he is not alive yet and so cannot be *deprived* of life in the relevant sense, though it can be *withheld* from him. I do not think it applies to the foetus as such, since it has as yet no conscious life (which is what we are talking about) and therefore cannot feel the loss of it or even the fear of that loss. If anybody thinks that foetuses do have conscious feelings sufficient to be put in this balance, I ask him to agree at least that their intensity is relatively small, and likewise those of the new-born infant. So I do not think that the harm one is doing to the foetus or the unsuccessfully operated upon new-born infant by killing them is greater than that which one is doing to Andrew by stopping him from being conceived and born. In fact I think it is much less, because Andrew, unlike them, has a high prospect of a normal and happy life.

13

Prediction and Moral Appraisal

13.1 An apology is perhaps needed for writing a simple paper about the freedom of the will. There has been no lack of subtle and sophisticated writing on this subject in recent times; but most of the easy pieces about it are now quite old, and as a result the standard postures are often rehearsed by students in forms that make the problem appear either more intractable than it is, or more simple. Two of these postures, Determinism and its opposite Indeterminism or Libertarianism, are still thought by many to be locked in a conflict which philosophers have been unable to resolve; and it is also thought that the conflict is of great practical significance, so that, for example, important policy decisions about the punishment of offenders or the education of children hang upon its solution. But in fact I do not think that many of those who have come down decisively on one of what they think are the two sides of the so-called 'Free will controversy' have been caused thereby to alter their opinions on any important practical question—or if they have, they have lacked reason. For as soon as we ask, what an extreme determinist or an extreme libertarian would have to say about practical issues as a result of embracing their doctrines, both are faced with the same dilemma. Either they say that the consequences of their views are something so utterly absurd as to cast doubt on the seriousness of anybody who maintains them; or they say that the consequences are no different from what the rest of us think— in which case they are left, in spite of their alleged dispute, in substantial agreement with one another and with the ordinary man.

This is, in short, one of the class of puzzles which used to be called 'pseudo-problems'—a very misleading expression, because if something is a problem for someone, it really is a problem for him and he needs to solve it. What the people who invented this term ought to have said is that there are different kinds of problems, of which only some admit of a 'yes'-or-'no' answer; others, such as this one, require instead a fuller understanding of the question itself, to see the pitfalls and ambiguities in it. The solution of this second kind of problem lies not in answering 'Yes' or 'No' to some question that is clearly understood, but in seeing that there are a number of different questions which had been confused with one another, and each of which, when clearly distinguished from the others, may admit of a fairly ready answer.

I myself have nothing much that is original to say about this problem. It seems to me that anybody who reads what Hume (1739: II. 3. i) and Mill (1843: VI. 2) say on the subject, and adds a judicious seasoning from the insights of Aristotle (1109^{b}30 ff.), can arrive at an understanding of the matter which will suffice for all practical purposes; and I have nothing to add, except possibly to give some explanations of why people have gone on being perplexed by it for so long. There are in fact a great many sources of this perplexity, of which I shall have space to deal with only a few. Of these, the most important are the following two. First, it is thought that there is some kind of incompatibility between the claim (supposed to be necessary for scientific work) that events in the world, including human bodily movements, are in principle predictable, and the claim that human actions are subject to moral appraisal. Secondly, it is thought that it is wrong or unjust to blame or punish people for acts which they could not but perform, with the consequence that, if human acts are predictable, it becomes unjust to punish or blame people for them. The two sources of perplexity are so closely linked that it might be thought that they are the same. However, if my experience is anything to go by, the unravelling of the first perplexity can prove insufficient by itself to remove people's worries about the second; and therefore something will have to be said about the second at the end of the paper.

13.2 What is the minimum that we have to know about the freedom of the will in order to be able to go on with the job of appraising human actions morally (or for that matter in any other way, for example technically), without wasting our breath? We have to know that there is nothing about human actions which makes them not a subject for such appraisal, in the same way as the movements of stars or hurricanes are not. Nobody makes a moral judgement to the effect that hurricane Shirley ought to have gone a hundred miles further east and not destroyed Miami; if we said this, the most we could mean would be, either that it would have been a good thing if the course of the hurricane had been different, or, in another sense of 'ought', that a different course was initially more likely or more to be expected. What, we want to know, is the difference—if there is one—between hurricanes and human beings that makes us think that we can properly say of a human being that he ought to have done something different from what he did? And are we right to make this distinction?

On the other side, we do not want to save the possibility of making moral judgements at the cost of rendering it impossible to make scientific predictions in cases where most people think it possible to make them. To put the point starkly at first: if, in order to preserve the propriety of moral judgements, we had to admit some kind of indeterminism in natural events which made it impossible to predict anything (even the movements of the stars), then that would be just as paradoxical in one way as it would be paradoxical in the opposite way if we made moral judgements impossible. We have to steer, if we can, between the Scylla of a determinism which would rule out moral appraisal of human actions, and the Charybdis of an indeterminism which would rule out scientific and other predictions.

But the matter is not so easy as this stark contrast might make it seem. For if there were such a stark contrast (if, that is to say, the world were divisible into things like stars whose movements were predictable but not morally appraisable, and things like people whose actions were morally appraisable but not predictable) then our problem would not be so difficult. But the contrast is not like that. As we shall see, a great many human actions (some would say all) are in principle predictable. Indeed, the most important (though not the most novel) point that I wish to make in this paper is that the problem is not to be solved by finding a class of events (namely certain human actions) which are in principle unpredictable. The problem is one, rather, of finding a way of reconciling the predictability with the moral appraisability of the same human actions. For it is quite clear that there are actions which we should all think we could predict and be right in thinking this, and about which, nevertheless, we also think it right to make moral judgements. It is not surprising, therefore, that most of the philosophers of any penetration who have discussed this problem have been trying to find a way of saying that human actions are, in principle, *both* predictable *and* morally appraisable. This seems to have been Aristotle's view (ibid.), and Spinoza's (1677: III), and Hume's (ibid.), and Kant's (1788: A169 ff. = 94 f.), and Mill's (ibid.). It is also that of Professor Stevenson (1944: ch. 14) and of a great many other good modern philosophers. It is only the more superficial thinkers who have held, either that human actions are predictable and therefore not morally appraisable, or that they are morally appraisable and therefore not predictable.

Our problem, therefore, can be stated as follows. What is the minimum that has to be conceded to the moralist, in order to make moral appraisals possible, and what is the minimum that has to be conceded to the scientist, in order to make science (including the human sciences) possible; and can we concede both these minima without inconsistency? I shall contend that, when we have correctly understood what these minimal requirements of the moralist and the scientist are, we can see that there is no inconsistency between them.

13.3 Let us take first, then, the moralist's side of the case. I will start with a way of stating it which has been extremely common in the literature, but which has certainly misled a great many people. It is said that, if we are to appraise an action morally, it must be the case that the agent *could have* acted otherwise (or, if the appraisal is of a proposed action, that he *could* act otherwise). It is certainly true that we do not normally say that a man ought to have done something when we know that he could not have done it, and that we do not normally ask whether he ought to do something if we know that he cannot do it. The reason is that, if I cannot do a certain thing, the question 'Shall I do it?' (in that sense in which it asks for a decision as to whether to do it) simply does not arise. And if the question 'Shall I do it?' does not arise, then the questions 'Ought I to do it?' and (later) 'Ought I to have done it?' do not arise either. But this is true only in what I have called the prescriptive use of 'ought'. On this, see *FR* ch. 4, in which I discussed this matter at greater length.

There are certainly uses of 'ought' in which I can say that I ought to do, or ought to have done, something, but cannot or could not. For example, I might say, 'I ought to have gone to the meeting, but I could not because there was no way of getting there in time.' And if we can say 'I ought to have, but I could not', it looks as if we can also ask whether I ought to have, although we know that I could not. But this is a non-prescriptive use of 'ought', because statements containing it are not intended as guides in answering any practical question of the form 'What shall I do?'.

This is not just because they are about actions in the past. There are past-tense 'ought'-statements which *are* intended as guides in answering practical questions. For example, if I am teaching someone to drive a car with an old-fashioned gear-shift, and I say to him 'You ought to have let the clutch in more gently', this is about a past action of his. But the purpose of saying it is to instruct him how to drive, not in the past, but in the future. This ties in with the feature of moral and other evaluative statements which has been called their universaliz-ability (see *LM* 155 ff., *FR* 10 ff., *MT* 21). It is because I am instructing him in the principles of good driving that I can say to him, about a past action, that he ought to have let the clutch in more gently, and yet say something that is of rele-vance to his future actions; I am pointing out that in this past action he broke a principle which he ought to follow in his actions. So, by considering this past action and my comment upon it, he learns something about what the principle is; and thus, when he comes again into a situation to which the prin-ciple is applicable, he is that much better able to decide what to do—I have taught him something.

So, then, it is not because the statement 'I ought to have, but I could not' is about the past that it is not prescriptive. Why it is not prescriptive can be seen if we consider its pre-sent- or future-tense version. Suppose that I had, before the occasion on which this action would have been done if I had been able and willing to do it, said 'I ought to, but I can't'. The reason why this use of 'ought' is not prescriptive is that, if

I cannot, then there is no place for the question 'Shall I?'. And if there is no place for this question, then there is no place for the prescriptive question 'Ought I?'. So, even if there is a place for the statement 'I ought', the 'ought' cannot, in that statement, be being used in a way that would make it an answer to the prescriptive question 'Ought I?' (that is to say, the question 'Ought I?', where 'ought' is being used prescriptively), because, as we have seen, no such question can, in the circumstances, arise. We may say, then, that, although it is true that 'ought' implies 'can', this is only true of certain of its uses, namely the prescriptive ones. And there is one other thing about this slogan that we must carefully notice. The word 'implies' in it does not mean the same as 'entails' or 'allows us to deduce logically'. The implication here is similar to that by which the statement that the King of France is bald implies (or, as Professor Strawson (1950) has said, presupposes) that there is a King of France; just as the question 'Is the King of France bald?' cannot arise unless there is a King of France, so the question 'Ought I to do it?' cannot arise (in the prescriptive use of 'ought') unless I can do it.

13.4 So, to sum up, a moral appraisal, if prescriptive (and of course not all moral appraisals are prescriptive, as I have explained in *FR* 22 n.), is out of place unless the person about whom it is made can, or could, do the action recommended. So far the usual way of putting the matter is perfectly all right. But the trouble begins when we ask what we mean by 'can' or 'could'. A popular move has been to add, after 'can', the qualification 'if he wants' or 'if he chooses' . The purpose of this addition is as follows. It is supposed to help us in finding a way of reconciling the making of moral judgements with the predictability of actions, as we want to do. For suppose that it is predictable that a person *will* want or *will* choose to do a certain action, and that *if* he wants or chooses to do it, there is no further obstacle to his doing it, so that we can say 'He can if he wants' or '. . . if he chooses' . If it is the case that he can if he wants or chooses, and that he does want or choose, then he not only can, but will do the action. For if, being able to do it, he did not, we should have to say that he did not, after all, choose or want to do it.

This is no doubt oversimplified. There are senses of 'want'

in which I can want to do a thing, and be able to do it, and not do it. For example, I may want very much to take the largest pie, and be able to take it (because I am served first), but not take it because I think it would be bad manners. What we have to say here is that, although I do want to take the largest pie, I want *more* to behave politely. So when we say that if a person wants, and can, he will, what we mean is that if that is what he most wants to do, and can, he will. We have also to understand 'want' here in a wide sense to include all motivations; it has to include, for example, what is called the motive of duty as well as the baser passions. 'Most wants to' has, that is to say, to be taken as meaning, in general, 'is most highly motivated to'. It is not illegitimate, if we take 'wants' in this general sense, to say that what a person most wants to do, he will do if he can, and that this is analytically true in virtue of the meaning of the word 'wants' as so understood.

Let us say, then, that, if it is predictable that a person will want to do a certain thing and if he 'can if he wants', then he will, and it is predictable that he will. So if the condition for the proper making of moral appraisals is that the person in question can if he wants, this condition is not incompatible with the predictability of his actions; for we may be able to predict what he will want, and so what he will do, and yet it will be true that he could have done something else *if* he had wanted (although we are able to predict that he *will* not want anything else, and will want to do this).

13.5 We have now come to the point at which the whole discussion can very easily go off the rails if we are not prudent. In order to keep it on the rails, we have to be careful what we say in answer to an objection which will at once be made to what has just been said. It will be objected that for the proper making of moral appraisals it is not sufficient to require that the agent can if he wants, or could have if he had wanted. It is necessary further, the objectors say, that he could have wanted, or not wanted. Let us take an example to make this clearer. The person in my previous example takes the largest pie. It is certainly true of him that if he had wanted to take a smaller pie he could have done so. So, we might feel like saying, it is all right to say of him that he ought to have taken a smaller one. But, say the objectors, could he have *wanted* to take a smaller one? We have to be able to answer 'Yes' to this question (they say) if we are to bring off the reconciliation trick. For the essence of the trick was this: we said that what he would want was predictable, and that therefore his action was predictable. But if what he would want was predictable, then he could not have wanted anything else. So (they say) if the moral appraisal is to be in place, we have to say, not merely that he could have taken it if he had wanted, but that he could have wanted. The assumption is that prediction, if legitimate, implies the certainty that the thing predicted will happen; and therefore it is inconsistent to claim, both that he could have wanted to take the smaller pie, and that his not wanting to do so was predictable.

The objectors thus try to reinstate, further back, the old irreconcilability between prediction and moral appraisal. They say that our attempt at reconciliation was a fraud. In order to evaluate this objection we have to ask whether the move the objectors made was legitimate. Were they within their rights in asking, not merely that the person should have been able to take the smaller pie if he had wanted, but that he should have been able to want to take it, before we can morally appraise his action in not taking it?

I will first give a prima facie reason for saying that the move was not legitimate. If we look at the function of moral appraisal, we can see why, for it to be in place, an agent must be able to do the act appraised if he wants, but why it is not required that it should be unpredictable whether he will want or not want. We have seen that prescriptive 'ought'-statements (which are the kind that 'imply "can"') function as guides to action. Another way of putting this is to say that to accept, or sincerely assent to, such an appraisal, or to any other kind of prescription, is to want, or in general be motivated, to act accordingly. It must be noted (but briefly, for the point ought to be familiar) that to say this is neither to endorse what may be called the 'verbal shove' theory of the meaning of appraisals and prescriptions, against which I have repeatedly argued (e.g. H 1951, 1971*a*) nor to identify appraisals with one particular kind of prescriptions, namely simple imperatives (an identification which is rejected in many places in my writings, starting with *LM* 2). Now an appraisal would seem to lose all point if the agent whose act is appraised is going to do the act *however* he is motivated, or *whatever* he wants; in that case, acceptance or rejection of the appraisal would make absolutely no difference to his action, and its utterance by another could not guide his action. But if to be motivated by an acceptance of the appraisal would make a difference to his action, then the appraisal obviously has a point, even if it is predictable whether he will accept it, and in general how he will be motivated. For example, if I say to somebody 'You ought', and he comes to agree with me and think that he ought, and acts accordingly, the saying and thinking that he ought has obviously played a role in the process that led to his action and therefore had a point. This begins to explain why it is legitimate to demand, before appraisals are in place, that the agent should be able to act on them if he wants, but illegitimate to demand that his motivations should be unpredictable.

13.6 But before we can understand this fully we shall have to dig deeper; and I can think of no better place to start than with Aristotle's discussion of voluntary action in *Nicomachean Ethics III* (1109^{b}30 ff.; and see 2.8, 9.6). He there says that before we can call an act voluntary, and therefore appraise it morally, two conditions have to be satisfied. One of these does not concern us here, namely that the agent should know what he is doing. The other condition, which does concern us, is this: the origin (*archē*) of the action has to be *in* the agent. The word I have translated 'origin' is one of the key terms in Aristotle's theory of action, and indeed in his logic as well. It means the origin of any train of reasoning or thought.

In theoretical logic, it often means some kind of premiss. In Aristotle's theory of practical reasoning, or of thought about what to do, the *archē* or origin or principle (the word is derived from the Latin '*principium* (beginning)', the literal translation of '*archē*') is a desire (or more generally motivation) to do something of a certain kind. This is expressed in various ways as a principle (for example, the desire to eat something sweet might be expressed in the principle 'Let me eat whatever sweet thing is available'). Aristotle's theory of the origin of action is summed up in his doctrine of the so-called practical syllogism: if somebody thinks 'Let me eat whatever sweet thing is available' and also thinks 'This is an available sweet thing', these two thoughts, put together, will lead to the action of eating this thing (1147ᵃ29). In other words, the desire to eat something sweet, coupled with the perception that this is a sweet thing, together lead to the action. This is the Aristotelian version of the 'drive–stimulus–response' theory which is still current among psychologists; and something like it must, it seems to me, be true, and indeed analytically true in virtue of the meaning of 'desire'.

The *archē* or origin of the action is the desire to do a thing of a certain kind, or, expressed in words, the principle 'Let me do a thing of a certain kind'. I have deliberately expressed it in the form 'Let me . . .' (the first-person imperative), although Aristotle puts it normally in forms which are translated 'I should' or even 'I ought'. This is in order to make clear that the *archē* is not itself a moral appraisal—to suppose that, would be to make nonsense of several passages in the text. It is this *archē* which has to be 'in' the agent if his action is to be voluntary and thus morally appraisable. This means that, on Aristotle's view, an action does not have to be uncaused or unpredictable before we can appraise it morally; its causation has to be of a certain special kind. The action has to be explicable by reference to a desire, or, to put it generally, a motive, *in* the agent. Aristotle's examples make this fairly clear. To enlarge upon one of them, he draws a contrast between voluntary actions and actions done under constraint, as for example when my ship is blown on shore by contrary winds and there breaks up. In the second case my action (if it can be called an action) in landing in that territory is not voluntary; if I had been exiled from the territory I could not justly be punished for being on it. Nor can the action be morally appraised; and the same applies if somebody carries me there by overpowering force.

In these latter cases the explanation, and therefore the causation, of the action has nothing to do with anything 'in' me; if one wants to explain the action, or to predict it beforehand, one has to consider, not anything about me, but something about, in the first case the properties of winds and of ships, and in the second case the motives, not of me, but of the people who are carrying me. The reason why, if the explanation goes outside me in this way, *I* am not to be appraised morally for it is that such a moral appraisal would be an appraisal of *me* (of *my* character). This character is the combination of all the dispositions that I have, each of which provides the *archē* for actions in appropriate circumstances. For example, because I have the disposition to like sweet things, I eat this thing which is sweet. Thus the fact that I eat it shows something about me, my dispositions or my character. On the other hand if I were forced to swallow the sweet thing, the fact that I swallowed it would show nothing about me or my character or my dispositions.

If Aristotle is right in drawing the distinction just where he does between the actions which are morally appraisable and those which are not—and I myself think that, broadly speaking, he is right—then the objection which we were considering is not well taken. The objection was that it was not sufficient, for the making of moral appraisals of actions, that the doer should have been able to act differently if he had wanted. It is necessary also, the objection said, that he should have been able to want something different from what he did want. But if Aristotle is right, the question 'Could he have wanted something different from what he did want?' is irrelevant to the question of the voluntariness of his action. To call it voluntary and appraise him morally, we have to regard it as indicative of the sort of man that he is. But it is so indicative if the action is the direct result of *his* desires and motives and character and dispositions, not of something outside himself. If he does the action because that is what he most wants to do, the fact that he does it shows us what he most wants to do, and that, in turn, shows us what is his disposition with regard to the particular circumstances in which he is, or what sort of man he is.

Suppose, for example, that a man runs away in battle. Suppose, further, that he could have stayed and fought if he had wanted to—nobody dragged him away. This tells us that he was the sort of man to run away in circumstances of that sort. Let us suppose that the circumstances were not especially terrifying as battles go. Then we shall be able to say of this man that his action in running away in those not very frightening circumstances was a sign that he was a coward. To call him cowardly is to appraise him morally. The question 'Could he have wanted to stay and fight?' is not relevant to this moral appraisal. Let us suppose that it was predictable, knowing his parentage and upbringing, that he would grow up into the sort of man who, in a battle of this degree of frightfulness, would want to run away more than he wanted to stay, and would therefore run away. This makes no difference to the fact that he is the sort of man who runs away in such circumstances—i.e. a cowardly man.

13.7 Aristotle's account ties in with what I said earlier was a prima facie reason for rejecting the objection we are considering. But there is a difference between Aristotle's approach and our earlier one which I may be accused of ignoring unless I now mention it. I do not think that the difference has much bearing on the present argument, though in other contexts it is important. We were speaking earlier of those moral appraisals which have the function of directly or indirectly guiding actions. But Aristotle is talking about the moral appraisal of agents and their characters. His interest is in the conditions under which we hold people to be blameworthy. I do not think that these two kinds of moral appraisal (what we might call the action-guiding and the character-assessing kinds) are as unrelated as might appear at first sight; but fortunately we do not need to discuss what their relation is, because for the purpose of the present argument we can ignore any relation that they may have to each other, and deal with them separately. That is to say, we can treat as separate the problem of whether the predictability of actions is compatible with the making of action-guiding appraisals of them, and the problem of whether the predictability of actions is compatible with the making of character-assessing appraisals of their agents. And then we can say that the latter problem is dealt with by Aristotle's account which I have just been summarizing, and that the former problem is dealt with by the prima facie reason mentioned earlier for rejecting the objection we are considering—a reason which I shall in a moment be trying to make more secure. Later, I shall indicate how treacherous the notion of blameworthiness is.

Confining ourselves then for the moment to the action-guiding role of moral appraisals, i.e. their role in offering guidance in answering questions of the form 'Shall I do this or that?', we have seen already that such appraisals are out of place when no question of this sort arises. In the case of the man who is driven on shore by contrary winds, no question arises like 'Shall I land on this shore?'. Therefore the prescriptive advice 'You ought not to land on this shore' is out of place. It is in place only when a question arises which it could be a help in answering. On the other hand, take the man who is wondering whether to run away in battle. He is asking himself the question 'Shall I run away?'; and therefore the advice 'You ought not to run away' is in place. Not only is he asking the question; what he does will depend on what answer he gives to it.

It is here that the difference lies between the two cases, and not in anything to do with predictability. It may be the case (I think it is) that in both examples we might have been able to predict what he would do. That is a feature common to the two cases. The difference lies in something else. It is that, in predicting that the man will be driven ashore, I have to look only at the fact that he is on a ship of a certain sort and that the winds are in a certain quarter, and of gale force; whereas in predicting that the man will run away, I have to take into account the fact that *he* is a man of a certain sort, that he is asking himself the question 'Shall I run away?', and, because he is a man of that sort, with that combination of desires and other dispositions, he will answer it in the affirmative, and will therefore run away. That is why in the latter case, but not in the former, I can appropriately say to him 'You ought not to run away'. For, even if it is predictable that he will run away, and I can therefore be sure that he will not take my advice, that does not stop it being good moral advice. For he is asking the question 'Shall I run away?', towards answering which the advice *would* be helpful, if he were not, predictably, going to reject it. In the same way it may be true and in point to make a factual statement to someone even though it can be predicted that he will not believe it, whereas it is neither true nor false, and certainly not in point, to make a so-called statement which purports to answer a question which does not, in the circumstances, arise.

We must also remember here the universalizability of moral appraisals, already alluded to. Even though *he* is not going to take our advice, a situation could occur which was like this

one, except that the agent *was* disposed to heed the principle
to which we are implicitly appealing. It is true that the situation will then not be exactly similar to this one, because the
disposition of the agent makes a difference. But it may all the
same be *relevantly* similar, because the dispositions of agents to
follow or not to follow moral principles are not, in general, relevant to the morality of their *acts*—an act is wrong whether or
not I want to do it. So a moral appraisal of the act in this situation in which it is not going to be heeded may bear usefully
upon some other relevantly similar situation in which it may
be heeded, and be action-guiding for that situation.

If the objection is now made that if *all* acts were predictable,
the appraisal could *never* be heeded—i.e. that in any relevantly
similar situation upon which it bore, the agent's motives and
actions are going predictably to be such that the making of the
moral appraisal is going to make no difference to them, this is
simply and obviously false. For in those other situations the
making of the appraisal and its coming to the notice of the
agents will be a factor in the situation. Without it, they might
have acted in one way; with it, they may act in a different
way. So the making of it has a point. The objection would
only hold if the making of appraisals had no effect in the
world; but this is not so.

I will illustrate by yet another example the point that predictability does not destroy freedom in the sense in which this
is required for moral appraisal. I am driving from Oxford to
London, and there are two equally good routes. I come to the
point where I have to choose my route, and there is somebody
sitting beside me who knows me well and can predict which
route I will take (perhaps I have told him why I prefer it, or
perhaps he has observed that I always take it at a certain time
of day or in a certain state of the weather or of my temper).
Does the fact that he can predict what I will decide remove
from me the need to decide? Not in the least. I am asking
myself the question 'Which route shall I take?', and what I do
depends on the answer I give to it. I am not a mindless
automaton or a zombie or subject to post-hypnotic suggestion.
And if a moral question arose about the decision, as it might
(perhaps if I chose one route, I should be tempted or constrained to exceed the speed limit in order to keep my

appointment), I can properly ask myself 'Which route ought I (morally) to take?'. When I reflect, I can see no reason, in the predictability of my decision, to deny that this question arises and has to be answered. Even if my passenger were to tell me his prediction, I still have to answer the question 'Which route shall I take?' and perhaps the question 'Which route ought I to take?'; and after I have answered them we shall know whether his prediction was correct or not. If it was correct, none the less I had to answer the questions. And it is the fact that we have to answer such questions that gives moral and other appraisive language its use.

13.8 I must end by saying something about blame. The word is highly ambiguous. From the way philosophers sometimes speak of moral appraisals generically as 'judgements of praise and blame' one might think that to make an adverse moral appraisal was always to blame somebody; but if this were so, how could we say, as we certainly can say, 'He ought not to have done it, but one can hardly blame him because, etc.'? In the *Oxford English Dictionary* the following five senses of the verb 'to blame' are listed:

1. to find fault with, to censure: the opposite of *to praise*;
2. to address with rebuke, to reprove, chide, scold (obs.);
3. to bring into disrepute or discredit (obs.);
4. to charge, to accuse (no citation after 1649);
5. to lay the blame on, reproach, to fix the responsibility on, to make answerable.

I shall in a moment briefly allude to sense 2 ('chide, scold'), but shall otherwise ignore the senses which are not current (2, 3, 4). This leaves senses 1 ('censure') and 5 ('fix the responsibility on'). Perhaps enough has been said, following Aristotle, about sense 1; I hope I have provided grounds for saying that, in order for us appropriately to find fault with or censure somebody for an act, the act does not have to have been unpredictable. If the act was indicative of the sort of person he was, because the motivation of the act lay in *his* dispositions, then, if that was a bad sort of person to be, we can accordingly find fault with him.

This leaves sense 5. It is commonly thought that it would be unjust or unfair to blame people in this sense (i.e. make them answerable), and also to chide or scold them (sense 2), if their acts were predictable. Now, when a claim is made that it would be unjust to do something, we ought to ask why it would be unjust—that is to say, what is the principle of justice (to use Professor Rawls's expression—1971) which makes it unjust, and what is the basis of that principle. This raises the general question of how we should select principles of justice (see H 1978, *MT* ch. 9). There is room here only for a quick survey of some of the more plausible candidates for ways of selecting principles of justice, to see whether any of them comes anywhere near supporting the view that it is unjust to make people answerable for actions unless the actions are unpredictable.

I am myself an adherent of a kind of utilitarianism (there are of course many kinds, some of which are so easily demolished that it is thought, too hastily, that *all* kinds are easily demolished). My own view is that we should select principles of justice on the ground of their acceptance-utility—i.e. that we should adopt those principles whose general acceptance within a society would leave the members of that society, all in all, best off. It is clear that such a view will not support the thesis that it is unjust to hold people responsible for their acts unless the acts are unpredictable. For if this thesis were written into a principle of justice, it would become impossible justly to make answerable for their acts a great many people whom we now do make answerable—acts which could easily have been predicted. And so the whole system of law would break down, to the great harm of nearly everyone in society.

However, it will not do to rest the argument merely on utilitarian premises, because then it will not convince anybody but utilitarians. It might be equally well based on a theory of the ideal-observer type, which yields results similar to certain forms of utilitarianism. I can see no reason why a fully informed and impartially benevolent observer should adopt a principle of justice which made it unjust to punish predictable acts. Indeed, a certain degree of malevolence would be required to make somebody adopt such a principle, in view of its disastrous consequences. If God is the ideal observer, the same holds for him. And if, as I have argued elsewhere (H 1973), Rawls's theory when deprived of purely intuitional support collapses into utilitarianism, he also would have to reject such a principle.

Could the upholder of such a principle appeal to any variety of ethical naturalism in its support? I think not. Most naturalistic definitions of the moral words are either of a utilitarian sort (they make some kind of utilitarianism true by definition) or else they are attempts to write into a definition or into the meanings of the moral words the opinions of the common man. In the first case, even if naturalism were a tenable ethical theory, no more support would be forthcoming for the principle than from utilitarianism of any other sort. Neither will it get any support in the latter case; for one thing is certain, namely that the common man operates with ideas of justice according to which it is in order to punish acts which could have been predicted. It is being done the whole time without protest by the common man; it is only the philosophers who have scruples.

Lastly, what about ethical intuitionism, the last refuge of moral philosophers who have become bankrupt of arguments? Are there moral intuitions which require us not to blame or punish predictable acts? Not, certainly, the intuitions of the common man, for the reason just given. Nor my own intuitions as a philosopher either. If there are philosophers whose intuitions make them uphold the principle of justice which I am attacking, it may be merely because they are the victims of the confusion which I have been trying to clear up in this paper. But intuitions unsupported by argument are in any case not to be relied on. If anybody claimed to have intuitions contrary to mine, I would content myself with asking him to try to become clearer about the whole matter, with the hope that he would then agree with me.

14

Health Care Policy
Some Options

14.1 I have argued elsewhere (H 1993*a*, 15.2 and refs.) that a viable ethical theory is going to have to contain elements drawn both from the utilitarians and from Kant. There is in my view no inconsistency between a carefully formulated Kantianism and a carefully formulated utilitarianism. It is the purpose of this paper to try out such a theory on a pressing practical problem, that of how health care should be provided and distributed. I will start with some discussions of distributive justice in general. For only when we have decided what distribution of goods in general, equal or unequal, is just or right, can we go on to the particular question, well phrased by Norman Daniels (1985: ch. 1), 'Is health care special?'. But I shall not spend much time on the general question.

Utilitarianism of the Kantian sort which I defend can justify a moderate degree of equality of distribution of goods (probably much greater than prevails in the United States). The reasons are basically two (5.5, H 1978, *MT* ch. 9). The first is that the diminishing marginal utility of most goods and of money, over the ranges that matter, makes it the case that to deprive a poor man of a certain amount of money or goods will do more harm to him than to deprive a rich man of the same amount. This can be used to justify a certain degree of redistribution of goods and money by progressive taxation, and this in fact happens in nearly all countries, including the United States. Whether the progression is steep enough, or too steep, is a political question that fortunately I do not need to broach. There are other factors, also connected with utility, that militate against a too equal distribution, such as the need for incentives to make people give of their best to society; if they

Published in different form in Spanish, *Agora* 8 (1989). Not published before in English.

got no benefit for themselves, they would not be so keen to do it.

The second main Kantian utilitarian reason for seeking moderate equality is the disutility of envy; if people think that other people are much richer than they themselves are, but have done little to earn their greater wealth, they will be envious; and envy is a festering sore in society which can only lead to dissensions, disaffection, and in extreme cases rebellion, all of which harm everybody in society and frustrate everybody's ends.

If we ask whether health care is special, we have to consider first whether these considerations apply to it. It is often argued that it is not special: if we had a system of progressive taxation which redistributed wealth to the optimum extent, then could we not let people, now enjoying the degree of equality that they ought to enjoy, *buy* whatever health care they thought they needed, thus boosting their autonomy?

14.2   A digression is necessary in order to explain this concept (see also 2.7 f. and refs.). We must be clear that 'autonomy' is not being used here in its Kantian sense. It means simply 'being left free to make one's own decisions on matters affecting one's own future'. I wish to argue that autonomy in this sense is not a value independent of utility: it owes its value to its utility: first to the fact that people usually, though not always, want it for its own sake (in Kantian terms, that they have it as an end), and secondly to the fact that if you leave someone to make his own choices he will usually, though not always, make them more wisely than other people can make them for him, so that people's ends are more likely to be achieved in this way.

Some philosophers, however, treat autonomy as a separate value, independent of utility or of the furtherance of people's ends or interests. They argue that there are cases in which, by infringing autonomy, one could do better for a person than if one let *him* decide. We may take as an example the relations between doctors and patients; this illustrates on a small scale the problem of the relation between the individual and any claimant to paternalistic authority. In some cases, these philosophers think, one should allow the patient to decide on the treatment, even if all in all it is against his interests.

But this defence of autonomy is superfluous, if it can be sufficiently defended without requiring it to be an independent value. This can be done in two complementary ways. The first is by pointing out that many people most of the time do want very much to make their own autonomous decisions about their treatment, as about other things. This is not always the case: some patients want to have anxiety lifted from them by letting the doctor decide what is for the best, and to force autonomy on such patients would be a cruelty. But probably the majority of patients do want to have the final say in their treatment, and this majority includes nearly all philosophers who write on this subject, so that they tend to neglect the others. And even most ordinary people do not *like* to be powerless in the hands of their doctors. This is one reason why autonomy in itself is usually in the patient's interest; to be given weight in this way it does not *need* to be an independent value.

The second reason is that autonomy is very often, perhaps in the great majority of cases, a *means* to arriving at decisions which are best for the patient. This is because most normal patients know best what they are trying to get out of life, which varies enormously from one patient to another. For this and similar reasons, a doctor will often not know what is best for *this* patient. Therefore, if the patient is competent and not completely unintelligent (and this can be said of most patients), it is likely to be best for the patient if he himself, after being informed of the medical facts by the doctor, has the last word. So the best general rule is to respect the patient's autonomy.

There are exceptions which have to be made: the case of the incompetent patient, where the question arises, who should decide if the patient cannot; the case I mentioned where the patient wants to be spared anxiety and a wise decision can be made without his intervention; and there are others. Also, there are things the doctor knows and cannot fully explain to the patient because they are too technical, especially if the patient is not very clever, or is frightened out of his wits. The doctor's superior knowledge of the medical facts and probabilities to some extent weighs against the patient's superior knowledge of his own life plans. There are thus considerations that should make us accept a general rule to respect autonomy, and considerations which should cause us to make exceptions to this rule. I do not believe anybody thinks that autonomy is an *overriding* value, except a few philosophers.

So there are two good reasons for having a rule to respect the autonomy of patients, and indeed to respect the patient's *right* to autonomy, subject to the sorts of exceptions I have been speaking of. It will be for the best to have such a rule and to treat it as compelling, so that a doctor will feel he has sinned if he infringes it without very strong reasons. We do not need to make autonomy an independent value to justify the sanctity that all good doctors attach to it in practice. In terms of my own theory, critical thinking can easily justify its adoption as a firmly held intuitive principle.

14.3 We can return now to the argument mentioned earlier, which says, in effect, 'Get the overall distribution of wealth right, and then treat health care much like groceries'. We have to ask whether the value of autonomy can be used to support such a policy. Obviously what is in question here is not the autonomy of patients in relation to their doctors, but the autonomy of individual citizens in relation to the State. Will an appeal to such autonomy bear the weight put on it? The 'groceries' example gives us a clue. We do not actually leave even the distribution of groceries just to the market. Most countries, including most Western countries at least since the eighteenth century, have recognized a duty not to let people actually starve to death. Now, most countries do much more than that for their poor, though again there is political argument about whether they do enough.

There is a similarity which we must notice between welfare food distribution and health care. Malnutrition and illness are both *very great* evils. One of the main reasons why we think health care special is the same reason which makes us think the prevention of starvation and malnutrition special: that serious illness and starvation are such great evils (such great disutilities, to use the jargon) that it is worth forgoing a good deal of other benefits in order to eradicate or at least diminish them. Indeed, they are the same kind of evil, and overlap; starvation and malnutrition are causes of illness, and all three are causes of extreme suffering and often of death.

Those who argue for a market system for the sake of autonomy (which they often insist on to a much higher degree than utilitarian or Kantian or any other sensible arguments could justify) ignore the fact that the very poor, whatever they in prudence *should* do, and whatever they in theory *could* do, will inevitably not always make sufficient provision either for their future medical needs, or even for a rainy day when the groceries run out. Try telling a poor mother, whose children are dying for lack of food or medical attention, that if she had been more provident she would not have been brought to this pass. This is a case where autonomy can be pushed beyond the limits of utility. In such cases, provided that there are not other adverse effects, such as the destruction of incentives, utility will be served by the State making provision which the poor person has (quite understandably) neglected to make.

To this we must add the thought that a compassionate society, which does not let people starve or die of curable diseases just because they are poor, is probably a better society to live in than the other kind for *everybody* in it. It is not a source of happiness to see others in such misery. And if we do not mind that, widespread illness is also a weakness in the economy.

But, of course, this touches only the fringe of our main problem. All civilized countries, and all civilized philosophers, probably agree that provision ought to be made for routine medical care of the very poor who otherwise will not get it; and this includes preventive medicine. But to accept this is not necessarily to accept the desirability of a *universal* system of health care, like the British Health Service, which everybody can use, supported by taxation. To justify such a more ambitious kind of public health provision, further arguments are needed, and they are complicated ones. They may even be applicable to some countries and societies and not to others; but I will try to be as general as I can. I must add that I am not well versed in these complexities, even as they affect Britain, let alone the USA. All I can do is just list some arguments that are often advanced, and comment on them.

14.4 There are some very important differences between the health care systems in the USA and Britain. The USA has in the main a private system, in which those who are insured either at their own expense or at that of their employers can receive good treatment up to the limits allowed by their insurers. Even some very rich people, when they have expensive ailments or need expensive surgery, can ruin themselves and their families. For the poor who have no insurance there is a system financed out of taxes which does something for them; but it does not go far. Old age pensioners get help through a different arrangement, also financed by taxes, which is no more generous. In all, it is a system which favours the rich, and even for them is not satisfactory.

The British system, by contrast, is financed mainly by taxes, and anybody can get all the treatment that the system allows, which is fairly good. Treatment is free, except that fairly small payments are required for drugs, and other larger ones for dental treatment and spectacles. But for really costly treatments there is, within the Health Service, a kind of informal *triage*. One is unlikely in practice to get renal dialysis on the Health Service if one is over a certain age. In other cases not considered urgent, such as hip replacements and hernias, one can get free treatment but there is a long waiting list, which one can circumvent by going private. That is why many people insure themselves privately as in America, or are insured by their employers. But this insurance costs much less than in America, because most treatment even of the insured is obtained free through the Health Service.

On the whole people in Britain like the Health Service, and do not want to go over to a system like the American. But the British system is in some financial danger because of the escalation of costs, and the Conservative government has been introducing reforms which give a bigger role to private medicine, and to internal competition within the State sector. Nobody knows yet how these reforms will work out, but it is safe to predict that things will not remain as they are.

We are discussing this question at a time when both of our countries are in pretty much of a mess with our health care provision. In Britain the Health Service worked, and to a great extent still works, extremely well. So well, in fact, that when I have a choice I usually save up my health problems till I get home to Britain, although I have a fairly good insurance policy in the USA. Admittedly, we have been especially favoured in Oxford; our GPs have been close personal friends and good at their job, and all the specialists one might consult are my colleagues in the University and, if not personally known to me, part of a much closer-knit community than the University of Florida. When I might have had to have my carotid artery attended to, it gave a lot of comfort to know that the Professor of Surgery who would have done it was like me a fellow of Balliol College. Other areas of Britain are not so fortunate, but they are all at least adequately served.

But, as in America, the rising costs of health care have brought on a crisis which is now involving the doctors and politicians in acrimonious battles. The costs have risen for many reasons, all of which apply to both countries, but to different degrees. One is the development of expensive new technologies. Another is the changing age-distribution of the population, with more elderly people needing medical care (though the financial effect of this may have been exaggerated). Another is inflation: doctors, and even more nurses, to say nothing of ancillary workers, need much more money to maintain their standard of living in real terms; and when those in other jobs are even increasing their real affluence, it is hard to say to nurses that they should be dedicated enough to put up with a reduced standard. The result is the growth of unionism and strikes, which it is hard to condemn, but to avert which greatly increased pay will have to be provided. Another factor, which as yet affects the USA more than Britain, is the escalation of malpractice awards and thus of malpractice insurance premiums. One must also say that doctors in America, in contrast to nurses in Britain, have managed to get for themselves a fairly high degree of affluence.

Another important factor in Britain is that expectations are rising. In earlier generations people were often afraid of doctors, or of their bills; now they go to them much more readily. Preventive medicine may gain in some cases, but at a heavy cost in doctors' time.

14.5 All these factors have meant that there is simply not enough money to pay for what people think is needed in the way of health provision for everybody. Basically it is the same problem in both countries; and even the solutions sought are beginning to converge. Let us consider some of these. One says: 'Granted that we have to provide for the poor: why not *just* provide for the poor and let all above the poverty level, or at least all above a certain minimum level, insure themselves?'

The trouble with this solution is that it creates a two-class health system which will inevitably produce envy, the evils of which I have already stressed. Do we want to live in a society where the poor get the bare minimum of attention and the rich can have everything they can pay for, including some treatments which are probably quite unnecessary for their health?

However, a less extreme solution of the same general sort might be accepted from the Kantian utilitarian point of view. If the standard of health care available to everybody were brought up to a decent level (say, to the level now available in the Health Service in Oxford to the general public, which I do not think is much below that available to dons like me), then is it so bad if, as happens in Britain already, those who want extras like private beds, expensive heart transplants, and transport home by air ambulance if they fall ill when vacationing in the Azores, provide for it by insurance if they can. Though I normally use the Health Service in Britain because it is so good, I have been privately insured for forty years or more, initially by my college. It insured me on the ground that if I needed non-emergency operations I could get them immediately in the vacation, and not join a waiting list and have perhaps to be off duty during term. On the left of British politics, there has been a lot of very silly and very damaging campaigning by the unions against private pay beds; their near-abolition in some places in the interests of a bogus egalitarianism has in fact caused heavy financial loss to the Health Service.

But there is another consideration which tells in favour of a nationalized public health service and against an insurance system: efficiency. Under the old dispensation in America, before they had DRGs and HMOs (diagnosis related groups and health maintenance organizations—see below), I was told that in a typical large hospital one entire floor might be taken up with accounting staff, producing the figures to satisfy the insurance companies that the money they were being asked for was really due and necessary. The insurance system was notoriously an incentive for hospitals, competing with each other for custom, to spend whatever they would like to spend. The British Health Service, for all its other inefficiencies, at least avoids this one, of which I can speak from personal experience in the USA. I do believe that the fact that the British spend a much lower proportion of their gross domestic product on health care, while not being obviously less healthy, may be due to our reliance mainly on a public tax-funded system with reasonably good accounting procedures. Whether DRGs and HMOs have improved matters in the USA, it is probably too early to judge, and I certainly cannot. The former classify patients according to their conditions, and pay for treatment at a standard rate for the condition; the latter are rather like smaller private versions of a health service: the patient insured under them has a regular general practitioner to whom he has to go in the first instance before being referred to a specialist or hospital; this family doctor thus acts as a gatekeeper rather like his British counterpart, and this may keep down costs by avoiding unnecessary referrals.

So there is an argument on grounds of efficiency for having a more than minimal public health service available to everybody, even if people are allowed to insure to provide the frills. If we accept this, our problems are not over, but at least the arguments will be about questions of degree, not about rather unreal questions of principle. That is what the utilitarian approach, sensibly used, can do for us. We shall have to go on arguing about *how much* the public service should provide, and how much should be left to private insurance; and about whether the two systems should be kept separate, doctors and nurses and hospitals being required to opt for employment in one or the other system but not both, or whether they should be allowed to take in each other's washing and charge competitive prices. In a full account, one would need also to look at the systems in use in continental European countries, and in Canada; in the latter, there is universal health provision by the State, but the relations between it and private health provision are different from those in Britain, and more restrictive. The system is said to give much satisfaction. But there are also attractions in a more relaxed mixed system like the British.

14.6 We shall have, further, to decide what to do about the extremely expensive technologies that are now available. We are reaching a stage at which the most costly of them cannot be provided at the public expense for everybody without diverting tax funds from other uses which we shall in practice be unwilling to forgo. In Britain now, for all the huge public political support there is for the Health Service, we have been, as I said, forced into a kind of *triage* (very well and humanely administered, I think) for kidney dialysis patients. Paradoxically the USA, which in general is much more inclined to private health provision, has made dialysis available to all kidney patients whatever their means; but Congress is not going to—it hardly can—repeat this generosity with all other life-threatening conditions.

My guess is that both countries will in the end converge on to some system which gives everybody (whether through insurance or by public provision out of taxes) access to health care considered adequate for all ordinary needs, and for all ordinary emergencies, but which looks rather carefully at some very new and very expensive technologies, making the most expensive of them available only to those who are able and willing to insure against the need for them. I do not see how we can do better than that in the present circumstances. As the technologies get cheaper, they can be made more generally available. This certainly is what the utilities, as I see them, seem to justify. But, as I said, I am not very well versed in the details of these problems, and have had to content myself with giving what I think is the best philosophical basis for their solution, leaving it to others to apply it to the various difficulties that all who seek to provide an adequate health service are faced with.

15

Why I am only a Demi-Vegetarian

15.1 The 'Why' in my title promises an explanation as well as a justification; so I can usefully begin with a little dietetic autobiography. I am speaking only from my experience, and not as an expert dietician. I had a normal British upbringing until I found myself in 1940 in the Indian Army. There I acquired a strong taste for curries, including the delicious *dāl* (lentil) curries that our Punjabi soldiers filled their *chapātīs* with. When in 1942 I found myself a prisoner of war after the fall of Singapore, we all knew that we were going to have a thin time, and most of us expected that we would suffer in health by eating little or no meat. But this turned out not to be the case. Our dietetic experiences can be divided into three periods. In the first, in Singapore, we had plenty of polished, or white, rice, a few musty rice polishings, and a very little meat, fish, and vegetables. There was not much ground to grow vegetables in; and a pig farm which the Japanese made us set up did not prosper. During this period we suffered a number of deficiency diseases owing to an unbalanced diet, there being too much carbohydrate in proportion to the other ingredients. But none of our troubles were attributed to lack of protein.

Then, when we were sent up for eight months to work as coolies on the Burma Railway, we got very little food altogether, and suffered from a lot of all kinds of diseases owing to our debilitated state and the numerous infections that were going around. Between 20 and 40 per cent of the groups I was in died (I do not know the exact figure, but there is relevant information in Dunlop 1987). When we got back to Singapore, we had for the first time larger vegetable gardens, and grew sweet potatoes, of which we ate mainly the leaves, Ceylon or Malabar spinach, kangkong (a kind of water convolvulus), tapioca (or cassava), and small quantities of other vegetables. At

Not published before.

the same time our rice ration diminished to very little. The result was that we stopped suffering from deficiency diseases, because our diet, though insufficient in quantity, was now well balanced, and we got small quantities of legumes for protein. So insufficient was it that we were getting not much over 800 calories a day, and became very thin. I came out of prison in 1945 weighing about 30 pounds less than my pre-war weight of 150 pounds, and made it up in a month. I now, at age 73, weigh about 165 pounds, which is at the bottom of the ideal weight-range for my height. Since we did not appear to have suffered from lack of meat, I had become disposed to be a vegetarian, and had acquired a great love of growing vegetables, which had probably saved our lives.

When my wife and I married in 1947, we talked about our diet, and I wanted to eat only vegetables, not for the reasons usually advanced nowadays, but because rationing was still in force in Britain and it seemed sensible to leave the meat for those who thought they needed it. But my wife argued that when we had children they ought to be given meat to make them grow strong; and so, having no really convincing arguments to set against this, I gave in, and we resumed a normal British diet, growing as many of our own vegetables as we could, in continuation of the 'Dig for Victory' movement that had been popular during the War. At first we had little land and I had no time to travel to and from a rented vegetable patch. When we moved out into the country in 1966, we had a large and beautiful garden, but the vegetable garden attached to the property had been retained by the previous owner to expand his honey business. There are a few fruit trees, but it seemed a shame to dig up the flower beds and lawns; so in the end we got ourselves a vegetable patch five minutes' walk away and became almost self-supporting in vegetables. This made us feel good, and seemed to improve our health, and we have ended up eating very little meat at all. Very recently, when the swimming pool that we had inherited with the property perished from old age, we filled it with soil, gave up the other patch, and now grow most of the vegetables we need within the curtilage.

So we became demi-vegetarians largely by accident, and without having any of the moral reasons usually given (though, as I said, it did make us feel good to be growing such a large proportion of what we were eating). It was only relatively recently, under the influence of Peter Singer (1975) and other animal liberationists, that I have started to take seriously these usual moral reasons for not eating meat. I began then to contemplate becoming a full vegetarian, but was unable to convince myself that it was morally required. I did for a time give up eating fish (which in any case my wife intensely dislikes) on the ground that fish are nearly always killed cruelly; but I started eating them again after I had been persuaded (wrongly, I now believe) by a physiologist colleague that fish lack the part of the brain that mediates suffering.

15.2 So far I have not tried to give any philosophical arguments for my views. I have to repeat that, as a moral philosopher, I am pretty confident that the best ethical theory is a combination of Kantianism with utilitarianism (1.6, 11.4, 12.1, and H 1993*a*). Such a combination is thought by many philosophers to be impossible, because, misled by partisan expositors of Kant, they think that his theory is quite incompatible with any form of utilitarianism. This is, I am sure, wrong. Kant's theory of the Categorical Imperative is quite compatible with a form of utilitarianism such as I am able to defend on formal logical grounds; he was not a utilitarian, but only because his rigorist upbringing when young had imbued him with some very strait-laced moral opinions which he tried unsuccessfully to defend by his theory, but which very few moderns, whether they are utilitarians or anti-utilitarians, would accept—for example, that suicide is as wrong as murder, and that capital punishment of murderers is morally obligatory. He also thought that the only reason for considering the sufferings of non-human animals was that cruelty to them harmed the moral character of humans. On this point, however, he was put right by his follower Leonard Nelson (1956: 136), who argued on Kantian theoretical lines that all animals are equal in their right to consideration.

The ethical theory on which I would base moral arguments can thus be called both Kantian and utilitarian. It is also compatible with the doctrine of *agapē* which is the basis of Christian ethics (1.6 and refs.; H 1992*b*: ch. 3). What it requires is that we should treat the ends of others as of equal weight with our own ends (Kant himself says explicitly, in relation to humans, that his Categorical Imperative requires this—1785: BA69 = 430). This is what it is to love them as ourselves, and to count everybody for one and nobody for more than one, as Jeremy Bentham bade us (Mill 1861: ch. 5, *s.f.*). So the argument about vegetarianism, if we accept such a theory, is going to boil down to an argument about how this would require us to treat non-human animals.

15.3   By this time I have become fairly confident in the Kantian utilitarian ethical theory that I have espoused, which is very similar to that of Singer. Neither he nor I talk much in terms of animal rights, as do some other vegetarians like Thomas Regan (1982). The reason is not that utilitarians cannot use the concept of rights—they can certainly find a use for it in their theories (see 10.2 and refs.)—but that what one needs to say about treatment of non-human animals can be put much more clearly in terms of duties to them than in terms of rights which they have.

Given this confidence, which I did not have before, it seemed to me that I ought to go into the moral question more fully and see whether the demi-vegetarianism that my wife and I were following ought, morally, to be abandoned in favour of full vegetarianism. I have come to the conclusion that there is insufficient reason for our taking this step, and I will now give my arguments for that view.

The arguments about meat-eating divide naturally into categories, of which I will deal with the less difficult first, in order to get them out of the way. There are first the dietetic arguments that I have already mentioned. I am quite convinced by my own experiences that one can live more healthily without meat, but not that one can live without protein. My wife now shares this view, and our children are grown up. That is not to say that meat is not a valuable source of protein, so that, if there are other reasons for producing some, they would be supported by dietetic considerations. Against this, it is now said that a diet containing a lot of animal products, especially fat, is bad for the cardio-vascular system, and I believe it. This, however, is a reason only for eating selected meat in small quantities, not for leaving it out of one's diet altogether. It is also a reason for avoiding other animal fats such as milk products, and also eggs; but I find it hard to believe that moderate consumption of these foods does one any harm. And the dieticians are now saying that we ought to eat fish. I have learnt recently that I have mild diabetes, like many people of my age, and I have to control it by diet; but I do not think this has altered the argument very much. The conclusion that I reach from these dietetic considerations is that it is right from the health point of view to eat very little meat, but not none at all. So far, then, my wife's and my present practice seems to pass muster.

15.4 Next, we have to consider the economic arguments, which tend to the same conclusion. There is a very good reason for saying that in conditions of food shortage it is more economical to grow food in the form of vegetables direct from the ground, than to grow fodder, feed it to animals, and then eat the animals. The reason is that enormously much more food is produced in the first way. From this point of view, it seems a scandal that so much land in America, Australia, and even Europe is given over to fodder crops. In theory, if it were devoted instead to growing human food, it would be much easier to feed the starving millions outside these regions.

To this, however, some important qualifications have to be made. It is often suggested that the present grain and other food surpluses in these regions should simply be distributed to countries where people are starving. The main objection to this is not financial, since the accumulation of food 'mountains' is a severe financial drain on the economies of countries that practise it. The trouble lies the other end; the effect of distributing food surpluses in this way, let alone producing even more human food by switching from animal husbandry, would be to ruin what remains of the agriculture of the recipient countries, and so put an end to any hope of their becoming self-supporting. There must be an answer to this problem, but I do not know what it is. If there is an answer, then economic considerations provide a reason for eating very little meat, but not, as we shall shortly see, for eating none.

The other qualification is that there are substantial, though not enormous, areas of the world which are suitable for pasture but unsuitable for crops. The reason is usually that the ground slopes too much, so that cultivation would result in soil erosion. Other areas are too arid and subject to wind erosion for crops, but will support some stock. When my daughter was working at an experimental farm in Jamaica, her Jamaican director, who had an impressive grasp of local problems, showed me with pride the two new breeds of cattle that they had achieved, suited to the Jamaican climate. The first was a Brahmin–Channel-Island cross called Jamaica Hope, bred for milk production. The second was called Jamaica Red Poll, also Brahmin-crossed, bred for beef production. I said to him, 'Why beef cattle in Jamaica, where people are short of food? Would it not be better to grow crops?' He replied that much of Jamaica is mountainous, and that one can pasture cattle on the slopes, provided that one does not overstock them; but that ploughing would be impossible or disastrous. So he thought that cattle could be an important source of protein for Jamaicans.

I also know a farm, to which I shall be recurring later, on the Cotswold escarpment in England, where the cattle graze the slopes which are too steep for it to be sensible to plough them. The owners, a brother and sister, Richard and Rosamund Young, are devoted organic farmers and claim that the stock is necessary to maintain the soil's fertility; this adds another reason for keeping animals. It is arguable that such land should be devoted to dairy cattle and the production of wool; but if economics favours meat production, there would be no argument here for not producing beef, bacon, or lamb, but only for confining such use to land that will not grow crops economically or even at all.

15.5   Our arguments so far favour demi-vegetarianism but not full vegetarianism. But of course they are not the most important arguments from the moral point of view. If there were moral arguments for full vegetarianism that I found convincing, based on our duty to respect the interests of other animals, I should think that I ought to give up eating meat altogether. Before addressing such arguments, it may be helpful to explain more exactly what I mean by 'demi-vegetarian'. I did not invent the term. I have been told by Onora O'Neill that it is used by the market researchers who serve the meat trade. It means someone who, while not being a full vegetarian, let alone vegan, eats little meat, and is careful what kinds of meat he (or she) eats. Usually the selection is on dietetic grounds (lean meat rather than fat, fish rather than meat, etc.); but no doubt moral considerations come in too. She told me that the market researchers and the trade are much more worried about the growth of demi-vegetarianism than of vegetarianism proper. The reason is that demi-vegetarianism is catching on in Britain in a big way, whereas there are still relatively few full vegetarians. That the meat trade has something to fear from demi-vegetarianism was brought home to me when I found displayed in a vegetable shop a pamphlet headed 'WHAT DEMIVEG CAN DO FOR YOU', and singing the praises of the demi-vegetarian diet from a health and culinary point of view. So evidently what is bad for the butchers is good for the greengrocers. But more of this later.

My wife's and my own practice is to buy little or no meat or fish for ourselves to eat at home, to support ourselves so far as we can on our own vegetables (which is hard if one lives half the year in Florida and half in England, though we are gradually learning how to do it). When we have guests who we think will not like to eat no meat, we buy some; and we allow ourselves to eat meat in restaurants when there is no obvious alternative. When we eat in other people's homes, we tend to say that we are demi-vegetarians (it makes good conversation—and propaganda—explaining what this means), and ostentatiously ask for a half helping of meat and lots of vegetables. The result is that all told we eat extremely little meat by ordinary standards, since we do not eat out much except when travelling. So our practice is supported by the arguments so far.

15.6   The moral arguments from the duty to respect animals' interests fall into two sub-classes which it is important to distinguish. The first concerns the alleged wrongness of *killing* animals, regardless of whether this involves suffering or not. The second, and to me more persuasive, one concerns the wrongness of *causing suffering* to animals, whether or not one kills them. The first kind of argument tells against eating meat and fish of all kinds; but the second does not tell against eating meat and fish unless rearing or killing them involves their suffering; but it also tells against eating animal products such as milk and eggs, if those are produced in ways involving suffering. I will take first the arguments against killing as such.

For utilitarians like Singer and myself, doing wrong to animals must involve harming them. If there is no harm, there is no wrong. Further, it has to be harm overall; if a course of action involves some harms but greater benefits, and there is no alternative with a greater balance of good over harm, it will not be wrong. We have to ask, therefore, whether the entire process of raising animals and then killing them to eat causes them more harm overall than benefit. My answer is that, assuming, as we must assume if we are to keep the 'killing' argument distinct from the 'suffering' argument, that they are happy while they live, it does not. For it is better for an animal to have a happy life, even if it is a short one, than no life at all. This is an old argument, and there are well-canvassed objections to it (e.g. Singer 1975: 254 f.); but I do not think they succeed. First, it is claimed that mere existence is in itself not a benefit. But this is irrelevant; I am not claiming that mere existence is a benefit in itself, but that it is a necessary condition for having the benefits that we can have only if we are alive. It is beneficial not in itself but as a means to these.

Secondly, it is claimed that, even if the benefit which existence makes possible is a real benefit, its absence is not a harm. For in order for it to be a harm, the state of not having it must be preferable to the state of having it. But in order for it to be preferable, we have to be able to *compare* one state with another. But, the objection goes on, we cannot compare the state of not existing with the state of existing, because non-existence is not a state accessible to us for comparison; we cannot imagine it, or say what it would be like; so the comparison cannot be made. To this we can answer that happy existing people are certainly glad that they exist, and so are presumably comparing their existence with a possible non-existence; so what the objection says is impossible actually happens.

This is a very complex question metaphysically speaking, and I shall not go into it here (see 6.2 f. and refs.). I will cut the argument short by simply assuming that the combination of Kantianism and utilitarianism which I have said I hold is the right way to reason about moral questions. I shall assume further that the 'total' variety of utilitarianism is the most defensible one—that is, that which holds that what we have to do is to maximize the total amount of preference-satisfaction

that is had in the world by beings capable of forming preferences, and distribute it impartially between these beings, giving
to each, within the available resources, in accordance with the
strength of its preferences, and not favouring any preference
simply because it is ours or that of a group specified in terms
of ourselves (e.g. our family, sex, race, or species). I have discussed total and average utilitarianism in 5.1.

From the point of view of such a theory it would seem that
the issue about *killing* animals, as distinct from causing them
suffering, resolves itself into, not the question of whether it is
all right to kill animals, but the question of how many live animals, of different species including the human, we ought to
cause there to be. To be more accurate, I shall have to introduce the concept of a QALY, or quality-adjusted life year.
The quality-adjusted life years that an animal enjoys are the
number of years lived by that animal, multiplied by a factor
corresponding to the average quality of life enjoyed during
those years. This concept has been employed in assessing the
merits of different medical treatments; for example, if a treatment will give n years of life of average quality q, it is assessed
at nq QALYs; and if an alternative treatment will give m years
of life of average quality r, it is assessed at mr QALYs; and the
first is to be preferred if nq is greater than mr. Of course, the
probability of these outcomes has also to be factored in, and
the procedure involves judgements about quality of life (from
the point of view of the person who has it) which are hard to
make.

All the same, this does represent a good model of what we
ought to be trying to do when we make clinical decisions. The
fact that QALYs are not easy to quantify or measure numeri-
cally is not so important; after all, before weighing machines
with numerical scales were invented, people could all the same
pick up two sacks of corn and tell which was the heavier. They
could not formulate the result in pounds and ounces, but they
knew what they were doing. I think that the model does represent pretty well what I am trying to do when I am choosing *for
myself* whether or not to have surgery for a particular condition.

If we can apply this concept to our problem about vegetarianism, what we ought to be doing is to maximize the amount

of quality-adjusted life years or QALYs of sentient beings. And I do not believe that we should be doing this if we refrained from eating animals. The reason is that if we gave up eating animals the market for meat would vanish, and no more animals would be raised for meat-production. Such animals as there were would be either wild, or kept as pets, or kept for other economic purposes such as milk, egg, and wool production. And it is certain that there would be very many fewer domestic animals than at present live. This thought gives me pause when I walk in the fields around my home in England, and see a great many apparently happy animals, all destined to be eventually eaten. As it happens, they are mainly pigs, who would certainly not be kept except for the bacon market.

Let us, to make the position clearer, consider some more extreme, though not fictitious, cases. In our village there is also a trout farm. The fish start their lives in moderately commodious ponds and have what I guess is a pleasant life for fish, with plenty to eat. In due course they are lifted out in buckets and put immediately into tanks in the farm buildings. Purchasers select their fish, which is then killed by being banged smartly on the head and handed to the customer. I am fairly certain that, if given the choice, I would prefer the life, all told, of such a fish to that of almost any fish in the wild, and to non-existence.

Again, suppose that one were able to keep animals in ideal conditions under one's own supervision, as the Youngs whom I mentioned earlier do, and then kill them to eat without causing them suffering (at least more suffering than they would have from a 'natural' death); would I consider that one had done those animals a service by bringing them into existence to have that sort of life and death? The Youngs, I am sure, would answer 'Yes'; and they claim to have reconverted some converts to vegetarianism. They do not slaughter their animals themselves, but have made what they think are satisfactory arrangements with the local public abattoir, and always accompany their animals there to see that they suffer the minimum of fear. They claim that even their pigs never squeal— which is remarkable, because pigs, being highly intelligent animals, nearly always know when something nasty is in the offing. The Youngs' pigs, I must add, are the most well-liking

pigs I have ever seen, and the same can be said of their sheep.
If all farm animals were as well looked after as theirs, there
would be no complaints about cruelty involved in animal husbandry.

15.7   To this question of cruelty, then, I now turn, as the
second of the two headings under which moral questions about
the treatment of animals have to be considered. I must at once
admit that some animal husbandry practices are quite scandalous. The problem is, how best to get them improved, and
in particular what effect on their improvement can be had by
abstaining from eating meat. I find this a highly complex and
difficult question, and to its complexities are due my remaining
doubts about whether I ought to become a full vegetarian. On
the face of it, the immediate effect of my not, on a particular
occasion, buying meat is to reduce, very slightly, the demand
for that kind of meat. It will not directly save the life of any
animal, because the animal in question has been killed already.
Any effect on the lives of the animals, including the quality of
their lives, is bound to be indirect; and I find it extremely hard
to assess it. I wish I were more of an economist, which is what
one needs to be to determine the effects of one's actions in the
market. However, I will try to make some guesses, under several headings.

First, there is the obvious effect, that a reduction in the market for meat lowers the price, and this, if many people do the
same, may force out of production the least efficient marginal
producers. We have therefore to ask whether these will also be
the ones that treat their animals best, or worst, or a mixture. It
might seem at first sight as if it would be the factory farms that
would survive, because they are said to be the most efficient in
the narrow commercial sense of that term. But I do not
believe that this is the whole story, if only because the Youngs
told me that they do quite well out of their farm in spite of
treating their animals so admirably. The reason is that their
meat and milk is so good that it earns a substantial premium.
So, they say, does their wheat, grown by organic methods; but
I am inclined to take all claims by organic farmers with a
pinch of salt, and so am prepared to expect the financial collapse of farms like theirs if vegetarianism or even demi-vegetarianism spreads in a big way.

However, there are other equally important considerations. Demi-vegetarians have one very powerful advantage over full vegetarians when it comes to influencing the market. Since they eat little meat, but do eat some, they would be in a quite strong position to influence animal husbandry practices if they could get enough information to enable them to make use of their power. By selecting carefully the meat that they did buy, they might help to cause those practices to be abandoned which occasion most suffering to animals.

The obstacle to this is the extreme difficulty of finding out reliably where one's meat (and for that matter one's eggs and milk) come from. Even so-called free-range eggs are often nothing of the kind—or so it is said. Living in a country village, my wife and I are better placed than most people to find out the sources of what we eat. I think we usually know where the eggs we eat come from; and we are on good terms with the local butcher, who has an interest in philosophy, and once attended a discussion on vegetarianism with my students at one of the seminars I have given in our home. Almost the only thing we ever buy from him is an occasional turkey, which he assures us is free range; it certainly tastes like it, and I think with turkeys one can tell the difference. I am pretty certain that one of the most important reforms to agitate for, if one is the agitating sort, is a law requiring full disclosure of the sources of all foodstuffs. Even a non-governmental certification scheme, such as the Royal Society for the Prevention of Cruelty to Animals is said to be considering, would do a great deal of good.

Another way in which our eating habits can influence the treatment of animals is by their propaganda or publicity value. It might be urged in favour of full vegetarianism that to make a stand in this simple way against meat eating will bring home to people how awful some animal husbandry practices are, and so lead to public revulsion against them and thus possibly to legislation forbidding them. In my moral philosophy as a whole I do lay stress on the utility of having firm general principles of this sort, and not making complex cost-benefit calculations about particular cases; these calculations are bound to be unreliable and may even involve self-deception (2.3 f.). But a steadfast full vegetarianism is not the only possible firm principle. One might even take against this position the line which its upholders could rightly take against veganism, if they were utilitarians. It is hard to be sure—indeed, it is on the face of it unlikely—that complete abstention from eggs and milk will do much for the welfare of animals (it is certainly likely to reduce their numbers). A firm abstention just from meat and fish is better. But is it not possible that a large reduction in one's consumption of them, coupled with as much selection of sources as is possible, would do even more?

On the question of the propaganda value of the rival policies, then, there can be different views. Here we have to ask what we are trying to achieve by our propaganda. It must be remembered that, if what I have said about the morality of killing animals is correct, our aim should be to bring it about, not that no animals are killed, but that the quantity multiplied by the quality of animal (including human) life is maximized. We therefore do not want everyone to be full vegetarians. Rather, we want there to be enough meat-eating in the world to sustain the number of animals that there ought to be, whatever that is. I shall come later to the even more difficult question of where this optimum lies. It is an open question whether it would be best and most quickly achieved by there coming to be a few full vegetarians, while the rest of us ate as much meat as most people in developed countries do now, or whether it would work better if there were much larger numbers of demi-vegetarians (with varying degrees of deminess).

I am inclined to think that these possibilities would work equally well, and that therefore the most material consideration is how easily each of them could be achieved. And I also think that we are more likely to persuade very large numbers of people to become demi-vegetarians (it is happening already) than to convert enough people to full vegetarianism to have the same effect on the market and on public opinion. But I am open to conviction on this.

15.8 But now we come to the most difficult question of all. How many animals ought there to be, and what proportions of these should be allotted to the various species? If one is not a specist (and I hope I am not) it is purely the quality multiplied by quantity of life that has to be considered, and not the fact that one of the competing species is our own. (I use the term 'specist', formed by analogy with 'racist', instead of the intolerably clumsy word 'speciesist' which seems to be becoming current.) I do think that humans are capable of a higher quality of life than *some* animals (earthworms, for example). I also think that some animals (oysters, for example) have no conscious experiences, so that we cannot sensibly ask what the quality of their lives is (they have none in the relevant sense). This presupposes an answer to the question of whether life can have quality, in the morally relevant sense, even if it is not conscious. There is also the further question, pressing for environmentalists, of whether plants and even non-living beings have a value that needs to be weighed in this balance. I have made a beginning of addressing both these questions in H 1987*b*, and shall leave them on one side now, although, once one has opened up the question of how many animals there should be of various species, this aspect of the matter has to be considered.

Ecological considerations will obviously be very important here. The ecology determines what combination of various species, and in what numbers, *can* coexist on this planet; and till we have settled that, there is no point in asking how many there *ought* to be. But, assuming some sort of answer to the equally difficult question of how we assess the quality of life of various species under various conditions, how do we determine the optimal numbers? Before going any further, it is important to distinguish between two entirely different ways in which humans can make use of other animals for food. I shall call them 'predation' and 'husbandry'. In predation the animals (fish are the most obvious example) live in their wild state and are hunted by man for food. In husbandry the animals are domesticated and kept more or less confined, and then slaughtered for food as required.

The effects of predation vary, but in general it can perhaps be said that, *provided* that there is not over-fishing or over-hunting (that is, provided that the stock of animals is not depleted), the hunting or fishing makes no difference to the numbers of animals (this is indeed a tautology). But we still have to ask what would happen if there were no predation by man. The answer must be that the populations would rise to the limit imposed by other predators, parasites, and diseases, and by the

available space and food supply. My conclusion is that predation is all right within limits (which are frequently transgressed
by fishermen, to their own ultimate ruin). However, the methods of predation need careful watching to avoid cruelty—
though we have to bear in mind that, in the wild, animals
often die miserable deaths from 'natural' causes, and that other
predators, parasites, and diseases are even less merciful than
man. Therefore, in spite of now disagreeing with the physiologist colleague I mentioned earlier, I feel inclined to eat fish in
moderation when my wife lets me, but have misgivings about
those caught with rod and line. I have misgivings about all
kinds of predation, but they may be mistaken.

Before leaving the subject of predation, it is worth mentioning that it is urged by some people that in large tracts of
Africa more economical use could be made of the land by
having game preserves, with controlled predation by man,
than by grazing cattle. I cannot judge of this; but it is claimed
that more meat would thereby be produced more economically, with less soil erosion. If this is so, it would also solve
some moral problems, if, as I have suggested, predation is
morally less suspect than at any rate most kinds of husbandry.

Husbandry presents more difficult moral problems, some of
which I have mentioned already. At the best, the fish farm,
and the Youngs' farm on the Cotswolds that I described earlier, seem to me to be all right, and most forms of factory
farming all wrong; but all kinds of farm in between need careful discussion in detail which I have no room to give them. If
the most fundamental issue is one of numbers, then we might
consider an extreme position (Derek Parfit's 'repugnant conclusion' applied to all animals and not just to humans—see 5.1
ff.). This would require us to increase the population of both
up to the limit at which the *total* (not the average) utility or
preference-satisfaction was maximal. That is to say, we should
increase numbers even at the cost of decreasing quality of life
provided that the total utility or amount of QALYs resulting
from the increased numbers at this lower level of quality was
thereby increased. Obviously the argument is going to have to
be even more complex in order to take in other animals.

At the other extreme we might argue that QALYs would be
maximized if we adopted a much more primitive life-style,

requiring the use of a lot of land per person and therefore a greatly reduced population of people (and probably of animals too, compared with what can be kept in intensive husbandry), and so had what some would try to persuade us is a much superior quality of life. I do not myself favour either of these extremes; but where, in between them, the optimum policy lies I could not decide without a great deal more information about the ecological possibilities than I, at any rate, have. I am very much in favour of experiments in living, and I think that what we achieved in our prison camps in Singapore was a quite successful one; but if, once set free, any one of us had been willing to go on with it just as it was, I should have been extremely surprised. However, I brought something away, especially my love of growing and eating vegetables. And I acquired some gastronomic arguments for at least demi-vegetarianism which I still think powerful.

15.9 I will try now to sum up my very tentative conclusions. First, there are good dietetic and economic arguments for demi-vegetarianism, but they do not support full vegetarianism. Secondly, the moral argument based on the wrongness of *killing* animals collapses completely in the face of the objection that by accepting it we should in practice *reduce* the number of animals, and thus the total amount of animal welfare. Thirdly, the *sufferings* of animals in most commonly practised forms of animal husbandry are scandalous; but the best way of improving matters is not easy to find. I am inclined to the view that, though homage must be paid to the courage of the full vegetarians who stand out completely against meat-eating, and though they undoubtedly do a lot to propagate better practices, more could perhaps be done if a much greater number of people could be converted to demi-vegetarianism, and if they had more easily available the information they need in order to select those animal products that are produced by methods which minimize suffering to animals. I think that there are some, and that controlled predation is one of them; but the factual questions involved here are so complex that I hesitate to discuss them, not being an expert in these matters.

Lastly, the question of how the numbers of various species should be apportioned within the available resources and ecological limits is an immensely difficult moral question, whose solution requires *both* an understanding of some rather deep philosophical issues which I have dealt with elsewhere, including the papers I have referred to, *and* a grasp of the enormously complicated ecological issues which affect the answer. Nobody that I know of has mastered both these groups of issues; few philosophers have even begun to master the ecology, and few ecologists and other environmentalists have even begun to understand the logic of the arguments, and the pitfalls which beset them. So there is everything to be said for the two disciplines getting together.

REFERENCES AND BIBLIOGRAPHY

References of the form '1.1' are to the numbered papers and sections of this volume. Other references are to date and page-number, unless otherwise indicated. References beginning *'LM'*, *'FR'*, and *'MT'* are to *The Language of Morals* (H 1952), *Freedom and Reason* (H 1963), and *Moral Thinking* (H 1981) respectively. References beginning with 'H' are to the first part of the bibliography; the rest, beginning with the author's name unless this is clear from the context, are to the second. Full bibliographies of the writings of R. M. Hare are to be found in H 1971*a* (to 1971), *MT* (1971–81), H 1988 (1981–7). H 1992*a* and H 1993*c* contain complete and up-to-date bibliographies in German of all his philosophical writings.

1. Writings of R. M. Hare

1949   'Imperative Sentences', *Mind* 58. Repr. in H 1971*b*.
1951   'Freedom of the Will', *Ar. Soc.* supp. 25. Repr. in H 1972*b*.
1952   *The Language of Morals* (Oxford UP).
1955   'Universalisability', *Ar. Soc.* 55. Repr. in H 1972*b*.
1963   *Freedom and Reason* (Oxford UP).
1971*a*   'Wanting: Some Pitfalls', in *Agent, Action and Reason*, ed. R. Binkley *et al.* (Blackwell). Repr. in H 1971*b*.
1971*b*   *Practical Inferences* (Macmillan, London).
1971*c*   'The Argument from Received Opinion', in his *Essays on Philosophical Method* (Macmillan, London).
1972*a*   *Applications of Moral Philosophy* (Macmillan, London).
1972*b*   *Essays on the Moral Concepts* (Macmillan, London).
1972*c*   'Rules of War and Moral Reasoning', *Ph. and Pub. Aff.* 1. Repr. in H 1989*b*.
1972*d*   'Principles', *Ar. Soc.* 72.
1973   Critical Study: 'Rawls' Theory of Justice: I and II', *Ph. Q.* 23. Repr. in *Reading Rawls*, ed. N. Daniels (Blackwell, 1975) and in H 1989*a*.
1975   'Euthanasia: A Christian View', *Philosophic Exchange* 2 (proc. of Center for Philosophic Exchange, Brockport, NY). Repr. in H 1992.
1976   'Ethical Theory and Utilitarianism', in *Contemporary British Philosophy* 4, ed. H. D. Lewis (Unwin). Repr. in *Utilitarianism and*

Beyond, ed. A. K. Sen and B. A. O. Williams (Cambridge UP, 1982), and in H 1989*a*.

1978   'Justice and Equality', in *Justice and Economic Distribution*, ed. J. Arthur and W. Shaw (Prentice-Hall). Repr. in H 1989*b*.

1979*a*   'What is Wrong with Slavery', *Ph. and Pub. Aff.* 8. Repr. in *Readings in Applied Ethics*, ed. P. Singer (Oxford UP, 1986), and in 1989*b*.

1979*b*   'Universal and Past-Tense Prescriptions: A Reply to Mr Ibberson', *Analysis* 39.

1981   *Moral Thinking* (Oxford UP).

1984   'Supervenience', *Ar. Soc.* supp. 58. Repr. in H 1989*a*.

1986   'Punishment and Retributive Justice', *Ph. Topics* 14, ed. J. Adler and R. N. Lee (U. of Arkansas P.). Repr. in H 1989*b*.

1987*a*   'An Ambiguity in Warnock', *Bioethics* 1.

1987*b*   'Moral Reasoning about the Environment', *J. of Appl. Ph.* 4. Repr. in H 1989*b*.

1988   'Comments', in *Hare and Critics*, ed. D. Seanor and N. Fotion (Oxford UP).

1989*a*   *Essays in Ethical Theory* (Oxford UP).

1989*b*   *Essays on Political Morality* (Oxford UP).

1991   'Are there Moral Authorities?', in *Ethics in Reproductive Medicine*, ed. D. R. Bromham *et al.* Also in 1992*b*.

1992*a*   *Moralisches Denken*, German translation of *MT*, with complete bibliography of author's philosophical works (Suhrkamp).

1992*b*   *Essays on Religion and Education* (Oxford UP).

1993*a*   'Could Kant have been a Utilitarian?', in *Kant and Critique: New Essays in Honor of W. H. Werkmeister* ed. R. M. Dancy, proc. of conference at Florida State University, 1991 (Reidel). Also in *Utilitas* 5 (1993).

1993*b*   'Utilitarianism and Deontological Principles', in *Principles of Health Care Ethics*, ed. R. Gillon (Wiley).

1993*c*   Replies to 23 critics (in German) in *Zum Moralischen Denken*, ed. C. Fehige and G. Meggle, with complete bibliography of author's philosophical works (Suhrkamp).

2. Other Writings

ANSCOMBE, G. E. M. (1985), 'Were You a Zygote?', in *Philosophy and Practice*, ed. A. P. Griffiths (R. Inst. of Ph. Lectures 19, suppl. to *Philosophy* 59, Cambridge UP).

ARISTOTLE, *Nicomachean Ethics* (refs. to Bekker pages).

BELLOC, H. (1908), 'Jim, who ran away from his Nurse and was eaten by a Lion', in *Cautionary Tales for Children*. Cited from 1923 collected edn. (Duckworth).

BENTHAM, J. (1789), *An Introduction to the Principles of Morals and Legislation*.

BLOCH, S. (1981), 'The Political Misuse of Psychiatry in the Soviet Union', and refs., in *Psychiatric Ethics*, ed. S. Bloch and P. Chodoff (Oxford UP).

—— and CHODOFF, P. (eds.) (1981), *Psychiatric Ethics* (Oxford UP).

BOORSE, C. (1975), 'On the Distinction between Disease and Illness', *Ph. and Pub. Aff.* 5.

—— (1976), 'What a Theory of Mental Health should be', *J. Th. Soc. Behaviour* 6.

—— (1977), 'Health as a Theoretical Concept', *Ph. of Sc.* 44.

—— (1981), Revision of Boorse 1977 in *Concepts of Health and Disease*, ed. A. L. Caplan, H. T. Engelhardt, and J. J. McCartney (Addison-Wesley).

—— (1986), 'Concepts of Health', in *Border Crossings*, ed. T. Regan and D. VandeVeer (Temple UP).

BRANDT, R. B. (1989), 'Hare on Abortion', *Soc. Th. and Practice* 15.

BUCKLE, S. (1988), 'Arguing from Potential', *Bioethics* 2.

BUTLER, J. (1726), *Sermon XII* and (1736), *Dissertation on Virtue*. Repr. in D. Raphael, *British Moralists* 1 (Oxford UP, 1969).

COGGAN, D. (1977), *On Dying and Dying Well*, Edwin Stevens Lecture 1976 (R. Soc. of Medicine).

DANIELS, N. (1985), *Just Health Care* (Cambridge UP).

DAWSON, K. (1988), 'Segmentation and Moral Status *in vivo* and *in vitro*: A Scientific Perspective', *Bioethics* 2.

DEVLIN, P. (1965), *The Enforcement of Morals* (Oxford UP). (For discussion see Hart 1962.)

DUNLOP, E. E. (1987), *The War Diaries of Weary Dunlop: Java and the Burma Thailand Railway* (Nelson, Melbourne).

DWORKIN, R. M. (1977), *Taking Rights Seriously* (Harvard UP).

FINNIS, J. (1973), 'Rights and Wrongs', *Ph. and Pub. Aff.* 2.

GLOVER, J. C. B. (1977), *Causing Death and Saving Lives* (Penguin).

—— (chmn.) (1989), *Fertility and the Family*, Report of EC Working Party (Fourth Estate).

HAMPSHIRE, S. (1972), 'Morality and Pessimism'. Repr. in his *Public and Private Morality* (Cambridge UP, 1981).

HART, H. L. A. (1961), *The Concept of Law* (Oxford UP).

—— (1962), *Law, Liberty and Morality* (Oxford UP).

—— (1967), 'Intention and Punishment', *Oxford Rev.* no. 4. Repr. in his *Essays in the Philosophy of Law* (Oxford UP, 1968).

HASLETT, D. (1974), *Moral Rightness* (Nijhoff).

HUME, Cardinal B. (1985), article in *The Times* (6 June, p. 12).

HUME, D. (1739), *A Treatise of Human Nature*.

KANT, I. (1785), *Grundlegung zur Metaphysik der Sitten*. Refs. to pages of original edns. and Royal Prussian Academy edn., given in translation, *The Moral Law*, by H. J. Paton (Hutchinson, 1948).

—— (1788) *Kritik der praktischen Vernunft*. Refs. to pages of original edn. and Royal Prussian Academy edn.

—— (1797) *Über ein vermeintes Recht aus Menschenlieben zu Lügen* (A301 = VIII. 423). Translation in T. K. Abbott, *Kant's Theory of Ethics* (3rd edn., Longmans, 1883).

KENNEDY, I. (1982), letter, *The Times* (11 Feb., p. 17).

LEWIS, C. I. (1946), *An Analysis of Knowledge and Valuation* (Open Court).

LOACH, K. (director) (1972), film *Family Life*.

LOCKWOOD, M. (1983), 'Sins of Omission? The Ethics of Non-Treatment in Clinical Trials', *Ar. Soc.* suppl. 57.

—— (ed.) (1985), *Moral Dilemmas in Medicine*.

—— (1988), 'Warnock versus Powell (and Harradine): When Does Potentiality Count?', *Bioethics* 2. Lockwood's rejoinder is in the same volume.

MECHANIC, D. (1968), *Medical Sociology* (New York, Free Press).

MELINSKY, H. (chmn.) (1975), *On Dying Well: An Anglican Contribution to the Debate on Euthanasia* (Westminster, Church Information Office).

MILL, J. S. (1843), *System of Logic*.

NELSON, L. (1956), *System of Ethics* (Yale UP and Oxford UP). First published in German, 1932.

NICHOLSON, R. H. (1986), *Medical Research with Children: Ethics, Law and Practice*: Report of Institute of Medical Ethics Working Group (Oxford UP).

PARFIT, D. (1973), 'Rights, Interests and Possible People'. Repr. in part in *Moral Problems in Medicine*, ed. S. Gorovitz (Prentice-Hall, 1976).

—— (1984), *Reasons and Persons* (Oxford UP).

—— (1986), 'Overpopulation and the Quality of Life', in Singer (1986).

RAMSEY, Bishop I. T. (chmn.) (1965), *Abortion: An Ethical Discussion* (Westminster, Church Information Office).

RAWLS, J. (1971), *A Theory of Justice* (Harvard UP and Oxford UP).

REGAN, T. (1982), *And All That Dwell Therein: Animal Rights and Environmental Ethics* (U. of California P.).

RICHARDS, D. A. J. (1971), *A Theory of Reasons for Action* (Oxford UP).

ROSS, A. (1958), *On Law and Justice* (*Om ret og retfaerdighed*), trans. M. Dutton (Stevens).

SEDGWICK, P. (1973), 'Illness, Mental and Otherwise', *Hastings Center St.* 1, 3.

SINGER, P. (1975), *Animal Liberation* (Random House).

—— (1979), *Practical Ethics* (Cambridge UP).

—— (ed.) (1986), *Applied Ethics* (Oxford UP).

—— and WELLS, D. (eds.) (1984), *The Reproduction Revolution: New Ways of Making Babies* (Oxford UP).

SPINOZA, B. (1677), *Ethics.*

STEVENSON, C. L. (1944), *Ethics and Language* (Yale UP).

STRAWSON, P. F. (1950), 'On Referring', *Mind* 59.

STÜRUP, G. K. (1968), 'Treatment of Sexual Offenders in Herstedvester, Denmark: The Rapists', Third Isaac Ray Lecture, *Acta Psychiatrica Scandinavica*, supp. 204 to vol. 44 (Munksgaard, Copenhagen).

SUMNER, J. W. (1987), *The Moral Foundation of Rights* (Oxford UP).

SZASZ, T. (1961), *The Myth of Mental Illness* (Harper and Row).

TATE, M. (chmn.) (1986), *Human Embryo Experimentation in Australia*, Senate Select Committee (Canberra, Australian Govt. Pub. Service).

TAYLOR, J. (1972), review of Loach (1972) in *The Times* (14 Jan., p. 8).

THOMSON, J. J. (1971), 'A Defense of Abortion', *Ph. and Pub. Aff.* 1.

—— and DWORKIN, G. (1968), *Ethics* (Harper and Row).

TOOLEY, M. (1972), 'Abortion and Infanticide', *Ph. and Pub. Aff.* 2.

VATICAN (1987), Congregation for the Doctrine of the Faith, *Instruction on Respect for Human Life in its Origin and on the Divinity of Procreation: Replies to Certain Questions of the Day* (Vatican City).

WALLACE, M. (1985), 'The Tragedy of Schizophrenia', correspondence and editorial, *The Times* (16–19 Dec.).

WARNOCK, Baroness M. (chmn.) (1984), *Report of Committee of Inquiry into Human Fertilization and Embryology* (HMSO, Cmnd. 9314). Repr. as *A Question of Life*, with new introduction and conclusion (Blackwell, 1985).

—— (1985), article in *The Times* (30 May, p. 12).

WEXLER, D. (1975), 'Behavior Modification and Other Behavior Change Procedures: The Emerging Law and the Proposed Florida Guidelines', *Crim. Law Bull.* 11. Repr. in part as 'One Proposed Legal Mechanism for Regulating Behavior Control', in his *Mental Health Law: Major Issues* (Plenum, 1981).

WILLIAMS, B. (chmn.) (1980), *Report of Committee on Obscenity and Film Censorship* (HMSO, Cmnd. 7772).

WOLFENDEN, Sir J. (chmn.) (1957), *Report of Committee on Homosexual Offences* (HMSO, Cmnd. 247).

INDEX

abnormal cases, *see* unusual and fictional cases
abnormal child 185–91
abnormalities 47, 87, 94–6, 136
abortifacients 183 f.
abortion v, 3, 6 f., 67, 90, 118, 147–84, 189
Abraham and Hagar 101
absolutism 5–8, 15–17, 22, 113, 172
act and omission 9, 161, 164
actual and hypothetical or potential situations, people 67–9, 153, 163–5, 174
  see also hypothetical acts; potentiality
actual world and abstract diagrams 70
administrative model for control of prisons 52 f., 65 f.
adultery 99–107, 113, 120
affection of parents for foetus, infants 91, 93, 159, 183
agapē, *see* love of neighbour
AID 99–104
American and British systems of health care 213–17
amoralism 176–8
anaesthesia 50, 95, 140, 168, 171
anencephaly 87
animals, non-human: interests of 82, 95, 112, 131, 135, 221, 225–35
Anscombe, G. E. M. 130
anti-psychiatry 31
  see also Szasz, T.
appraisal, moral 192–208
archē 200–2
argument:
  rigour in a. 1 f.
  good and bad as. 3, 98, 125, 129–32, 147 f.
Aristotle 2, 27, 31 f., 65, 103, 140, 164, 193, 195, 200–3, 206
artificial insemination, *see* AID

attitudes 8 f., 11–14, 47, 53, 61, 93, 104 f., 109
authority:
  of doctor 25 f., 45
  of Bible 108
autonomy 210–13
  see also liberty
aversion therapy 27, 44, 46 f., 50–66

Belloc, H. 103
Bentham, J. 122, 222
'bird in the hand' argument: foetus further down the track 91, 159, 183, 189
blame 206–8
Bloch, S. 22 f., 31
Boorse, C. 32, 36–41
Buckle, S. 129
Burma Railway 75 f., 219
Butler, J. 107 f.

'can if he wants' 197 f.
Canada, health care in 217
castration 62
casuistry 28, 123
ceteris paribus clauses, other things being equal 28, 34, 39, 42 f., 45, 67, 90, 153 f.
character 202, 221
  c. appraisal and action-guiding appraisal 121, 127
chastity 157, 181
Chodoff, P. 22 f.
Clapham omnibus 106
cleavage arrest 129
codes of conduct 19
  see also guidelines; prima facie duties; principles
committees, ethical, governmental and official 52 f., 84, 95 f., 109–17, 125–9, 143 f.
compassion 213

(

competence of patient 25, 51, 56–9,
    64, 211
confidentiality 23 f.
confinement, involuntary 21, 51, 57
conscience 17, 19, 107 f., 184
    see also intuitions
consent, informed 25–8, 51, 56–9,
    63–5, 95, 101 f., 116, 135, 137,
    139–46
consequences 56, 72, 93, 114, 122,
    178
    c. of legislation, of moral princi-
    ples 7, 18, 28, 94, 100, 103, 106,
    110, 116 f., 121–9
    c.-tialism 116, 123
Constant, B. 16
contraception, abortion, and
    infanticide 89–93, 159–62,
    182 f.
controlled experiments 2, 136, 139,
    145 f.
convictions, common moral, *see*
    intuitions
cost–benefit analysis 58, 230
    see also risks and benefits
costs of health care 214–17
'could have acted, chosen, wanted
    otherwise' 195–200
counter-intuitive conclusion 68,
    73–83
cowardice 202 f.
critical moral thinking 16–29, 92,
    160–2, 178 f., 212
cruelty to animals 132, 221, 229 f.,
    233
cure 32, 43–6, 48, 134, 137, 139

Daniels, N. 209
Dawson, K. 129
death, fear of 70, 79
demi-vegetarianism 219–35, *esp.* 224
democracy 118
demography 164, 183
deontologists 131, 173
descriptive properties, concepts 31,
    36 f., 45 f., 150
    d.-ivism 31
determinism 192–4

deviancy: behavioural, political 31,
    44–6, 57, 59–60
Devlin, P. 105, 112
diagnosis related groups 216 f.
diet 219 f., 222–5
disease 28–49
    mental d. 28 f.
distribution of wealth 78–82, 209 f.,
    212, 216
    between nations 82
Down's syndrome 182
duress, *see* force and duress
Dworkin, R. 26
dying and being killed 70, 91, 94
dyschromic spirochetosis 35

ecology 232–5
economic arguments 187, 212 f., 223,
    229, 234
education, bringing up children 7,
    17, 92, 192
efficiency in health care 216 f.
embryo:
    e. experimentation v, 109 f.,
    115 f., 125–30
    e. kitten 152, 154–6
    spare e. 95, 126–7
    see also foetus and embryo
emotivism 148
environmental causes 37–40
envy, disutility of 77 f., 210, 216
equality 78–82, 209
    see also distribution of wealth
ethical theory, use of 1–5, 20, 66,
    70, 198, 131, 147, 166 f., 172–4,
    185, 209, 221 f.
euthanasia 7–9, 12, 56, 185–91
evaluativity 28, 37
    see also descriptive properties
evolution of genes 38, 70
examples, use of in ethics 147
    see also unusual and fictional cases
exceptions to principles 21, 96,
    101–4, 113, 142, 159, 176–83,
    211 f.
existence 67, 69–75, 85–95, 127–30,
    157, 164–6, 173–6, 181 f., 189,
    226

e. compared with non-e. 70–5,
174–6, 226
thankfulness for e. 71–3, 164 f.,
174
experimentation:
on children 131–46
on embryos 109, 116, 125–30, 146
on humans 116

family-planning policy 89 f., 187
feelings:
as data for moral thinking 19, 105
f., 112 f., 142
see also affection of parents for
foetus
Finnis, J. 147
fish, eating 221–8, 231–3
Florida Guidelines 53, 144
foetus and embryo 3 f., 83–97,
148–84, 188–91
doomed or defective f. and e. 87,
96, 129, 152, 171 f.
f. or e. a person, human? 3 f.,
84–97, 103, 130, 115, 148–52,
168–72
suffering of f. and e. 152, 168,
171
see also embryo; experimentation
on children
force and duress 27, 65, 140 f., 201
free will 59, 192–208
freedom, *see* liberty
fuzzy concepts, *see* vague concepts

gametes:
moral status of g. 89–96, 116, 130,
189
union of g. not necessarily
adultery 99, 102
Glover, J. C. B. 9, 20, 112, 125
God's love, love of God 107 f.
Golden Rule 107, 153–8, 161, 163,
166
guidelines 12, 53 f., 95, 133, 144 f.
see also codes of conduct; prima
facie principles

Hampshire, S. 105

Hart, H. L. A. 122, 150
Haslett, D. 158
health 31–49
h. care 209–18
h. and illness, mental and physical
28, 31, 36, 43–5, 49, 57–9, 65
h. maintenance organizations
216 f.
Herstedvester 62
homosexuality 28 f., 44, 46 f., 52,
59 f., 106, 111 f., 118
'human' 3 f., 84 f., 93, 103, 130,
168 f.
see also 'person'
Hume, B. 110
Hume, D. 193, 195
husbandry and predation of animals
74, 223, 230, 232–4
hypothetical acts, cases, preferences
13, 21, 56, 133, 153, 164, 174,
177
see also actual and hypothetical or
potential situations

ideal observer 10, 21–4, 30, 56, 108,
153, 207
identity of person 84 f., 88, 164 f.
illness, *see* health
impartiality 7, 10 f., 17, 21, 23 f.,
53–5, 66, 89, 107 f., 178, 183,
207, 227
impartial spectator, *see* ideal
observer
individuation, *see* identity of
person
infanticide 7, 90–4, 96, 162, 185–91
'innocent' 3, 6 f., 17, 149, 161
insemination, artificial, *see* AID
insurance for health care 213–18
intention 3 f., 121 f., 127, 134, 149
direct and oblique i. 122
interests 7, 10–12, 15–17, 21, 23–6,
29, 34, 53–6, 58–62, 64–8, 82,
84, 86–91, 93–5, 108, 112, 119,
124, 141–3, 146, 151, 159, 163 f.,
176, 178, 183–8, 210 f., 224 f.
public i. 23, 27, 112, 150
internal state of organism 36–8

intuitions, i.-ism 56, 67, 69, 95, 105,
    108, 113, 115, 117, 125, 131, 141 f.,
    146–8, 155, 159, 207 f.
  i.-ive level 16–20, 22, 25 f., 66, 92,
    95, 160–2, 212
  logical and linguistic i. distin-
    guished from moral 20, 72
  place of i. in utilitarianism 105 f.
  i.-ive principles 54, 161 f., 179, *see
    also* prima facie
in vitro fertilization 94 f., 98–106,
    109, 113, 125, 130

Jamaica 75, 224
judges and legislators contrasted
    with psychiatrists 28, 55,
    61–3
judicial model for control of prisons
    52
justice and utility 54 f., 62, 66, 145,
    184, 207 f., 209

Kaimowitz's case 51
Kant, I. 10, 16, 61, 66, 70, 115, 153,
    172 f., 178, 185, 195, 209 f., 213,
    216, 221 f., 226
Kennedy, I. 144
Kenny, A. 157
killing:
  and causing suffering to animals
    225–9
  and letting die 9, 127; *see also* act
    and omission

lawyers, duties of to clients 119
legislation, morality of 119–27
levels of moral thinking 12, 16, 20,
    22–7
  see also critical, intuitive levels
Lewis, C. I. 158
lexical ordering 16
liberty 21, 24–7, 29, 46 f., 58, 64, 74,
    140 f., 148, 170
  see also autonomy
lies, truth 7, 17
Loach, K. 47
Lockwood, M. 84–97, 111, 136
love of neighbour 107–9

Mackey's case 50
mala in se and *mala prohibita* 120
Maralinga atomic tests 124
marriage 100 f., 140, 148
means, using people as 114 f.
Mechanic, D. 35
mental and physical illness, *see* health
Mental Health Act 47
method in medicine and philosophy 1
Mill, J. S. 193, 195, 222
multilateral situations 158
murder 3 f., 7, 17, 60, 103, 109, 118 f.,
    149 f., 162, 169 f., 179 f., 221
mutations 38 f.

natural:
  n. function 36 f., 40 f.
  n. kind terms 33
  n. law 119–21, 124
  n.-ism, ethical 208
negative features of acts 176
Nelson, L. 221
neonates, treatment of, *see* infanticide
Nicholson Report 95, 115 f., 132 f.,
    143

O'Neill, O. 224
order, preservation of 55, 66
'ought', prescriptive uses of 196–9,
    204
own patient, duty to, *see* partial
    principles, duties

Parfit, D. 67 f., 89, 233
partial principles, duties 22 f., 55, 61
paternalism 210
  see also autonomy
Paul, St 108
'person' 130, 150–2, 169–71
  see also 'human'
placebo effect 135, 139
Plato 2, 31
pluralism 118, 124
political correctness vi–vii
Pope 181
population policy v, 67–9, 73–82,
    89 f., 156, 163, 175, 181 f., 232 f.

possible people v, 67–83
  see also potentiality
potentiality 84–97, 112, 116, 128 f.,
  152–6, 159, 162–5, 168, 171–4,
  187–90
Powell, E. 110, 113
practical syllogism 200
prediction 105, 193–208
  p.-ability of motivations 198 f.
preferences 26, 56 f., 61, 67, 70–3,
  105, 176–81, 226 f., 233
prejudices, *see* intuitions
prescriptions 22, 69 f., 175, 185–99,
  204
  past-tense and timeless p. 71 f.,
    173–5, 196; *see also* universal p.
  p.-ive words 42
  p.-ive uses of 'ought' 196–9, 204
  p.-ivism *see* universal p.
pressure groups 124–6
prima facie duties, principles, rights
  16, 18 f., 22, 95, 142, 166, 175
principles, general and specific 6–8,
  12–14, 19–24, 28 f., 53–5, 65 f.,
  100–4, 113, 142, 145, 160–2,
  179
priority between duties, *see* lexical
  ordering
prisoner patients 27 f., 50 f., 54–66
private and public health care
  provision 213–18
procreate:
  decisions to p. 72, 88 f., 159–61
  duty to p. 156 f., 160, 163–5
  p.-tion is choice 89 f.
prognosis, role of doctor in 25 f., 56,
  187–9
promises 7, 140
propaganda 113, 124 f., 225, 230 f.
property rights in own body 148
proxy decisions 48, 95, 116, 145 f.
prudence 57, 176, 213
pseudo-problems 192
psychiatry 15–31, 36, 46–9, 55, 58,
  60–6
  abuse of p. 28, 31
public's right to protection 23 f.
  see also interests, public

punishment 50–2, 58, 60 f., 64, 192,
  221
  cruel and unusual p. 50 f., 60 f.

quality of life, QALYs 82, 89
  of non-human animals 227 f.,
    233–4
questions not arising 195, 197, 204–6

rational contractor 10, 153
Rawls, J. 10 f., 207
realists, political 119
rebellion 79 f.
Regan, T. 222
repugnant conclusion 68, 233
research, therapeutic and non-
  therapeutic 134–8, 142
retrolental fibroplasia 136
revisionism 28 f.
  see also deviancy
rich fool parable 86
Richards, D. 10
rights 15 f., 24–30, 52–6, 84 f., 132 f.,
  141–5, 147–51, 154, 164, 169 f.,
  174, 183, 212, 221 f.
  r. as trumps 26
  r. and utilitarianism 24, 26, 28,
    30, 132 f., 141 f.
rigour:
  in argument 1 f.
  in research 135
  see also controlled experiments
risks and benefits 114, 133, 138 f.,
  143 f., 189
  see also cost–benefit analysis
Ross, A. 120
rules of thumb 19, 54

schizophrenia 44, 47 f.
Sedgwick, P. 35
self-defence, killing in 177
sexist language vi–vii
Singapore 75–7, 219, 234
Singer, P. 20, 109 f., 116, 221 f., 226
sins and crimes 104, 119 f.
slavery 75, 79 f.
slippery slope, slide 6, 35, 45 f., 101,
  104, 161 f., 180 f.

Socrates 2
soil erosion 223 f., 233
Soviet Union, abuses of psychiatry in 31
space, living 74, 233
special pleading, cooking 17, 19, 54, 131 f., 142
species-typical function 37–40
specism, speciesism 231 f.
Spinoza, B. 195
states of world and transition between them 68, 73, 75–7
Stevenson, C. 195
Stürup, G. 62 f.
submerged class 78 f., 81
suffering 7, 26, 35, 166, 172, 189, 212
  s. of non-human animals 221, 225–30, 234
  s. of foetus 95, 151 f., 168, 171
suicide 25, 58, 79 f., 147, 221
Sumner, L. W. 53, 141, 149
superhuman moral thinker, *see* ideal observer
surrogate motherhood 106, 109 f., 114 f.
Szasz, T. 31, 36, 44 f., 57–60

Tate Committee 96, 126, 128 f.
Taylor, J. 47
technology:
  in health care 215, 217 f.
  of *in vitro* fertilization 126, 129
tenses and moods 71 f., 85 f., 88, 153, 196
Thomson, J. J. 147 f., 155
tier systems 51
token economies 51
Tooley, M. 116, 152, 154–6, 159, 161 f., 172
triage 214, 218

underclass 78 f., 81
Unités d'Habitation 74
universal:
  prescriptions, principles 10 f., 13, 20 f., 70–2, 179, 196

prescriptivism 10, 153, 174, 185, 221
universalizability 73, 154, 176–8, 185, 196, 204
unusual and fictional cases 6, 92, 102, 155
utilitarians, utilitarianism 5–8, 11–14, 17 f., 22–6, 30, 60, 66–70, 81, 83, 105–7, 109, 112, 116, 133, 141–6, 153, 163, 172 f., 178 f., 185, 188, 207–10, 213, 216 f., 221 f., 226 f., 231
  u. and intuitions 105 f., 141
  kinds of u. 67–9
utility, average and total 69 f.
utility as preference-satisfaction 67, 178

vague concepts 150
Vatican 130
  see also Pope
vegans 224, 231
vegetarianism 219–35
verbal disputes and manœuvres, disputes about words 4, 103, 151
verbal shove theory 199
voluntary action 200–2
voluntary and involuntary treatment, confinement, experimentation 21, 29, 50 f., 57, 138

Wallace, M. 47
'want', senses of 197 f.
Warnock, M. 84, 93, 105, 109–17, 125
wedge, thin end of: *see* slippery slope
weighing duties 15
Wells, D. 109 f., 116
Wexler, D. 50–4, 58 f., 65, 144
Williams, B. 111 f., 117
wisdom of the ages 106
Wittgenstein, L. 42
Wolfenden, J. 111 f., 117

Young, R. and R. 224, 228, 233

zygote 130, 183